Lay Theories

*Everyday Understanding
of Problems in the Social Sciences*

Lay Theories

Everyday Understanding
of Problems in the Social Sciences

by

Adrian Furnham
Lecturer in Psychology
University College London
Gower Street
London

PERGAMON PRESS
OXFORD · NEW YORK · BEIJING · FRANKFURT
SÃO PAULO · SYDNEY · TOKYO · TORONTO

U.K.	Pergamon Press plc, Headington Hill Hall, Oxford OX3 0BW, England
U.S.A.	Pergamon Press, Inc., Maxwell House, Fairview Park, Elmsford, New York 10523, U.S.A.
PEOPLE'S REPUBLIC OF CHINA	Pergamon Press, Room 4037, Qianmen Hotel, Beijing, People's Republic of China
FEDERAL REPUBLIC OF GERMANY	Pergamon Press GmbH, Hammerweg 6, D-6242 Kronberg, Federal Republic of Germany
BRAZIL	Pergamon Editora Ltda, Rua Eça de Queiros, 346, CEP 04011, Paraiso, São Paulo, Brazil
AUSTRALIA	Pergamon Press Australia Pty Ltd., P.O. Box 544, Potts Point, N.S.W. 2011, Australia
JAPAN	Pergamon Press, 5th Floor, Matsuoka Central Building, 1-7-1 Nishishinjuku, Shinjuku-ku, Tokyo 160, Japan
CANADA	Pergamon Press Canada Ltd., Suite No. 271, 253 College Street, Toronto, Ontario, Canada M5T 1R5

Copyright © 1988 Adrian F. Furnham

First edition 1988

Library of Congress Cataloging-in-Publication Data

Furnham, Adrian
Lay theories: everyday understanding of problems in the social sciences/by Adrian F. Furnham.
p. cm—(International series in experimental social psychology; vol. 17)
Bibliography: p.
1. Attribution (Social psychology) 2. Common sense. 3. Belief and doubt. I. Title. II. Series: International series in experimental social psychology: v. 17. HM291.F86 1988
300'.1—dc19   88-9857

British Library Cataloguing in Publication Data

Furnham, Adrian, 1953-
Lay theories: everyday understandings of problems in the social sciences.
(International series in experimental social psychology).
1. Society. Theories
I. Title II. Series
301'.01

ISBN 0-08-032694-3 Hardcover
ISBN 0-08-033970-0 Flexicover

Printed in Great Britain by A. Wheaton & Co. Ltd., Exeter

FOR ALISON

Who holds some very strange theories

The object of all psychology is to give us a totally different idea of the things we know best.

PAUL VALERY *TEL QUEL,* 1943

The point of philosophy is to start with something so simple as to seem not worth stating, and to end with something so paradoxical that no one will believe it.

BERTRAND RUSSELL *LOGIC AND KNOWLEDGE,* 1956

Foreword

Two events led me to become interested in lay theories, the topic of this book. The first occurred while doing my doctorate in Oxford. I joined a small group who were interested in attribution theory, at the time the most popular topic in social psychology. Many of the contributors to the group — Frank Fincham, Miles Hewstone, Jos Jaspars and Mansur Lalljee — criticised the predominantly American research for being too asocial as experiments were concerned specifically with how individuals explain or attribute the causes of other individuals' behaviour (and their own). Many in the group attempted to "socialise" attribution theory in a number of ways by looking at such things as inter-group attributions, focusing on the context of attributions, and by examining the social nature of what is attributed.

I, like everybody else, was expected to give an informal lunch-time seminar. Although I was interested in how situational or contextual features shape explanations for social behaviour, I began to be more interested in how people explain social phenomena. A chance event led me to ask how people explain poverty. Fortunately, I found two other interesting studies in the area, which I partly replicated. I found the topic fascinating and proceeded to expand the research project into how people explained the origins of wealth, and the causes of unemployment. Clear results, social relevance and considerate journal editors led me to continue and extend research to other areas: How do people explain delinquency? What do people think causes alcoholism? Although my data collection was primarily through interview and thence questionnaire, the media of course prove a rich source of ideas. The causes of unemployment, delinquency, drug addiction, mental illness are frequently discussed on chat shows, debated in the columns of the quality press, dictated in party political broadcasts. Whereas most psychological studies, particularly those in attribution theory, had been concerned with the *process* of arriving at explanations, I became more interested in the *content* of these explanations, their structure and functions in particular. I became aware of other people working in this area, some like Sarah Hampson who was interested in lay theories of personality and others like Monika Henderson on how people explain antisocial behaviour.

Obsessionally regular visits to four university libraries, all a stone's throw away from my office, helped in the collection and classification of books, papers and reports that were the basis of this book. When the pile reached over three feet in height it seemed necessary for some proper cataloguing, which of course meant reading the papers. It was Michael Argyle who suggested that I might do a book on the topic and make the reading I was doing more focused.

The second reason I became interested in lay theories originated from my training in, amongst other things, social psychology. I, like all other social psychologists, in general departments of psychology in Britain, have learned to become used to being the scapegoat for the relatively low prestige of psychology as a science in Great Britain. There are many reasons for this, not least of which is the popular interest in topics in social psychology compared with, say, psychophysiology, animal learning or memory. It is relatively easy to see the functional nature of the prejudice against soft psychology, of which, I believe for quite mistaken reasons, social psychology is supposedly the prototype. Added to this, some (mostly mistaken) social psychologists have turned their back on empiricism, so threatening the very basis of the scientific credibility of psychology in general.

Psychologists opposed to social psychology offer a number of explanations for their position: poor theories, trivial research topics, lack of progress, etc. But the criticism most frequently named by psychologist and layman alike is that it is all "common sense". I, therefore, became more and more interested in what is common sense — Who has more or less of it? How is it acquired? Can common sense account for counter-intuitive findings? etc. Discussions with students are particularly helpful in this regard and they frequently force one to attempt to articulate what one means and why. One student, I recall, gave some multiple choice questions — so beloved of the American examination system — derived from a standard introductory social psychology textbook to students not reading psychology. Unlike cognitive psychology, social psychology has not developed too many jargon terms and seldom uses ordinary terms in a specialist or technical way, so it was relatively easy to find questions that were easily understood and free of jargon.

The student was not convinced that her subjects would do very well on the test and I was, frankly, uncertain. In the event they got about half right. Of course this was not a great piece of research — the questions were not carefully selected, the respondents were hardly a representative group of the population as a whole, multiple choice is not always the best method to examine people's beliefs, theories or understanding, etc. But the task left me wondering why they had got some correct and some not? What distinguished a high from a low scorer? What was it about questions that showed floor and ceiling effects? In short, what determines the extent and range of psychological knowledge in the community? We are, of course, all psychologists anyway but some of us are clearly better than others. Of course we are also all economists, lawyers, meteorologists as well. What, therefore, determines the content and accuracy of a person's economic, or medical knowledge and beliefs?

These questions have not, of course, been fully answered, but they still fascinate me. Certainly writing the book has at least clarified for me, and I hope for others as well, what we know and what we do not know about lay theories and beliefs.

ADRIAN FURNHAM
Bloomsbury
London, 1987

Contents

1

Lay and Scientific Theories

1.1 Introduction

Many of the social sciences, such as anthropology, criminology, psychology and sociology, have the unusual advantage of offering an *explicit*, formal, "scientific" explanation for certain behavioural phenomena (i.e. the causes of delinquency, poverty, alcoholism, etc.) while at the same time studying the layman's *implicit*, informal, "non-scientific" explanations for the same behaviour. That is, while some social scientists may be interested in lay theories and beliefs about human behaviour, others research the "actual" causes of this behaviour. Despite the unique advantage to compare and contrast the structure, function and implications of these two types of explanation or theory, these two research areas have, in other disciplines, often developed independently of one another. For instance, in psychology over a decade of research has been dedicated to attribution theory, which is the study of perception or inference of causation, usually held by lay people about their own or others' behaviour. Yet simultaneously, psychologists in abnormal, personality and social psychology have been formulating theories and doing research into the actual causes of people's behaviour.

Of course it may be argued that the two are closely linked as people's theories of the causes of their own and others' behaviour are derived principally from self-observation (Bem, 1967). Hence the observation that psychologists study their own problems, or take up epistemological positions based on their own beliefs or experiences (Furnham *et al.*, 1985). Indeed it is possible to argue that *three*, rather than *two*, types of theories, perspectives or explanations may be involved (Hampson, 1982): the *explicit*, psychological (or social science) perspective; the implicit *lay* perspective (lay people's explanations for others); and the *self*-perspective (lay theories of the self). For the purposes of this book the last two will be considered together.

There are those who would argue that although research into lay causal beliefs about the origins, functions, etc., of various phenomena are interesting and potentially useful in therapy, etc., this research can and should never replace research into the actual causes of behaviour. Empirically tested, explicit formal academic theories of actual behaviour represent the most

1

important, valid, accurate and useful form of knowledge. Indeed behaviourists believe these cognitions (lay theories) to be epiphenomenal. For instance Skinner (1985) writes:

> I accuse cognitive scientists of emasculating the experimental analysis of behaviour by substituting descriptions of settings for the settings themselves and reports of intentions and expectations for behaviour. . . . I accuse cognitive scientists, as I would accuse psychoanalysts, of claiming to explore the depths of human behaviour, of inventing explanatory systems which are admired for a profundity which is more properly called inaccessibility. (p. 300)

Against this tradition are cognitive, clinical and social psychologists who suggest that lay theories — styles or patterns of attribution — both contribute to, and maintain, various behavioural states like depression. Hence many theories in psychology concerned with perceived control (learned helplessness theory; control of reinforcement theory; expectancy valence theory) stress that it is the *perception* of personal control, rather than control *per se*, that determines people's behaviour. Attribution theorists would assume that a particular attribution or style of attribution leads people to act in particular ways. Similarly self-theorists, who take a phenomenological approach, focus exclusively on the individual's unique own perception and interpretation of events. That is, they argue that behaviour which seems puzzling to an observer, may be perfectly understandable only when we know what the situation means to the individual.

The argument between these two approaches will be returned to later. What is perhaps more important is to explain differences between lay and scientific theories.

1.2 Differences between "Lay" and "Scientific" Theories

There are a number of criteria along which lay and scientific theories *may* differ. It should be pointed out that some "lay" theories have many of the positive qualities of scientific theories while some so-called scientific theories bear few of the acceptable criteria of a good theory. That is, it is not a four-legs-good, two-legs-bad problem where the dimensions of all scientific theories are good and those of all lay theories bad. Indeed philosophers of science have attempted to specify the criteria for choosing between "scientific" theories.

Valentine (1982) has listed eight criteria: scope, parsimony, clarity, logical consistency, precision, testability, empirical support, and fruitfulness. Not everyone would agree that they are the best or most relevant criteria, and there would probably be little agreement as to the rank order of those criteria. Furthermore, whereas some observers may agree with this criterion, they may not always agree with its implied other pole. Thus to take Valentine's (1982) first criterion of *scope*, she notes: "Both breadth and completeness of coverage *may* be considered advantageous" (p. 96) which suggests that some might argue that the greater the scope of the theory (in the style of grand theories) the better, while some would reasonably argue the complete opposite. This is not to suggest that there is *no* agreement as to the criteria by which one may judge theories but rather to note that agreement about them is far from perfect.

The following list of criteria is not exhaustive, nor is it meant to represent a rank order. Further it does not necessarily imply that it is always (or, in some cases, even often) true. However it attempts to represent some of the more important criteria that distinguish between a good "scientific" theory and a poor "lay" theory.

(1) Explicitness and Formality

Lay theories are often implicit rather than explicit, with tacit, non-specified assumptions or axioms. On the other hand some (but by no means all) scientific theories are *formal* in the sense that they are set in a logical, internally consistent manner. One of the finest examples of this is Hull's (1952) work which contains 17 postulates with 15 corollaries and 133 theorems. These are set out in a logical, progressive manner, many of which are expressed as mathematical formulae. Others more typically set out their theories in a less formal but nevertheless explicit manner.

By contrast lay theories are rarely explicit and practically never formal. If asked to provide an explanation (based on some theory) lay people can do so but rarely in an explicit formal manner. More often they do not know that their explanations are derived from particular sociopolitical, philosophical or economic traditions or paradigms.

(2) Coherent and Consistent

Because they are rarely, if ever, presented formally, lay theories are frequently ambiguous, incoherent and inconsistent. That is, people can hold two mutually incompatible or contradictory ideas or beliefs at the same time and not be particularly troubled by that inconsistency. On the other hand, scientific theories should be, and usually are, both coherent and consistent. They are coherent in the sense that they usually apply to a specific domain of phenomena and make propositions that "fit together". They are consistent in the sense that they are not mutually contradictory. Of course it has been pointed out that some writers contradict themselves over time, as their theories develop and change, but rarely does any acceptable scientific theory have inconsistent or contradictory theories within it. Indeed, psychologists have long been obsessed with balance, consistency and dissonance, and they have developed an array of consistent theories of consistency to explain how, when and why people are inconsistent in their beliefs.

Lay people on the other hand often hold mutually inconsistent beliefs. For instance they might endorse the work and leisure ethics simultaneously (Furnham, 1984a) or believe in both nationalisation and privatisation (Furnham, 1985a). One may argue that these "superficial" inconsistencies may be resolved at a specific level — for instance one may believe in the nationalisation of vital industries (transport, energy, defence) and the privatisation of service industries (communications, health, etc.) hence resolving this apparent inconsistency. Whilst this may be occasionally true it seems that people are frequently made uncomfortable by inconsistencies, though they are rarely aware of them. That is, lay people are infrequently aware of the inconsistencies, incompatibilities, non sequiturs in their pet theories of behaviour.

(3) Verification vs Falsification

Although not universally accepted, many epistemologists accept Popper's principle of falsification as the criterion of science. On the other hand, the layman often seeks for verification rather than falsification. To put it another way, lay theories often rely on principles of inductivism while scientific theories usually rely on deductivism.

For Popper and many others inductivism and the search after verification, which is very often the "method" of lay people, is unscientific. Inductivism suggests that people must accumulate evidence (by observation or experiment) and thereafter make inferences or posit theoretical statements. But for deductivists no amount of accumulated evidence that all A's are B (blacks are musical; extroverts are sociable) proves that this is true. According to the principle of falsifiability, a theory must be able to be disproved and holds until it is disproved. For the deductivist, hunch and common sense, as well as experiment and observation must be converted into hypotheses which, once the strict conditions for their falsification have been established by deductive logic, must be tested by a sustained search for *negative* instances.

There is considerable evidence to suggest that in attempting to establish certain facts lay people are nearly always inductivist in that they search for confirmatory rather than disconfirmatory evidence (see Chapter 2). Whilst this may be true of the initial stages in scientific research, it is infrequently the case once theories have become established.

(4) Cause and Consequence

Lay theories often confuse cause and effect. That is, because lay theories are so often correlational in nature they cannot infer cause, yet frequently do so. Lay people frequently see a relationship between two variables — an increase in television viewing and an increase in delinquency; a decrease in church attendance and an increase in divorce, etc. — and then infer unidirectional cause based on an implicit theory. As is frequently pointed out, observing a relationship between A and B may be due to A causing B; B causing A; bidirectional causation between A and B; the relationship between A and B being moderated by a third variable C which indirectly relate to both A and B.

Of course, scientists are like laymen and frequently fall into this trap or tend to prefer causal explanations based on correlational results to support their pet theories. This is particularly noticeable in the case of moderator variables. For instance, Eysenck (1965) has argued that a correlation, albeit well established, between smoking and disease does not itself prove a causal connection. For instance it may be that people who are genetically predisposed to smoke are also genetically predisposed to certain diseases or that smokers have different "lifestyles" to non-smokers so that though chronologically the same age they are biologically older and hence more at risk. Though hotly contested this moderator variable approach is quite reasonable and a good example of the weaknesses of inferring cause simply from correlation.

(5) Content vs Process

This issue will be more fully discussed in the next chapter, though some mention may be made here. Many academic theories are process rather than content oriented whereas the opposite is frequently true of lay theories. Consider theories of human nature. Academic theories of the aetiology of personality and individual differences are frequently concerned with processes whereby people tend to differ one from another on various dimensions — intellectual or cognitive reactions, emotional responses, etc. Most lay theories, on the other hand, are content oriented in the sense that they are primarily descriptive of types or categories. One can, in fact, observe this in the development of thinking about personality. Most early attempts were essentially attempts at taxonomies based on observation. Some people have subsequently been supported by empirical evidence (for instance the ideas of Kant and Wundt) while others have not (like much of the work of phrenology). Further, often early content oriented theories are tautological as they do not attempt to describe the process whereby the types arise.

Again not all lay theories are content oriented, and not all scientific theories are process oriented, as we shall see. These are not mutually exclusive. However, it may be fair to point out that as description frequently precedes explanation and lay theory frequently precedes scientific theory, lay theories are often descriptive and content oriented while scientific theories are explanatory and process oriented.

(6) Internal (Individualistic) vs External (Situational)

According to Heider (1958) people are the prototypes of origins: that is, most often seen as the causes of events. In other words people generally underestimate the importance of external or situational factors in explaining behaviour. This has been described by Ross (1977) as the fundamental attribution error which refers to the fact that lay people frequently infer broad personal dispositions (traits) and expect the consistency of behaviour (across situations) and stability of behaviour (over time) across widely disparate situations and contexts. In other words, when attempting to explain *others'* social behaviour, lay people tend to ignore or play down situational forces and constraints preferring to locate the "causes" of human behaviour in an individual's personality, motives etc.

The layman then is a psychologist (because he/she focuses on individual behaviour) rather than a sociologist (because he/she focuses on societal or structural forces). Consider the example of vocational choice. Sociologists see vocational choice as constrained and dictated by social forces like class, education, race, etc. Psychologists, on the other hand, like the layman, tend to focus on needs, personality and other internal motives in the choice of jobs. Whereas a lot of sociology attempts to explain individual behaviour in terms of macro and micro sociological forces, psychology (more personality than social) attempts to explain individual behaviour in terms of individual pathology, genetics and learning. It is not surprising, therefore, that psychologists are more interested in heredity than sociologists.

(7) General vs Specific

Some theories tend to rely on a few superordinate concepts or axioms which are very broad constructs that can "explain" a wide variety of types of human behaviour. This is not the same dimension as simple vs complex as it is quite possible that general theories are complicated and specific theories simple. An example of a general approach may be Eysenck's concept of introversion–extraversion which may relate to behaviours as diverse as learning style, mate selection, drug use, sexual experience, etc. These broad-band theories may be contrasted with narrow-band and specific theories which do not attempt such complicated endeavours.

Whereas it may seem that academic theories tend to be specific and lay theories general, Jaspars (1983) has argued the opposite. He found that through the logical inductive inference process people are able to offer clear theories or explanations for specific phenomena, but that people do not generalise. It is possible that prior expectations and various motivational determinants shape people's explanations and theories rather than a reasonable generalisation from the specific to the general.

What may be occurring, then, is that lay people formulate theories or explanations for specific phenomena based on the information that they receive or seek but do not generalise to abstract theoretical principles. That is, there is no "bottom-up", "data-to-theory" process whereby specific observations build up into a *general* theory, but smaller "mini-theories" for very specific events.

(8) Strong vs Weak

Eysenck (1960) has distinguished between weak and strong theories in science. Strong theories have a number of identifiable characteristics. They are based on numerous accurate observations made by many different people. They bring together various sub-fields in which quantitative laws have been discovered; the phenomena in question were relatively clear-cut and unambiguous; mathematical relations were not of a very complex order; and predictions were straightforward and precise. Also strong theories have interdependency, in that it is rarely possible to change one postulate without changing others. Weak theories do not share these characteristics, but are useful in directing research to problematic areas. Weak theories frequently do not have precise, trustworthy data, hence they direct scientists to accumulate good evidence. Thus, every strong theory probably started out as weak, but obviously not every weak theory necessarily becomes strong. The fact that the evidence for weak theories is poor and occasionally equivocal does not necessarily mean that the theory is wrong and should be rejected. Eysenck (1960) writes:

> The best that can be expected is a set of low correlations, usually in the expected direction, but occasionally directly opposed to prediction; on such a foundation we can then begin to erect the infinitely complex set of laws and functional relationships, concepts and definitions, which will ultimately, shorn of ambivalences and ambiguities, constitute that proper science of behaviour and personality which so obviously does not exist at the present time, except possibly as a foundation for a palimpset. (p. 315)

It may be argued that few existing theories in the social sciences could be described as strong, though nearly all aspire to it. Clearly most lay theories are weak and the majority weaker than the explicit academic theories that exist.

There may well be other dimensions upon which one could differentiate lay and scientific theories, e.g. parsimoniousness, operationalisation. But rather than stress the difference between the two it may be as wise to stress similarities. Lay theories *overlap* with scientific theories; they *function* in similar ways, indeed the one may be seen as an outgrowth of the other. Lay people can, and do, formulate theories that are explicit, coherent and falsifiable, as do "scientists" who are frequently far from infallible in their own model-building.

1.3 The Study of Lay Theories of Human Behaviour

The study of lay implicit beliefs has many facets. Indeed these facets do not differ greatly from those of people studying or reviewing professional or explicit beliefs. For instance Pervin (1984) has identified the four crucial features of all theories of personality as structure, process, growth and development, and psychopathology which provide a way of comparing and contrasting different theories. There are a number of important areas of research in the psychology of lay theories of human behaviour.

(1) The Aetiology or Development of Lay Beliefs

It is impossible to understand fully the nature of lay theories without understanding their origin. Whereas developmental psychologists have always been interested in how, when and why children learn about physical concepts of mass, time and space, and to a lesser extent about how they come to understand aspects of society (economics, politics) very little work has been done on children's understanding of individual needs, motives, emotions, etc, i.e. meta-learning. Some have speculated on the origin of lay beliefs. For instance Sarbin *et al.* (1960) has listed four main sources: induction or experience; construction or inference and deductions from observations; analogy or extrapolation from specific encounters; and authority or acceptance of ideas from others, the media, etc. Although there has been some work on children's moral and cognitive development which has attempted to identify stages of development there is no parsimonious theory which can account for why people hold different, contradictory or similar lay beliefs. What is needed is to establish which socialisation experiences and maturational processes contribute to the establishment of which specific, stable beliefs about human behaviour. Equally, it is important to know how these beliefs develop and change once they have been established. Some of the most promising work in this field has taken place in the fields of economics and politics (see Chapters 6 and 8). Stacey (1978, 1985) has considered both political and economic socialisation in Western societies and has attempted to define when children acquire these concepts and what socialisation experiences are important.

Clearly much needs to be done on children's and adolescents' beliefs about other individuals and the society in which they live.

(2) The Relationship between Lay Beliefs

Just as reviewers have attempted to classify formal academic theories of personality into various categories *and* specify the relationships between them, so it is possible to examine the relationship between various lay belief systems. Furnham and Lewis (1986) have noted that there are three equally important but distinct areas of research on the relationship between lay beliefs concerning different issues. The first is the relationship between specific beliefs within an individual or group. For instance, do people who hold radical economic beliefs have different views about the "nature of man" from those who hold conservative economic beliefs (Furnham *et al.* 1985). People may also hold various beliefs about different aspects of social life whose implications or assumptions are mutually contradictory, but not realise that. One may therefore look at the relationships between lay beliefs on conceptually related topics, looking for contiguity, overlap and contradiction. Thirdly, one may look at the relationship between lay beliefs and behaviour. The vast body of psychological literature on the link between attitudes and behaviour suggests that this is a complicated and subtle relationship but that certain predictions may be made.

There exist many excellent attempts to discriminate between and taxonomise various lay beliefs in specific areas and then see how they interrelate as well as relate to other issues. Good examples are Forsyth's (1980) work on ethical, ideological and moral judgement and Paulus's (1983) work on spheres of perceived control.

(3) The Function of Lay Beliefs

Much of cognitive social psychology is concerned with how people make sense of the social world. That is, various belief systems (locus of control, just world, Protestant work ethic beliefs) are said to serve to make the world a stable, orderly and predictable place. The function of these beliefs is probably to establish a cause-and-effect relationship between phenomena, which in turn enables one to apportion blame, praise or responsibility. For instance, Lerner (1980) argues that just world beliefs are functional and essential, in fact they are ways of adapting to a world in which one feels relatively helpless by attributing absolute virtue to the legal system. He notes:

> Much of the previous discussion portrays the "belief in a just world" as inextricably bound up with the person's motives and goals. People want to and have to believe they live in a just world so that they can go about their daily lives with a sense of trust, hope, and confidence in their future. If it is true that people want or need to believe that they live in a world where people get what they deserve, then it is not surprising that they will find ways, other things being equal, to interpret events to fit this belief. (p. 14).

Similarly Gans (1972) has proposed a functional analysis of poverty which implies that the existence of, and explanations for, poverty fulfil a number of important functions. For instance the poor may be labelled and punished as deviants in order to uphold the legitimacy of dominant social norms. Also poverty helps to guarantee the status of the non-poor, in that they remain a relatively permanent measuring rod for status comparison.

Functionalist theories, though somewhat unfashionable, provide useful insights into why people maintain and change their lay beliefs. It has been objected that functional theories are teleological, and thus incur the logical error of placing the cause of an event after it in time. However, this takes place in any self-regulating system with a negative feedback loop. For example, in a thermostat the behaviour of the system leads to the goal of a certain temperature being attained, though the goal was actually set before this temperature was reached. There is no mystery once the mechanism has been described. It has been objected that functionalism encourages or reflects a conservative bias by emphasising the positive functions of every aspect of the status quo. Advocates of social change can try to bring about alternative institutions to meet the same needs, or to meet them better, and to avoid areas of dysfunction in society. Functionalism does, however, contain a warning for reformers — that existing institutions may be serving hidden functions, and it is important to understand these hidden functions before attempting change. Thus, if lay beliefs serve unspecified or not well understood functions they may well be very difficult to change.

(4) The Stability and Consistency of Lay Beliefs

The question of how and when individual lay beliefs change is of considerable interest to psychologists, advertisers and politicians. The temporal stability of both micro- and macro-sociological beliefs has important implications for how these beliefs may be changed. The stability of beliefs refers to their similarity over time, while consistency of beliefs refers to their similarity across situations. Thus the stability and consistency of lay beliefs about social behaviour have implications for how they are measured. For instance, if lay beliefs are fairly inconsistent and influenced greatly by the context in which they are gathered (e.g. market interview) it is important to make reference to the context when evaluating the evidence. Similarly, if they are relatively stable over time, results from surveys and interviews may be safely generalised to predict future beliefs.

If cultural factors influence lay beliefs, changes in the culture — e.g. it becoming more or less permissive — may well affect many lay belief systems. People's beliefs not only change over time but may be expressed differently in different situations. People may describe their understanding of how a particular feature or process (e.g. influenza, inflation) relates quite differently to an adult and to a child. Also, depending on the nature of the person, he or she might express beliefs and attitudes that he or she feels most congruent with, or attractive to, the people in the situation rather than what he or she actually believes (Snyder, 1979). What needs to be researched is what factors account for each lay belief, about human behaviour, being either stable or unstable over time, and consistent or inconsistent across situations.

(5) The Consequences of Lay Beliefs

Lay beliefs — like attitudes and explanations — do have consequences for the development of other beliefs and for behaviour. Central to a great deal of the early psychological work on attitudes is the concept of balance. Balance, congruity and dissonance each assume that people are motivated to be, and to appear, consistent, while an awareness of imbalance or unconsistency is tension producing and not easily tolerated, so that attitude change is a principal tool for resolving inconsistencies. Thus if one major core belief changes, for whatever reason, others related to it are also likely to change. For instance, Furnham and Bland (1983) found, as predicted, that Protestant work ethic beliefs are closely related to more general conservative social attitudes. They also argued that if work ethic beliefs are on the decline one might expect conservative social attitudes to change likewise, and as there is no evidence of the latter one should not necessarily infer the occurrence of the former.

Secondly, lay beliefs have behavioural consequences. As Furnham and Lewis (1986) have noted, lay economic beliefs can actually affect economic variables just as much as economic variables may affect economic beliefs. Consumer sentiment has consequences for consumer demand, in that if people believe high inflation is likely to continue they may spend rather than save and have high wage demands, which partly accounts for the continuance of high inflation. Similarly Katona (1971) found that public pessimism about the economy showed a sharp decline about 6–9 months *before* a major recession. Of course it is impossible to tease out cause from correlation when examining lay beliefs and behaviour and it is probable that some form of reciprocal determinism operates.

Finally, lay beliefs may have other consequences. For instance, they may affect a person's self-concept and/or the way they interpret their own behaviour.

(6) The Changing of Lay Beliefs

Central to social psychological research on attitudes and beliefs are theories of attitude change and consequent suggestions as to the best methods of changing them. There are a number of different approaches including learning and reinforcement theories based on behaviouristic ideas of stimulus–response learning, social judgement and consistency theories which stem from Gestalt tradition, and functional theories which place most emphasis on human needs. These theories place different emphases on both the causes and methods of change, and are in large part mutually exclusive. Applied research in the area of racism and religious prejudice has revealed the difficulty of attitude change because of the complexity of the process and the number of internal and external factors involved. Yet there are cases of quite sudden and surprising change in beliefs as a result of various happenings. Sudden inflation, the collapse of a bank, increasing unemployment, sudden personal wealth, may each serve to change lay economic beliefs. There are many examples of how religious experiences change people's lay belief systems.

(7) The Manipulation of Lay Beliefs

There is a wide range of groups of people interested in changing lay beliefs about the economy, their own health and minority groups. Politicians, advertisers, health educators and pressure groups all attempt to change beliefs and behaviours to suit their own ends. Often their aims are to change specific beliefs or to encourage a change in one particular behaviour (e.g. how to vote, what to purchase). However other groups are interested in changing people's entire theories about general phenomena. There is a whole range of techniques known to laymen, advertisers, salesmen, etc., which have been shown to be successful — in appropriate circumstances — for this task. These include ingratiation, conformity pressure, using multiple requests (i.e. foot-in-the-door approach and door-in-the-face tactic), inducing guilt or pity, etc. The manipulation of lay beliefs may also be observed in extreme situations of brainwashing, torture, etc.

(8) The Structure of Lay Beliefs

Many social scientists have attempted to classify belief systems into discrete categories or along various dimensions. For instance Furnham and Lewis (1986) have suggested that lay economic beliefs may fall nicely into four quadrants, described by two dimensions: individualistic–collectivistic; tough-minded–tender-minded. The first dimension would reflect right-wing, conservative capitalism, free enterprise beliefs vs left-wing, radical, socialist, state control beliefs, while the second dimension would reflect economic policy implications with tough-minded beliefs emphasising state, legal or political action, while tender-minded beliefs would emphasise passive, consensual or conventional, rather than interventionist policies. The terms "wet" and "dry", already in current usage in Britain, may be used interchangeably with tough- and tender-minded views to avoid confusion with Eysenck's work.

Eysenck (1981) however has developed a more general system looking at the structure of social attitudes in terms of two dimensions. His system is set out in Fig. 1.1, which shows how attitudes to a wide range of issues fall nicely into a two-dimensional structure. There are, of course, other dimensional solutions for other beliefs. Despite numerous differences and subtle distinctions in the structure of lay beliefs there appear to be many common solutions.

(9) Lay Beliefs about Social Behaviour vs Social Scientists' Beliefs about Lay Behaviour

As has already been discussed, whether thay make it explicit or not, many academic social scientists hold various beliefs about the behaviour (and beliefs) of lay people. Economists devise sophisticated models of the economy based upon axiomatic beliefs about an individual's purchasing, saving, etc., strategies. Similarly health educators devise instructive posters and other material based on what they think lay people believe about their health.

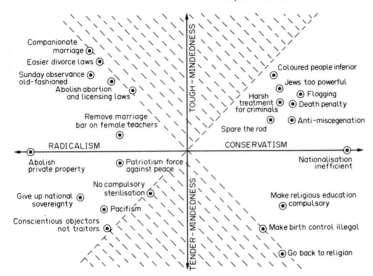

FIG. 1.1. Distribution of Attitudes with Respect to Tough-Mindedness and Radicalism. Reprinted with permission from Eysenck, H. (Ed.) *The Psychological Basis of Ideology* Lancaster: MTP Press.

Politicians hope to present themselves in accordance with the belief systems of prospective voters.

There has been very little work on the reasons for social scientists' views of human nature and human behaviour though these are often implicit in the schools of thought within various academic disciplines.

1.4 Some Definitional Distinctions

If one is to discuss lay theories of human behaviour it is important to describe the features of a theory and distinguish between similar concepts such as theory, model and law. Indeed there are a whole range of possibly relevant terms which may be used. These include: adage, aphorism, attribution, axiom, belief, corollary, creed, definition, dictum, doctrine, explanation, guess, heuristic, hunch, hypothesis, idea, law, maxim, metaphor, model, motto, observation, paradigm, postulate, principle, proverb, rule, rumination, theory, truism, etc. Although dictionary definitions may prove interesting they are seldom very useful in making careful working distinctions. For instance consider Chambers' *New English Dictionary* definitions of some of the more commonly used terms:

Hypothesis: A proposition or principle put forth or stated (without any reference to its correspondence with fact) merely as a basis for reasoning or argument, or as a premise from which to draw a conclusion; a supposition. A supposition or conjecture put forth to account for known facts, especially in the sciences, a provisional supposition from which to draw conclusions that shall be in accordance with known facts and which serve as a starting-point for further investigation by which it may be proved or disproved and the true theory arrived at.

Law: In the sciences of observation a theoretical principle deduced from particular facts, applicable to a defined group or class of phenomena, and expressable by the statement that a particular phenomenon always occurs if certain conditions be present.

Model: A description of structure; something that accurately resembles something else; an archetypal image or pattern.

Paradigm: A pattern, an example, exemplar.

Principle: A fundamental truth or proposition, on which many others depend; a primary truth comprehending or forming the basis of, various subordinate truths; a general statement or tenet forming the basis of, or ground of, or held to be essential to, a system of thought or belief; a fundamental assumption forming the basis of a chain of reasoning.

Theory: A scheme or system of ideas or statements held as an explanation or account of a group of facts or phenomena; a hypothesis that has been confirmed or established by observation or experiment and is propounded or accepted as accounting for the known facts; a statement of what are held to be the general laws, principles, or causes of something known or observed.

From the few terms selected it appears that these may be arranged in some sequential order reflecting developments. Hence a hypothesis, which may contain a model or paradigm, precedes or is part of a theory which may or may not develop into a principle or law. Eysenck (1981) in fact spelt out this relationship (see Fig. 1.2)

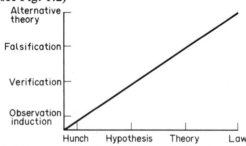

FIG. 1.2. Demarcation Theories of Science: A Unified Point of View.
Reprinted with permission from Eysenck, H. (1981) *A Model for Personality.*
Berlin: Springer-Verlag.

He writes:

At an early stage of development, we are reduced to fact-collecting on the basis of vague hunches, serendipitous discoveries of unforeseen regularities and inductive generalisations. When sufficient data have been collected along these lines, we are in the position of being able to put forward hypotheses of relatively small compass, and now the emphasis shifts to verification; unless we can verify these hypotheses, at least within the confines of certain parameter values, it is unlikely that they will be pursued further or interest other scientists. Given that this stage is successfully passed, we enter the realm of theory-making proper, and now falsification becomes the most important aspect of our experimental work. When a given theory is firmly established, it becomes a scientific law, and now the paradigm has become settled; only a revolution, sparked off by the accumulation of anomalous findings, and the emergence of an alternative theory, will dethrone such a theory. Thus what constitutes a scientific approach will depend on the degree of development of a particular field; too rigorous a demand at too early a stage may well prevent the proper development of a discipline from ever taking place, just as too lenient a requirement at a later stage of development will prevent the discipline from growing up and assuming its rightful place. (p.2)

Earlier Hull (1943) has attempted to spell out the nature of scientific theory. He argued, from his strongly hypothetico-deductive principle thus:

> Scientific theory in its ideal form consists of a hierarchy of logically deduced propositions which parallel all the observed empirical relationships composing a science. This logical structure is derived from a relatively small number of self-consistent primary principles called postulates, when taken in conjunction with relevant antecedent conditions. . . . Empirical observation, supplemented by shrewd conjecture, is the main source of the primary principles or postulates of a science. Such formulations, when taken in various combinations together with relevant antecedent conditions, yield inferences of theorems, of which some may agree with the empirical outcome of the conditions in question, and some may not. Primary propositions yielding logical deductions which consistently agree with the observed empirical outcome are retained, whereas those which disagree are rejected or modified. As the sifting of this trial-and-error process continues, there gradually emerges a limited series of primary principles whose joint implications are progressively more likely to agree with relevant observations. Deductions made from these surviving postulates, while never absolutely certain, do at length become highly trustworthy. (pp. 381–382)

However it should be pointed out that there is no accepted agreement as to the use of these various terms. For instance Valentine (1982) has provided rather different definitions for various terms: a *hypothesis* is a tentative law; a *postulate* is an assumption of a theory not intended to be subjected to empirical test; a *system* is a general theory plus metatheoretical recommendations; a *law* refers to a relatively well established statement of regular predictable relations among empirical variables. She appears to be satisfied with Marx's (1976) definition of a *theory* as a "provisional explanatory proposition, or set of propositions, concerning some natural phenomena and consisting of symbolic representations of (1) the observed relationships among (measured) events, (2) the mechanisms or structures presumed to underlie such relationships or (3) inferred relationships and underlying mechanisms" (Valentine, 1982, p. 90). Similarly she quotes Simon and Newell (1956) to distinguish models from theories: the former (models) are (a) useful rather than true (heuristic aids, rather than complete descriptions), (b) less data sensitive (disconfirming evidence is damaging to a theory but not necessarily to a model) and (c) they are more susceptible to Type II errors (more liable to make false claims).

The use of these "epistemological" terms is open to fad and fashion. Furthermore certain terms may become linked with specific people or schools. Thus the term paradigm seems inextricably linked with Kuhn's ideas.

There are therefore no hard-and-fast definitions in this area. Thus terms like model and paradigm or principle and theory may be used interchangeably by some writers. Philosophers of science on the other hand in an attempt to bring order into this area have attempted to taxonomise or specify different types of models, theories, etc. For instance Marx (1970) has distinguished between three types of theory (depending on the relationship between theory and data: *deductive* theory — theoretical generalisations are induced from observations and predictions of future observations are deduced from theoretical hypotheses; *functional* theory which is a restatement of the data, with both data and theory being given equal weight; and *inductive* theory where theoretical statements are simply summaries of empirical findings. But as most reviewers and lexicographers note, "theories" have many meanings. Lacey (1976) in his *Dictionary of Philosophy* has noted:

> Theory has various meanings: (i) One or more hypotheses or lawlike statements (either of first two senses), regarded as speculative. (ii) A law about unobservables like electrons or evolution, sometimes called a theory because evidence about unobservables is felt to be inevitably inconclusive. (iii) A unified system of laws or hypotheses, with explanatory force (not merely like a railway timetable). (iv) A field of study (e.g. in philosophy; theory of knowledge, logical theory). These senses sometimes shade into each other. (p. 110)

Another way of looking at definitions is to consider their function. Thus Selltiz *et al.* (1959) note that "the intention of a theory in modern science is to summarize existing knowledge, to provide an explanation for observed events and relationships, and to predict the occurrence of as yet unobserved events and relationships on the basis of explanatory principles embodied in the theory" (p. 481). Valentine (1982) notes that theories serve to summarise and organise data by bringing order and coherence to material. They also are attempts at explanation and serve a heuristic function of guiding research. However, she does note that some (particularly Skinner) have put forward a case against theories, arguing that they create new problems by giving a false sense of security.

1.5 How Does One Measure, Assess or Investigate Lay Theories?

The social sciences as a whole offer a plethora of methodologies for studying social behaviour, each with its own distinct advantages and disadvantages. Some of the more powerful techniques, however, such as laboratory and field experiments, seem less useful for looking at lay theories than other methods.

Different methodologies may be profitably used to investigate lay theories of human behaviour, such as those based on *self-report*, those derived from *test data* and those actually concerned with observing *behaviour*, as well as others. These methodologies are by no means exhaustive or mutually exclusive, and may well overlap considerably. Other methods include ethno-methodology and ethogenics

(1) Self-Report

An obvious way to "get at" lay theories of behaviour is through listening to, or recording the answers to, specific questions. This may be done through questionnaires and surveys (i.e. pen-and-paper exercises) as well as interviews (i.e. face-to-face interviews). Each may differ according to the amount, type and quality of information available, though, of course, one may use more than one methodology at the same time. Therefore, as Furnham (1983a) and Forgas *et al.* (1982) did, one can simply ask "What causes people to become rich?" and do a content analysis on the answers, which may or may not reflect theories; but they also gave people various explanations (classified *a priori*) which they were requested to rate. Both yielded comparable data.

The use of questionnaires with either open-ended or closed questions has obvious advantages and disadvantages. Some of those that have been psychometrically assessed and may be useful for investigating general lay beliefs about human nature may be seen in Chapter 2. Questionnaire measures have, however, been constantly criticised, sometimes justly and sometimes not. Essentially there appear to be four criticisms of frequently used questionnaires, check lists and interview schedules. The first is the problem of *response sets* — social desirability bias, faking good or bad, acquiescing with their perceived demands of the researcher, etc. Though this is an extremely frequent objection aimed particularly at personality inventories, and may well be far less relevant when investigating lay theories. In any event, the extent to which response sets threaten the validity of self-report measures has been challenged by Furnham (1986a). The second objection is the limitation of self-report data in that people may *tell more than they know* (Nisbett and Wilson, 1977) or simply be unable to report on certain features such as their needs, motives, etc. Once again it is not always clear to what extent this objection applies to studies on lay theories except, perhaps, the cognitive processes involved in their maintenance. Thirdly, there are inevitable *sampling problems* when using self-report measures such as questionnaires (but not interviews) which are by definition limited to the literate. Indeed interviews are also biased to the articulate. Thus, better educated, higher socioeconomic classes may be over-researched while illiterate or marginally articulate people are neglected. It may well be that the latter group holds qualitatively as well as quantitatively different theories that do not get sufficiently researched. Finally, there is always the problem in standard questionnaires of imposing the researchers' own cognitive constructs on to the respondents, rather than allowing them to reveal the range and content of their *own constructs*. This is a well-known objection, favoured by followers of Kelly (1955) and his personal construct theory.

Once again, this is probably less true of studies in lay theories, where open-ended questions are frequently used in which subjects may respond entirely in their own words.

Some researchers such as Harré (1984) would aim to gather "accounts" which are full and free descriptions of social episodes which could be used to reveal people's understanding of the world in general.

(2) Test Data

A number of different types of tests may be used to attempt to ascertain lay theories or knowledge. Consider, for instance, the possibility of using studies of *memory*. Many studies have supported the selective recall hypothesis which suggests that people remember information better if it is congruent with their attitudes, because the attitudes or beliefs act as a type of organising framework which tends to promote the encoding and retrieval of attitude-support material. This has been demonstrated with religious, political and sexual stimulus material, though not all attempts have supported the hypotheses. A recent study by Furnham and Singh (1987) tested the hypothesis by getting males and females to listen to a tape that listed 30 "facts" about sex differences (15 pro-female; 15 pro-male). They were also tested on their attitudes towards women. In accordance with the hypothesis they found that males and those subjects with more negative attitudes towards women, recalled (free and cued) less pro- and more anti-female items and vice versa.

Thus, by giving lay people material to process (read, watch, listen to, etc.) and then asking then to recall as much as they can of it, various organising schema may become apparent which shape other theories.

A second (relatively obscure) test method involves asking people to *deliberately dissimilate* in tests (that is, not necessarily give the correct or preferred answers but the one they expect a particular type of person to give). For instance, if a person is asked to respond to a test as they believe an accountant might, and their resultant profile is that of an obsessive, boring, non-spontaneous person, one may argue that this is the stereotype the respondent has about accountants. Similarly, if, when asked to fake good respondents, they produce a healthy, adjusted, intelligent, etc., profile, one may argue that they have understood the underlying dimension investigated by the researcher (Furnham, 1986a; McCarthy and Furnham, 1986). Similarly, if a person can *predict* their score accurately on a test (of personality, ability, skill, etc.) one may conclude that they are familiar with the concept being tested.

Thus if you asked non-alcoholics to "pretend to be an alcoholic" and then interview them regarding their drinking habits and motives, as well as other features of their social behaviour, one might elicit the full subtlety and complexity of their beliefs and theories about alcoholism. Furthermore, if they were required to predict their score on some alcoholism related test, this too may yield interesting insights into their theories of the manifestations of alcoholism.

There are numerous other ways in which test data might be used to investigate lay theories. These include using selective attention tests, measures of preconscious processing. A method which appears to be attracting more attention and is highly relevant in this field is the development of prototypes. Horowitz *et al.* (1981a,b) devised a method for developing prototypes of depression, which change with experience and are theoretical standards against which examples can be measured. Each will have, of course, different advantages and disadvantages regarding the quality and type of information on lay theories.

(3) Observing Behaviour

Because of the problems associated with self-report some researchers have preferred to observe behaviour and infer attitudes, beliefs and theories from it. Thus, if a person is known to be attempting to lose weight and substantially reduces his or her intake of carbohydrates, one may infer that he or she believes carbohydrates are fattening. However, one cannot know much more than this, which itself may not be very informative. For instance, one cannot know whether the person believes carbohydrates are more or less fattening than proteins or animal fats; indeed one cannot even know whether the person knows what carbohydrates are or if he or she is just following instructions from a book as to what to stop eating. Simple observation of behaviour may not be very useful at all in researching lay theories for human behaviour, particularly as the relationship between attitudes and behaviour is known to be weak and mediated by many other factors.

Participant observation on the other hand may be much more useful, as one can observe contextual and social determinants of behaviour over time, which may lead to many more cues as to the nature of lay theories. However, as participant observation nearly always involves direct interaction between researcher and respondent, it could be seen to share all the advantages and disadvantages of the self-report methods.

It is, then, not surprising that most of the research reported in this book concerns self-report data.

1.6 Conclusion

In an attempt to make sense of the social and physical world to see it as stable, orderly, predictable and understandable, people develop theories or arrive at explanations for phenomena salient to their lives. Through observation, exposure to others, the media and personal experience people become familiar with "how things work". These theories — or belief systems — are frequently different from the sort of theories one may find in the physical or social sciences or the humanities, partly because they fulfil different functions.

There are enormous individual differences in the quality and quantity of theories that people hold. These differences occur partly as a function of experience (education, interests) but also as a function of necessity, e.g. farmers no doubt have more complex meteorological theories than shop-assistants, young parents more varied theories of child development than those choosing not to have children. Scientists and other academics, whose professions involve the refinement and development of theories, may be highly sophisticated in the exposition and testing of theories in their own area or discipline, but naive in their understanding of other phenomena. Hence, a brilliant physicist may have highly simplistic, even misleading notions about the causes of alcoholism, or the best predictors of academic excellence. Thus, one may be at once both naive and sophisticated, complex and simple. In other words a person may be a "scientist" with regard to theory about certain phenomenon, but a "lay person" in other areas. It is therefore not the aim of this book to draw clear distinctions between scientific method and theory (whether in the physical or social sciences) and lay theories. Nor can this be a discourse on the philosophy of science and distinctions between the natural and social sciences.

It has been argued that the distinction between lay and scientific theories is by no means clear. Various distinctions were made which may be useful in clarifying what may constitute a scientific, as opposed to a lay theory, though it should be admitted that many theories accepted as scientific do not fulfil these criteria, while many lay theories do. It was also suggested that the study of lay theories merited scientific research and various aspects of these theories were developed. For instance, it was argued that lay theories were both held and developed by people because they fulfilled various functions. Hewstone (1983) has suggested three functions of lay theories: the control function (to achieve some control through understanding of cause and effects in the physical and social world), the self-esteem function (to protect, validate and enhance feelings of personal worth and effectiveness) and self-presentation function (to gain public approval and avoid embarrassment). Thus it is quite possible that different theories fulfil different functions and misleading to suggest that all lay theories fulfil the same function.

Curiously, Maslow (1969) has listed what he calls cognitive pathologies which are "anxiety-instigated clinically observed expressions of our needs to know". It is suggested that these cognitive needs, such as intolerance of ambiguity a compulsive need for certainty and premature generalisation lead to the development of poor theories. For Maslow (1969):

> The path to the full truth is a rocky one. Full knowing is difficult. This is true not only for the layman but also for the scientist. The main difference between him and the layman is that he has enlisted on this search for truth deliberately, willingly, and consciously and that he then proceeds to learn as much as he can about techniques and ethics of truth-seeking. Indeed,

science in general can be considered a technique with which fallible men try to outwit their own human propensities to fear the truth, to avoid it, and to distort it. (p. 29)

Harré (1984) too is sceptical about the empirical methods used by psychologists and the theories they derive from them.

2

Common Sense and Human Nature

2.1 Introduction

Over the last decade or so, social psychology has been dominated by the study of social cognition which stresses that the way to understand complex social behaviour is through studying how people process, represent and utilise information about themselves, others and the social world. Cognitive social psychology also assumes that these processes are dependent on various other factors such as emotional states, motivation, contextual factors, as well as thinking styles or preferences.

There appear to be two basic strands to this research. The first concerns social categorisation and knowledge. Perhaps the best way to summarise this approach is to list the five general questions that Cantor *et al.* (1982) believe to be important in the area:

1. The Multiple Focus question: What are the various different overarching schemes that people use to organise and categorise social experience?
2. The Accessibility question: Are some organisations and constructions very accessible and frequently and easily used to structure and encode social experience?
3. The Structure question: How orderly, complex, and concensually agreed upon are the internal, cognitive representations of social experience?
4. The Content question: What kinds of information do we represent and store about social experience?
5. The Function question: How and under what conditions is social knowledge used in generating and planning social behaviour? (p. 33)

The second area of research — attribution theory — is concerned with how or why ordinary people explain events. Various theories have been developed and extensively tested, and various criticisms have been made of them.

Perhaps the two most relevant criticisms of the theories concern how much actual thinking or processing the layman does and whether the logical models developed are impossibly complex and sophisticated for the lay thinker. As there is so much evidence for error and bias sophistication in everyday thinking makes most models appear inappropriate. For instance, Hansen (1980) suggests that people make inferences and derive theories in the cognitively easiest ways. People look at problems with hypotheses and hence

22

look of confirmation of these expectations. If they find them, they look no further. They do not seek out and evaluate co-occurring factors if their expectances are confirmed. Others, such as Jaspars (1983a) have agreed that errors in common-sense reasoning are due not so much to misperceiving the information available, but are the consequences of the sequence of processing information. Rather than going from the general to the specific, common-sense explanations often start with the specific, but do not always correctly or appropriately generalise.

Secondly, much attribution theory research work has concerned everyday understandings of problems of physical causation and not social issues. Most lay theories are about intra-personal, inter-personal and social issues, yet the theories and research have neglected how people explain such things as delinquency, wealth, alcoholism, etc. In a sense, attribution theorists have concentrated on "man the psychologist" not "man the sociologist", ignoring how people come to understand sociological issues.

Others have attempted to draw together various strands in the above traditions. For instance Kruglanski (1980) has developed a theory of lay epistemology which assumes that all knowledge is comprised of beliefs with an orienting structure, specific content and supposed validity or truthfulness. All beliefs are validated by deductive logic (only if X, then Y) and confidence derives from logical consistency among propositions, while awareness of inconsistency results in doubt and confusion. He believes that all knowledge seeking behaviour follows a strict sequence — the formulation of a problem which may have several mutually exclusive propositions and problem evaluation or validity testing. It is an impressive attempt to devise a content *and* process model that evaluates and compares various attribution theories. He is not without his critics (Effler, (1984) and he does attempt to answer them (Kruglanski, 1984). However, it should not be thought that all this work on lay theories has revealed the superiority of "scientific" theories over lay theories. Curiously, one test of a psychological theory may be the extent to which it forms part of the layman's theory. Budd and Spencer (1986) demonstrate that Fishbein's attitude–behaviour theory forms part of a lay person's intuitive psychology of intention, and that this lay theory or intuitive psychology "may act as a source of response bias which motivates people to create consistency between the components of the theory of reasoned action when completing questionnaires which measure the model's constructs" (p. 109). In other words if people hold lay theories similar or identical to scientific theories, and if they see that these (latter) theories are being tested, they are likely to respond in a way which confirms them.

Others such as Reicher and Potter (1985) have argued that "scientific" theories of crowd events are erroneous, in part because they have taken the perspective of the outsider. Thus, formal theories stress the anonymity of crowd members and emphasise the negativity of crowd events, while crowd members themselves stress the meaningfulness of crowd action, solidarity and positive emotions. In other words, the perspective of the theorist be he or she "lay" or "scientific" inevitably effects the type of theory that emerges.

Finally, it has been suggested that many social psychological theories are in fact not even open to empirical investigation. Burton (1986) for instance, has argued that Heider's naive analysis of action is an empirical system of neccessary relations embedded in the language. Nearly all the research in this area has concerned itself with the content of the layman's knowledge and information processing. The concept of common sense reoccurs frequently and it is to this that we now turn.

2.2 Common Sense

To many laymen, the theories they come across in a number of the social sciences — psychology, management, sociology, criminology — are common sense. That is, the theories or findings are already well known, and hence the research is thought to be a trivial, expensive and pointless exercise describing or proving what we already know. Being sensitive to this criticism, which is naturally seen as misplaced, social scientists have often confronted this point at the beginning of their textbooks, warning readers of the dangers of common sense which lulls people into the false belief that they understand others (Lindgren and Harvey, 1981). Some have even provocatively mentioned the term "uncommon sense" in their papers and titles (Gammack, 1982).

For instance, McKeachie and Doyle (1966) begin their general psychology textbook asking how is a scientific explanation different from common sense, and present the following figure and explanation (Fig. 2.1).

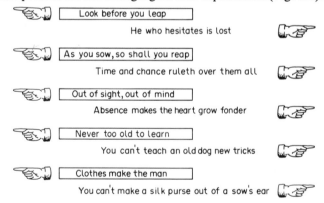

Look before you leap

He who hesitates is lost

As you sow, so shall you reap

Time and chance ruleth over them all

Out of sight, out of mind

Absence makes the heart grow fonder

Never too old to learn

You can't teach an old dog new tricks

Clothes make the man

You can't make a silk purse out of a sow's ear

FIG. 2.1. The Trouble with Folk Wisdom is that it Gives No Guide for Determining Which of Two Contradictory Sayings is Appropriate in a Particular Situation. Thus the Usefulness of Such Sayings is Quite Limited.
Reprinted with permission from McKeachie, W. and Doyle, C. (1966) *Psychology*. Reading, Mass: Addison-Wesley.

Thus, it is argued that common sense cannot tell us under which conditions each generalisation is true — for that scientific research is required (Fletcher, 1984). Others have attempted to persuade readers that *common knowledge* provides only inconsistent and misleading suggestions for understanding social behaviour by giving a short test. Baron and Byrne (1981), in their popular textbook on social psychology ask the following 10 questions each of which has a True–False response format: the numbers in parentheses indicate the number who got the answer correct by putting false in a study by Furnham (1985b)

1. In general, women conform more than men. (42%)
2. In bargaining with others, it is best to start with a moderate offer — one close to the final agreement desired. (63%)
3. In making decisions, committees tend to be more conservative than individuals. (18%)
4. Dangerous riots are most likely to occur when temperatures reach extremely high levels (e.g. around 95–100°). (54%)
5. The more persons present at the scene of an emergency, the more likely are the victims to receive help. (82%)
6. If you pay someone for doing something they enjoy, they will come to like this task even more. (46%)
7. In choosing their romantic partners, most people show a strong preference for extremely attractive persons. (51%)
8. If you want to get someone to change his or her views, it is best to offer this person a very large reward for doing so. (77%)
9. When a stranger stands very close to us, we usually interpret this as a sign of friendliness and react in a positive manner. (68%)
10. Most people feel sympathy for the victims of serious accidents or natural disasters and do not hold such persons responsible for the harm they have suffered. (8%)

They later assure the reader that research findings suggest that all these statements are *false*. Similarly in a book on *Organizational Behaviour* Baron (1983) offers a similar quiz, again where all the answers are *false*. Items include:

1. Unpleasant environmental conditions (e.g. crowding, loud noise, high temperatures) produce immediate reductions in performance on many tasks.
2. Directive, authoritative leaders are generally best in attaining high levels of productivity from their subordinates.
3. In most cases, individuals act in ways that are consistent with their attitudes about various issues.
4. Top executives are usually extremely competitive, hard-driving types.
5. Most persons are much more concerned with the size of their own salary than with the salary of others.

6. Direct, face-to-face communication usually enhances co-operation between individuals.
7. Most persons prefer challenging jobs with a great deal of freedom and autonomy.

Some have explicitly contrasted "scientific" vs "lay" accounts of events (Reicher and Potter, 1985). Others have taken specific proverbs and attempted to test them. Sigelman (1981) attempted to test — using General Social Surveys — the folk proverb "ignorance is bliss". From his fairly extensive and well-analysed study he argued for the rejection of the age-old notion. On the other hand Mischel and Mischel (1981) found that even 9- and 11-year-old children could predict some of the most basic empirical studies in psychological research.

Furnham (1983b) has suggested that the "common sense objection" may however take three forms. The first — that the findings are well known, intuitive, unsurprising, uninformative, etc. — has been discussed. The second is partly the obverse — that is, academic disciplines which investigate issues which are the "stuff of personal experience" (person perception, job motivation, love and attraction) have tended — either by use of excessive jargon or technical language, or the focusing on minute, esoteric, trivial or irrelevant aspects of social behaviour — to debase or corrupt common sense. That is, topics that are amenable to common sense should have explanations in terms of common sense.

A third, related, objection occurs when experimental findings or social science writings appear to contradict widely held views of human nature. Nearly all social psychological findings which have demonstrated that people are cruel, uninsightful, self-centred, compliant, antisocial have been criticised more than those that have painted the opposite picture (Milgram, 1974; Zimbardo et al, 1973). That is, where findings are against the consensus, or common sense, of people being basically good, altruistic, intelligent, etc., objections are made.

It is not only social scientists who have had to answer the "contrary to human nature" argument of lay people. Politicians too, particularly of the left, have attempted to counter the argument that human beings are solely motivated by competitive, self-interest, rather than co-operative sharing. In a book entitled *Why You Should be a Socialist* Paul Foot (1977) argues:

> What's good and what's bad in human nature is decided by the kind of society people live in. If the main purpose of society is to make a fortune for a few, then the virtues which society extols will be the virtues of the fortune-makers — meanness, competition, "to hell with your neighbour", "stuff your pockets never mind the other man's", "advance your children, abuse other people's", "love your God, Queen and country, hate the people around you".
>
> If society is controlled by the people who work, in the interests of the people who work, then society will encourage another side of human nature: co-operation and concern for others, pooling of skills and resources, stop the ruffian and exploiter. (p. 40)

Indeed, some Marxists believe common sense actors' accounts are epiphenomenal false consciousness. That is, despite the fact that people believe personality differences to be the causes of their own and others' behaviour it is really only economic factors that are the fundamental causes of human behaviour.

Stroebe (1980) has argued that many social psychological theories are intuitive and therefore not easily abandoned in the face of contradictory evidence. He mentions the complementary needs hypothesis which has not been replicated or supported in over two dozen attempts to test it. "Despite this devastating record, the theory is still presented in most attraction and social psychology textbooks. It just makes too much sense that, for example, somebody who loves to push people around should get along better with a spouse who prefers being pushed than pushing" (p. 186).

Thus the objection of "common sense" is fairly complex and may take various forms. Yet not all academics see this as a problem. Paradoxically, it is the "hard" scientists, who are most convinced that all science is just common sense. Huxley (1902) noted in an essay:

> Science is nothing but trained and organised Common Sense, differing from the latter only as a veteran may differ from a raw recruit: and its methods differ from those of Common Sense only as far as the guardsman's cut and thrust differ from the manner in which a savage wields his club . . . (p. 42)

Also Whitehead is reputed to have said that "Science is rooted in the whole apparatus of Common Sense thought". This idea of organised, disambiguated common sense is also supported by Rock (1979), who suggested that all the different academic theories of crime and delinquency are to be found in common-sense formulations:

> Common Sense can neither be wholly incorporated nor wholly abandoned. Rather it is typically subjected to a double form of exploitation. . . . Ideas of anomie, differential, association, relative deprivation, functional interdependence, conflict, and labelling theory may all be found in folk wisdom, early tracts, and conventional explanation. They represent parts of the common stock of everyday analysis. It is only the tendency of criminological discourse to become independent that renders such formulations academically novel and remarkable. They have to be restructured before they become available to criminological enquiry. Restructuring may resolve contradictions, unearth implications, and refine arguments. But it also sets up a barrier to participation in the larger conversation of ideas. The criminologist is at once unusually sophisticated and unusually simple. (p. 78)

Similarly, as Brickman (1980) has pointed out, because social science returns its findings to the general culture, they are apt to become more familiar and common sensical over time.

> A finding in social psychology cannot remain non obvious as people hear it again any more than a joke can remain funny to people who hear it again and again. More generally, we may propose that discoveries emerge from a region in which we disbelieve them into a zone in which we find them interesting, and then a zone in which we find them obvious, and eventually perhaps, into a further region in which we are again oblivious to them. (p. 12)

However, this view of the social scientist as a taxonomist and disambiguator of common sense cannot explain how counter-intuitive theories or ideas occur (Peters, 1960). As Gergen (1980) has noted: "This presents us with a special paradox: if one's understanding inevitably depends on existing interpretative modes, how can one engender 'interpretation' that is alien to the existing modes, If 'Common Sense' is employed as the instrument of understanding, how can one absorb an argument that violates 'Common Sense.' " (p. 263). Indeed one could ask how someone such as Freud developed so many completely counter-intuitive theories of human behaviour.

Furthermore, this position does not explain the many theoretical and methodological differences between social scientists. That is, if social science is simply common sense why do we find so much disagreement among social scientists? Of course, one might reply that the very contradictory nature of psychological theories proves that they are simply common sense because common sense is itself contradictory.

Other scientists have dismissed common sense as a source of ideas, let alone testable theories: some psychologists have been particularly dismissive of the importance of common sense. Skinner (1972) wrote: "What, after all, have we to show for non-scientific or prescientific good judgement, or common sense, or the insights gained through personal experience? It is science of nothing' (p. 160). Similarly, Broadbent (1961), Cattell (1965) and others have talked about prescientific or moralistic thinking which is to be ignored as wrong, unable to be proven, etc. Eysenck (1957) in his celebrated book *Sense and Nonsense in Psychology* states:

> This is only one example of what appears to be an almost universal belief to the effect that anyone is competent to discuss psychological problems, whether he has taken the trouble to study the subject or not and that while everybody's opinion is of equal value, that of the professional psychologist must be excluded at all costs because he might spoil the fun by producing some facts which would completely upset the speculation and the wonderful dreamcastles so laboriously constructed by the layman. (p. 13)

Thus for these eminent psychologists common sense is a dangerous area from which to draw ideas as they are often misguided or untestable. Even worse, various "common-sense" ideas may be based not on simple surmise but prejudice and political ideology. Moreover one can cite extensive literature that illustrates lay persons' "faulty" reasoning, e.g. the repeatedly observed failure of lay people to make appropriate use of disconfirmatory information in problem solving and the overwhelming preference for confirmatory strategies in logical reasoning tasks.

A slightly stronger and more popular criticism of social science as common sense is that often common sense notions are unclear, ambiguous, inconsistent, and occasionally contradictory. One way of illustrating this point is to produce contradictory idioms as done by McKeachie and Doyle (1966) (see page 2). Of course, it could be pointed out that both supposedly contradictory sayings may in fact be compatible, when they are made specific for certain circumstances. Thus, it might be that one is "never too old to learn" certain verbal tasks; however, when it comes to reaction-time skills, "you can't teach an old dog new tricks". Similarly, "out of sight out of mind" may apply to an acquaintance or distant relative but "absence makes the heart grow fonder" to a lover or close friends. However, the standard argument advanced is that of McKeachie and Doyle (1966) namely: "A major weakness of all these pre-scientific modes of explanation — superstition, Common Sense, and intuitive philosophy — is that contradictory predictions and explanations are offered without any means of resolving the differences" (p. 3).

This discussion begs the question as to what constitutes common sense. Indeed many are not sure what the term actually refers to (Schwieso, 1984). Although Descartes said that common sense is the best distributed commodity in the world, because everyone is convinced that they are well supplied with it, it remains quite unclear what it is. Different writers have described it differently: "the layman's conviction" (Kohler, 1947), "good sense" (Ryle, 1949), "intuitive philosophy" (McKeachie and Doyle, 1966), "prescientific good judgement" (Skinner, 1972). Schwieso (1984) has examined four terms: common sensation, ordinary intelligence, good sense and common opinion, which he argues have subtle different meanings but still offer no clear working definition of common sense. Fletcher (1984) has suggested that three aspects of common sense need to be delineated:

1. Common sense as a set of shared fundamental assumptions about the nature of the social and physical world. These assumptions are thought to be culturally unanimously held; never questioned, justified or even articulated; and which are the very stuff of philosophy. Examples are, according to Fletcher: that the world exists independently of our perception of it; that other people possess states of conscious awareness, that we are the same person from day to day.
2. Common sense as a set of cultural maxims and shared beliefs about the social and physical world. These assumptions in the form of proverbs, allegories and fables, are highly invariant across and within cultures as regards to whether they are known or believed. Examples include that severe punishment deters criminals, that the unemployed are lazy and that our country needs a powerful army to survive.
3. Common sense as a shared way of thinking about the social and physical world. These are tacitly known mental processes involved in explaining, interpreting and understanding the behaviour of self and others. Essentially this concerns all aspects of lay social cognition and the ways in which people process information about their world.

In the second part of his paper Fletcher (1984) is specifically concerned with how psychologists turn tacit common-sense knowledge into explicit knowledge. One way is through the conceptual schemes embedded in everyday language. "Conceptual analysis is only one way of assessing our common-sense cognitive schemata. Like all investigative techniques, it has its drawbacks and weaknesses, so that a range of other empirical investigative research strategies will be needed to explicate our common sense cognitive schemata" (p. 210). However, Fletcher argues that common sense is a valuable, but difficult and dangerous resource for psychologists precisely because it operates silently and implicitly in psychologists' thinking and analysis about lay people's common sense.

A related issue concerns what social scientists should know about common sense — in other words what aspect of everyday lay accounts should be investigated. For instance when considering lay or common-sense beliefs about the economy Furnham and Lewis (1986) argued that one needs to know the development, function, stability and consistency, consequences, change and manipulation and structure of common-sense beliefs about the economy. In psychology, the attribution theorists, notably Heider (1958) and Kelley (1973) have attempted to look not so much at the *content* of common sense but the cognitive *processes* involved. They are essentially attempts to explicitly formalise our common-sense understanding of causity and personal responsibility. Most attribution theorists appear to be impressed by the complexity of the process and the profundity of the content rather than being simply dismissive. Nearly all the psychological studies in social cognition have been process oriented, attempting to describe the process by which lay people make sense of (explain) their worlds. Yet as Sillars (1982) has noted: "The portrait of social actors depicted by attribution theory is plurastic. People are both reflective and spontaneous, rational and rationalising, logical and illogical. The current problem is how to integrate different processes" (p. 96). In fact White (1984) has suggested that psychologists are wrong in adopting statistical, logical and scientific criteria as optimal or necessary for the study of lay inference, when in fact the fulfilment of practical criteria is a much better criterion.

Whereas there appears to be a modicum of agreement as to how common sense explanations of action are to be researched in psychology — that is the nature of the questions to ask — the same cannot be said for philosophy and sociology. Wallis and Bruce (1983) have contrasted structuralist/functionalist and ethno-methodological approaches to common sense. The former, especially Marxists, discount common-sense explanations, particularly of political events, as merely epiphenomenal as all consciousness is determined by modes of production. The latter tend to assume the very opposite, namely that actors' common-sense accounts are all we can ever know about the social world. They criticise both and suggest that common sense and sociologists' explanations differ according to three criteria:

1. Sociologists are more routinely, regularly and professionally concerned with explanation than lay people.

2. Common-sense explanations are more superficial, and more easily satisfied.

3. Common-sense explanations are more concerned with the personal than with the general.

> For many who hold a traditional view of the scientific enterprise and wish sociology to possess the dignity of science, the absence of sharp distinctions between sociological and commonsense accounts will seem a great disadvantage. For ethnomethodologists who often accuse conventional sociology of resting, usually without acknowledgement, on common-sense conceptions and theories, the continuities to which we point merely confirm a weakness they had previously announced. For us, however, no shame attaches to the fact that sociology is — in its method, of course, rather than in its content or focus — only a more systematic form of common sense. Rather we are impressed by how well common sense has got along without sociology for all these years; how little the advent of sociology has added to the sum of human knowledge; and thus, how much there is to learn from what others affect to despise. (Wallis and Bruce. 1983, p. 105)

Few sociologists or psychologists have tried to explain the role of common sense in everyday thinking and behaviour. An exception is Smedslund who, in a series of papers, attempted to explain the origin and functioning of common sense and suggested that valid theories in psychology are explications of conceptual relationships embedded in ordinary language or common sense.

> By "common-sense psychology" is here meant "the network of concepts pertaining to psychological phenomena, imbedded in ordinary language". These concepts were acquired during our socialisation as persons, and, hence, are anterior to our observations and our theorising. Becoming a person means becoming a member of a society, and this again means functioning with an enormous amount of constraint, shared with the other members. There are severe limitations on what are acceptable ways of perceiving, acting, speaking, thinking, and valuing. Furthermore, these shared constraints form a highly organised system, such that, given one set of percepts, acts, sentences, thoughts or values, others follow necessarily or are necessarily excluded. Becoming socialised as a human being, therefore, involves acquiring an implicit psychology, which one cannot, as an individual, transcend. Psychologists are also persons, and, consequently, their observations, descriptions, and explanations must also conform with the common sense conceptual network". (Smedslund, 1978, p.13).

To illustrate his point he took Bandura's self-efficacy theory and translated it into a set of 36 common-sense theorems. Essentially Smedslund (1979) argues that (all) psychological theory constitutes a system of logically necessary, analytic theories, and he often chooses geometry or philosophical logic as an analogy. Therefore he tends to lament to the extent to which psychologists do not attempt to test their theories *logically* but rely on (pseudo) empirical support which is situation-and-culture-specific. In other words, attempts at sound empiricism are confounded by the prevalence of necessarily, logically true and false assumptions. For Smedslund (1979) psychological (but presumably other social sciences) studies have usually five major weaknesses:

1. *Aspirations to generality* which are usually unfulfilled.

2. A set of unrecognised, and hence unexplored, *analytic assumptions*.
3. A number of *logically incomplete assumptions*.
4. Assumptions disregarding commonly known facts which ignore important variations in subjects, laboratory and cultures as irrelevant features or constraints.
5. A low level of precision of theoretical analysis.

"We must recognise that theoretical psychology can only advance when it becomes truly legitimate to ask and pursue the following question: what is necessarily true in psychology" (p. 140).

In a very interesting debate in the *Scandinavian Journal of Psychology* in 1982, Sjöberg and Smedslund argued the role of common sense in psychological theory. Sjöberg (1982) has noted that common sense — a set of explicitly or implicitly held beliefs concerning human behaviour — differs between individuals, subcultures and cultures and changes over time and hence there is no such thing as *the* common sense. Common-sense beliefs are inconsistent, implicit, ambiguous, loose modes of thinking which provide *post-hoc* "explanations" not predictions and therefore offer little in the way of profound insight. Common sense has problems of content and process — erroneous in the former, illogical in the latter, and is hence not a promising source of psychological insight. Finally he criticises Smedslund's rejection of empiricism, critique of historicism and total reliance on logical analysis.

In his reply Smedslund (1982a) argues that Sjöberg has been using the term common sense incorrectly and that "a proposition in a given context belongs to common sense if and only if all competent users of the language involved agree that the proposition in the given context is true and that its negation is contradictory or senseless" (p. 23). Hence it is argued that the extent to which something is seen as common sense can be determined by how much consensus there is involved and hence discussion about the consistency, preciseness and stability of common sense can be dispensed with. He believes common sense to be stable, measurable and a necessary precondition for all communication. He believes that Sjöberg and many other psychologists are wrong in denying the importance of common sense because they maintain the unreflective presupposition that psychological language and psychological reality are independent realms. In other words psychological constructs must consist of explications of common sense or be translatable into such explications.

Curiously Smedslund (1982b,c) resorted to empirical studies to illustrate his point that many psychological theorems, when translated, are consensually accepted by a very high percentage of the population. In two studies he demonstrated that consensus about concrete predictions derived from theorems was generally high and argues that these widely held common-sense theorems are a kind of "calculus" used in everyday interaction.

Thus, in a sense, Smedslund is a natural language philosopher, translating psychological theories into simple everyday non-technical terms. If these natural-language theories are then seen to be logically correct and held widely this is described as common sense. He also makes the point that many psychological theories which claim to be empirically testable and falsifiable are, in fact, logically necessary and irrefutable in principle. They are in a sense like the "deep structure" of language which is true for all people. Smedslund is a little like a latterday Wittgenstein, who is remembered (or repressed) by some psychologists for his damning dictum "in psychology there is experimental method and conceptual confusion" (Wittgenstein, 1953, p. 232).

He also has his critics (e.g. Valsiner, 1985) but his work has made people think again about the role and importance of common sense in everyday behaviour (Smedslund, 1986).

Thus social scientists originally so dismissive of common-sense beliefs, accounts and explanations primarily on grounds of ambiguity, unfalsifiability and inferential errors are beginning to examine common sense in detail. Whereas psychologists seem particularly interested in the *process* of lay people explaining everyday events, sociologists seem more interested in the *content* of lay theories. Further philosophers have subjected social science theories to tests of whether they are common sense or not, and found that at heart many of them are perfectly understood by the layman.

Perhaps the greatest advantage of this current interest in common sense (or its many synonyms — lay epistemology, everyday accounts) is that it has encouraged social scientists to elucidate and systematise their theories and do more pre-empirical, logical analysis. In one sense the realisation that people are prone to numerous logical and inferential errors has encouraged social scientists to inspect their own theories for the same errors. This is particularly the case because recently psychology has become more concerned not with behaviour itself but rather with the accounts of behaviour (Shotter and Burton, 1985).

2.3 Human Nature

At one level it may be argued that all theories of behaviour depend on one's fundamental belief about human nature. These broader philosophies of human nature that people hold serve to make the world a more orderly, stable and predictable place. There is no shortage of philosophical speculation about the nature of man.

Jeremy Bentham (1748–1832) described man as a rational being, making choices and decisions in terms of enlightened self-interest. *Le Bon* (1841–1931) on the other hand stressed the irrationality and impulsiveness of men in crowds. *Hobbes* (1588–1679) viewed man as selfish, nasty and brutish, whose strivings had to be restrained by a powerful government. *Rousseau* (1712–1778) saw the restraints of his civilisation as the force that was destroying the nobility of natural man, the noble savage. Furthermore, there are numerous philosophical treatises which carefully compare and contrast some of the major thinkers of our time: Marx, Darwin, Freud, Levi-Strauss, Chomsky, etc. It may also be argued that the major schools of psychology — Skinnerian behaviourism, psychoanalysis and humanistic psychology — have quite different theories about the essential nature of man.

According to Wrightsman (1964):

> The most extended statements of human nature have appeared to treat at least nine broad issues: (1) What are the differing views of human nature, (2) How do these views explain behaviour in interactions among people, (3) How do the behaviours explained and predicted by philosophies of human nature compare to the actual ongoing, observable ways in which people act, (4) What types of societies and institutions are to be inferred from these views of human nature, (5) How do these societies and institutions compare with existing social structures, (6) Which of the views of human nature thus considered are most accurate, (7) Which behaviours are most congruent and which behaviours are least congruent with this view of human nature, (8) Where is it possible to place societal and institutional constraints upon behaviour, and how may these constraints be arranged to dampen or correct deviations and aberrations from human nature, (9) How can constraints be placed or removed in order to maximise the good in man's basic nature. (p. 13)

In his book Wrightsman (1964) attempts to systematise the various traditions in philosophic assumptions of human nature. He also attempts to spell out the implicit and explicit assumptions of prominent psychologists and sociologists regarding human nature. In doing so, he not unnaturally touches on issues such as the nature–nurture debate, how these philosophies of human nature develop, etc.

Experimental and social psychologists have attempted to specify *empirically* the basic dimensions that underpin the writings of philosophers, theologians, politicians, sociologists and others about the fundamental nature of "human beings". In doing so, they have attempted to spell out the determinants, structure and consequences of various "philosophies of human nature". For instance Wrightsman (1964) has devised an 84 item scale that measures six basic dimensions of human nature in his *Philosophy of Human Nature Scale* (PHN):

1. Trustworthiness vs untrustworthiness
   + = belief that people are trustworthy, moral and responsible
   − = belief that people are untrustworthy, immoral and irresponsible.
2. Strength of will and rationality vs lack of will power and irrationality
   + = belief that people can control their outcomes and that they understand themselves
   − = belief that people lack self-determination and are irrational.
3. Altruism vs selfishness
   + = belief that people are altruistic, unselfish, and sincerely interested in others

− = belief that people are selfish and self-centered.
4. Independence vs conformity to group pressures
+ = belief that people are able to maintain their beliefs in the face of group pressures to the contrary
− = belief that people give in to pressures of group and society.
5. Variability vs similarity
+ = belief that people are different from each other in personality and interests and that a person can change over time
− = belief that people are similar in interests and are not changeable over time.
6. Complexity vs simplicity
+ = belief that people are complex and hard to understand
− = belief that people are simple and easy to understand.

Two additional dimensions of the philosophies of human nature proposed by Wrightsman (1964) concern beliefs in the variation that exists among human beings. These two dimensions are similarity vs variability and complexity versus simplicity. However, Wrightsman's six dimension scale factor analyses into two major variables or subscales: *Positive–Negative* (strength of will, trust, independence and altruism) and *multiplexity* (variability and complexity) which are by-and-large independent of one another.

In research using the Philosophy of Human Nature Scale with people of different ages, sexes, races and occupations, Wrightsman and his colleagues have found that the average person believes human nature to be: (1) neither extremely trustworthy nor extremely untrustworthy; (2) somewhat rational and possessing a moderate degree of will power; (3) neither extremely altruistic nor extremely selfish; (4) somewhat more likely to conform to group pressures than to remain independent; (5) moderately variable and unique; and (6) moderately complex and hard to understand (Wrightsman, 1974; Wrightsman and Satterfield, 1967). The scale was developed in the early 1960s and a decade of research in America is summarised in Wrightsman (1974).

The scale has been used fairly extensively in other areas of research including cross-cultural research in the South Pacific (Stewart, 1983) and South Africa (Edwards, 1984). Furthermore the scale has been shown to relate predictably and systematically to values, religious and political beliefs, etc.

Others, too, have developed scales or measures which attempt general beliefs in human nature. There are various measures of Machiavellianism (MS), of which perhaps the best known is that of Christie and Geis, (1970). Taken from the writings of Machiavelli, the scale measures the extent to which people believe lying, cheating and deceit are acceptable when the ends justify the means. Items which score highly on this scale include "The best way to handle people is to tell them what they want to hear''; ''Anyone who completely trusts anyone else is asking for trouble''; and ''It is safest to assume that all people have a vicious streak that will come out when it is given a chance''. People who have a Machiavellian view of human nature tend to be competitive, manipulative, egocentric and amoral. Overall the scale tends to have acceptable reliability and predictive validity.

Thornton and Kline (1982) argued that the general syndrome of antisocial, anticonformist delinquency is partly attributed to delinquents' tendency to interpret other people as malevolent. Hence they devised the *Belief in Human Benevolence Scale* (BHB) which assesses the degree to which a person expects others to be generally benevolent and malevolent. The 20 item scale yields a single score: high scorers assert that people are unselfishly concerned for others' well-being, can be trusted not to exploit others and are likely to reciprocate kindness, whereas low scorers assert that people are selfishly (actively and maliciously) concerned with their own interests, will exploit others if given a chance and are unlikely to reciprocate kindness. The scale has not been extensively used but has been well psychometrised.

Another useful scale, not extensively used and developed for a specific purpose, *Beliefs in Human Nature Scale* (BHS) was devised by Furnham *et al.* (1985) to measure people's beliefs in the determinants (heredity vs environmental) in six human characteristics, physical characteristics (height, weight), psychological skills (sport, intelligence), personality (neuroticism, extraversion), beliefs (political, religious), psychological problems (alcoholism, schizophrenia) and physical problems (diabetes, asthma). These beliefs were shown to be related to sex, age, class, political opinion and education. Specifically, males more than females, younger more than older, middle-class rather than working-class, left-wing more than right-wing, and better educated rather than less well educated people tended to be more environmentalist.

Furnham *et al.* (1985) argue that they have developed a robust, multi-dimensional instrument for measuring beliefs in the determinants of human nature. These beliefs are strongly related to a person's *political* orientation in predictable and logical ways — left-wingers tend to attribute the origin of most human characteristics to the environment and right-wing people to genetic factors, though there are vast differences depending on the characteristic considered (e.g. personality vs physical characteristics). Thus, it may be possible to determine a person's political orientation by asking his or her views on the nature–nurture issue, or vice versa. Whereas many other variables — age, education, class, religion and sex are also important determinants of these beliefs in the origins of human characteristics they may be either confounding or mediating variables.

In addition to these three measures of human nature there are a number of other tests which, though less general, attempt to measure beliefs about aspects of other people and the world. For instance, one important dimension that has been considered is the extent to which it is believed that the world is just (where good people are rewarded and bad people are punished) or unjust (the rain falls on the just and the unjust alike).

There is a substantial literature on the *just world hypothesis* (Lerner, 1980; Rubin and Peplau, 1975) which may be stated thus: "Individuals have a need to believe that they live in a world where people generally get what they deserve. The belief that the world is just enables the individual to confront his physical and social environment as though they were stable and orderly" (Lerner and Miller, 1978, p. 1030). Studies on the determinants of just world beliefs have shown that believers in a just world tend to be more authoritarian, religious, have internal locus of control beliefs, believe in the Protestant work ethic and are more likely to admire political leaders/social institutions, and to have negative attitudes towards the underprivileged (Rubin and Peplau, 1973). A number of American studies have shown that believers in a just world tend to be hostile and unsympathetic towards victims of social injustice, especially in cases where their suffering cannot be easily alleviated — hence the desire to live in a just world leads not to justice but justification (Rubin and Peplau, 1975). This is not a theory of human nature so much as "more or less articulated assumptions which underlie the way people orient themselves to their environment" (Lerner, 1980). But it is, because the just world is one in which individuals "get what they deserve", that one can infer human nature from fate. People to whom fate has been kind tend to be perceived as energetic, friendly, generous, intelligent, kind, etc. while those who suffer at the hands of fate tend to be seen as cruel, lazy, stupid, unfriendly, ugly, etc. That is, fate, which is highly discriminating, distinguishes between those who are inherently good and those inherently bad.

There are a whole host of measures in psychology which relate to beliefs in human nature. For instance, Wilson (1973) discusses conservatism beliefs, many of which closely reflect assumptions about human nature. Similarly there are numerous measures of perceived control, each of which relates partly to views of human nature.

Apart from Wrightsman's (1964, 1974) work, and that of his disciples, surprisingly little work has been done in the social sciences on lay people's beliefs on human nature. The reason is most probably because of the generality, as well as incoherence and inconsistency of their views, as well as their poor predictability. Although a number of questionnaires have been devised to measure views on human nature they have had only modest success in predicting a person's beliefs or behaviours. Specific measures are nearly always more useful in predicting specific behaviours than general. Secondly, ideas about human nature are nearly all found in studies of political and moral beliefs as well as the nature–nurture debate, rather than as a separate issue.

Thus, whereas there is a plethora of philosophic treatises on human nature there is a paucity of empirical studies on lay people's views, though with good reason.

2.4 Two Approaches to Understanding Lay Theories
(World Views, Cognitive Systems)

Social scientists of all persuasions are interested in lay people's lay theories on world views. In the words of Helman (1984), a medical anthropologist:

> This world view enables man to locate himself spatially and historically, and provides a conceptual–perceptual structure beyond the limits of which few men transgress even in imagination. This cognitive system, shared with other members of one's culture or society, makes the chaos of life, understandable and gives a sense of security and *meaning* to people's lives. (p. 108)

Whereas some disciplines are interested in the cultural determinants and consensus of this world view, others are more interested in its structure and measurement.

Sociologists and anthropologists appear to be particularly interested in cultural and group determinants on the "actor's perspective" on his or her world; how these beliefs or views are "socialised" into members of the group; how these beliefs function to facilitate interaction with other groups and the natural environment; and how these views change over time. Psychologists on the other hand have been interested with the *content* of these belief systems and how they operate in practice — that is the *process* by which people understand and attribute the causes of behaviour. These two areas, whilst overlapping, represent rather different ways of understanding the problem of lay theories.

(1) Content

The content approach has been dedicated to describing the content and organisation of a belief system and the lay theories that go along with it. Some descriptions have been restricted to one topic like justice or morality, but others are much more widely conceived. A good example is conservative social attitudes which encompass ideas like authoritarianism, dogmatism and Machiavellianism. Indeed it is over 40 years since Eysenck (1947) first proposed a clear structure for social attitudes. Conservatism is conceived as a general factor underlying all social attitudes, much the same as intelligence is seen as underlying all abilities. Psychologists and sociologists interested in this topic have attempted to describe the content of this "factor". Wilson (1973) illustrated the conceptualisation of conservatism (the average of all the factors) but admits that it shows only half the picture because the other extreme (liberalism) has been left out (see Fig. 2.2). He also developed a theory for the conservatism syndrome. it is stated thus:

> The theory suggests that certain genetic factors such as anxiety proneness, stimulus aversion

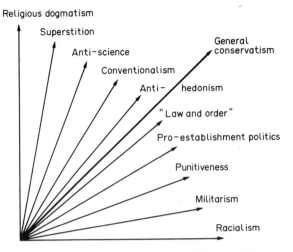

Fɪɢ. 2.2. Diagram to Illustrate Possible Arrangement of Attitude Clusters to Form
a General Conservatism Factor (Wilson, 1973, p. 10).
Reprinted with permission from Wilson, G. (1973). *The Psychology of
Conservatism.* London: Academic Press.

(sensitivity to strong stimuli), low intelligence, lack of physical attractiveness, old age, and female sex, and certain environmental factors such as parental coldness, punitiveness, rigidity and inconsistency, and membership of the lower classes, will give rise to feelings of insecurity and inferiority (low self esteem). For example, a child continually subjected to harsh punishment might eventually accept or "internalise" the low evaluation of himself that he perceives his parents or teachers to hold. Feelings of insecurity and inferiority may be expected to result in a generalised fear of uncertainty, the insecure individual fearing stimulus uncertainty because he perceives the environment as complex, changeable, and treacherous, and the individual with low self-esteem fearing response uncertainty because he lacks confidence in his ability to control events in his environment or make autonomous decisions regarding his own behaviour.

At the behavioural level the fear of uncertainty would manifest itself as: (1) a tendency to dislike and avoid uncertain stimulus configurations — innovation, novelty, risk, complexity, social disorganisation, etc., and (2) a tendency to dislike and avoid situations that involve a great deal of response uncertainty — conflict, decision-making, etc. These two groups of tendencies would be differentiated to some extent, the fear of stimulus uncertainty being associated more strongly with insecurity and the fear of response uncertainty being more closely tied with inferiority feelings. There would, however, also be a positive correlation between them because of their common genetic and environmental origins. The last step in the model suggests that this dislike for and avoidance of stimulus and response uncertainty would be manifested as an organised pattern of attitudes — that which we have labelled "the conservatism syndrome". (pp. 259–266)

The theory has been able to predict people's responses to jokes, art preferences and superstitious behaviour. It is set out diagramatically in Fig. 2.3.

It is argued, then, that people can be dimensionalised on this dimension of liberalism–conservatism, and that these beliefs have an ordering and simplifying function. Conservative beliefs act as a lens or filter on the world. Hence, one may derive hypotheses as to the lay explanations high and low scores would give for social phenomena. Thus, high scorers prefer a physical,

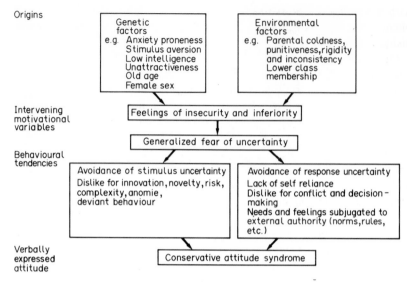

FIG. 2.3. A Theory of the Psychological Antecedents of Conservatism (Wilson,
1973, p. 261).
Reprinted with permission from Wilson, G. (1973) *The Psychology of
Conservatism.* London: Academic Press.

rather than a psychological, model to explain mental illness (Lillie, 1973). In
other words the lay explanations for various social phenomena of high
scorers on a measure of conservatism are likely to be very different from the
lay explanations of low scorers on the same scale.

Conservatism is only one of a range of "syndromes", "dimensions" or
individual difference variables considered by social and personality psychologists to relate to how people perceive and explain the world around them.
Others include: locus of control beliefs (Rotter, 1966); just world beliefs
(Lerner, 1980); the Protestant work ethic beliefs (Furnham, 1988a), etc.,
which are not surprisingly all related to one another in logical and predictable
ways (Furnham, 1984a).

This approach, then, is to systematically describe a belief variable, to
describe the organisation of attitudes in it, and to explain how this variable
relates to people's attitudes to, and explanations of, a wide range of social
behaviours.

(2) Process

This approach has been interested *not* in describing the content of a belief
system, but in describing the process that people go through in gathering,
ordering and selecting information to arrive at an explanation. This
approach is not so much concerned with the beliefs that people hold about the
social world, but how they assimilate facts and arrive at an explanation. Thus
researchers in this area, such as attribution theorists, have been concerned

with describing the processes lay people go through in explaining everyday phenomena such as why they (or others) pass or fail tests; why they like or dislike others, etc.

One such example is Weiner's (1985) theory of achievement motivation and emotion which is concerned with the perceived causes of success and failure. According to Weiner, when people attempt to explain their own success or failure for any behaviour these attributions have three common properties: locus of causality (internal vs external); stability (over time and across situations) and controllability (whether or not the outcome was controllable). Other dimensions of relevance include intentionality (of the action) and globality of causes. Thus, in arriving at an explanation a person will select these from the taxonomy set out below. Attributional decisions represent phenomenal causality (see Table 2.1).

TABLE 2.1. *A Three-Dimensional Taxonomy of the perceived causes of success and failure.*

| | Controllable | | Uncontrollable | |
	Stable	Unstable	Stable	Unstable
Internal	Stable effort of self	Unstable effort of self	Ability of self	Fatigue, mood, and fluctuations in skill of self
External	Stable effort of others	Unstable effort of others	Ability of others, task difficulty	Fatigue, mood, and fluctuations in skill of others, luck

Weiner (1985) further argues that the perceived stability of the cause influences changes in expectancies of future success as well as effective responses (e.g. anger, gratitude, guilt, shame) which in turn guide and motivate behaviour. Thus, a person's expectancy and affect, which are both mediated by causal attributions, influence the choice, the intensity and the persistence of behaviour. Thus, attributions of failure to lack of ability (stable cause) are debilitating, generating feelings of incompetence, while attributions to lack of effort (unstable cause) should or might enhance performance. This affect influences the use of causal antecedent which in turn influences causal descriptions which have psychological and behavioural consequences which in turn influence future attributions.

Weiner recognises that causes are inferred for specific events (and presumably theories are developed for general phenomena) on the basis of several factors which include specific issues (such as a person's past history, social norms prevailing, the pattern of performance, etc.); causal preferences of individuals based on their personal history; rules that relate causes to effects also known as causal schema; reinforcement history; communication from others; and presumably their "lay theories".

For Weiner the way in which one characteristically processes information to derive explanations, attributions and theories can have wide consequences, such as response to therapy, helping others, etc.

The content and process approaches are not antithetical but overlapping. It may well be that people with specific belief systems (e.g. conservative syndromes) have characteristic styles or strategies for processing data. Thus, for Weiner (1985):

> Perceived causality certainly will differ from person to person and within an individual over occasions. This is true not only for a specific causal inference, but also for the meaning or dimensional location of the cause. For one individual, luck may be perceived as an external, unstable cause of success; for another, luck is conceived as an enduring personal property. Indeed, a cause might convey different meanings in disparate contexts. But although the interpretation of specific causal inferences might vary over time and between people and situations, the underlying dimensions on which causes are "understood" or given meaning remain constant. That is, dimensions are conceived as invariant, whereas the location of any specific cause on a dimension is variable. (p. 553)

2.5 Information Gathering and Hypothesis Testing

In order to formulate a theory, a certain amount of information gathering and hypothesis testing needs to take place. Considerable psychological research has been concerned with how people draw inferences (usually about causality) from specific (pre-programmed) information provided by an experimenter. Logically, the inferential phase follows from the information gathering phase, which is a clearly necessary preceding phase. Thus, for instance, to select somebody for a job an interviewer collects information (from application forms, references, and the interview itself), tests certain hypotheses that are formulated during the interview and then makes his or her decision. Of course, how people choose to gather information differs widely; some may passively observe people in specific situations (over lunch, in a group discussion) while others may construct or manipulate situations to elicit specific responses — these include developing particular tests or questionnaires.

But it was not until comparatively recently that psychologists looked at the sort of questions lay people ask when gathering information and testing hypotheses. Most of the early systematic work in this field was undertaken by Snyder and his colleagues who were initially interested in the kinds of questions people ask to obtain information to test their hypotheses about another's personality.

Perhaps the study which attracted most interest was that of Snyder and Swann (1978), who hypothesised that an interviewer chooses information seeking strategies designed to confirm a pre-established hypothesis about the interviewee, and that this strategy actually affects the *behaviour* of the interviewee. In other words people often tend to cause self-fulfilling prophecies in their hypothesis testing at least in certain settings. That is, questions asked may search for confirmatory, disconfirmatory, or both kinds of information. Subjects were asked to select questions from a list which would best test whether a person was an extrovert or an introvert. The results strongly confirmed confirmatory (self-fulfilling) strategy, such that in the extrovert condition subjects asked more extrovert-orientated questions, while in the introvert condition, subjects asked more introverted orientated questions. According to Snyder (1984), in the gathering of information about social phenomena, lay people are clearly biased against the expression of answers that are indicative of the alternative, and this strategy traps them into confirming the hypothesis that they are testing.

Snyder has done a number of studies in this field, and the titles show the diversity of topics: Testing hypotheses about other people (Snyder and Campbell, 1980); testing hypotheses about human nature (Snyder *et al.*, 1982); testing hypotheses about the self (Snyder and Skryprek, 1981). In a review Snyder (1984) lists the impressive evidence for behavioural confirmation in social interaction. Four areas are pin-pointed:

1. *Beliefs about appearance* — there is considerable evidence to suggest that people assume that those who are physically attractive also have other desirable traits like sensuality, intelligence, kindness, sociability, and that people treat others as if this were so.
2. *Beliefs about gender* — sex role research has consistently demonstrated that sex role behaviours may be the product of other people's beliefs about the sexes.
3. *Beliefs about race* — there is some evidence to suggest that beliefs about different races may constrain the behaviour of people that causes them to behave in accord with those beliefs.
4. *Beliefs about job performance* — evidence suggests that selectors may allow their beliefs to influence the way they interview job candidates to make it more likely that those who fit their beliefs show up better in their job interviews than do job seekers who do not fit their beliefs.

For Snyder (1984) there are sequential behavioural confirmation processes which lead to self-fulfilling hypothesis testing. ''Reality testing'' becomes reality construction. In the first phase the person internalises and perseveres in the behavioural confirmation process by following two maxims — ''I am what I do'' and ''Believing means doing''. These beliefs guide questioning, which in turn prompts people to behave in ways that confirm these initial beliefs. Snyder believes that there are both behavioural and cognitive consequences of assumptions and hypotheses about other people and the self. In considerable detail he shows how our information processing (e.g. memory for events) and interpersonal behaviours are dependent on assumptions about the social world (themselves, others, the nature of specific jobs) as well as various hypotheses they develop. He concludes thus:

> These investigations have suggested that, whether individuals regard their beliefs as assumptions or hypotheses, whether their beliefs concern themselves or other people, social beliefs can and do channel the remembering of past events in ways that determine both the subjective and the objective reality of these beliefs . . . The things that individuals believe exert powerful

influences on they way they and other people live their lives. Beliefs and impressions do not exist in a vacuum. Instead, the processes of social thought are intimately woven into the fabric of social interaction and interpersonal relationships. The events of our lives are very much a reflection of our beliefs about ourselves and about other people in our social worlds. It is in this sense that beliefs can and do create reality. (p. 298)

Snyder's work has attracted considerable attention with both replications (Sackett, 1982) and refutations (Semin and Strack, 1980), as well as replications of both refutations and replications! (Meertens *et al.* 1984). Most studies are concerned to demonstrate how experimental artefacts in Snyder's repeated paradigm led him and his colleagues to draw the incorrect conclusions. For instance, Sackett (1982) performed four studies to test the generalisability of the *confirmatory hypothesis* finding. All four failed to support the hypothesis when experienced interviewers, rather than university students, were used; when the study was set specifically in an employment interview setting; and when traits like agreeableness or conscientiousness were tested. A fourth study showed, however, that the type of hypothesis held does affect the questioning strategy chosen by the subject, yet not the likelihood that the hypothesis would be confirmed, but that the evaluation made is determined exclusively by the information received regardless of the hypothesis. Curiously the subject adheres to the questioning strategy, even if the information consistently runs contrary to the hypothesis expressed. Four explanations are posited for the inability to generalise these results:

1. The hypotheses were not formed by the subjects but "given" to them and this may engender less commitment or interest.
2. The questions were likewise provided and not generated by the subjects.
3. The studies have concentrated almost exclusively on verbal behaviour and have ignored non-verbal behaviour.
4. The experience and training of the interviewer as well as the constraints of the situation may affect the questions asked which constrain, inhibit or promote the tendency to confirmatory hypothesis.

Thus the supposed ubiquitousness of the confirmatory hypothesis testing hypothesis has been challenged.

A similar approach has been taken by Trope and Bassok in a series of studies (Trope and Bassok, 1982, 1983; Trope *et al.*, 1984). They were particularly interested in the extent to which people can take into account factors affecting the hypothesis testing value of behaviour, or the extent to which its probability depends on possession of the personal disposition under consideration. The strategy of asking questions to the extent that the answers are diagnostic for discriminating between the hypothesis and the alternative was termed, by these authors, as the diagnostic strategy. They argue that the information gatherer selects questions that elicit subjectively "diagnostic" answers and, hence, questions are preferred for their diagnostic/discriminatory features regardless of whether the features are probable or improbable under the hypothesis. In the first of their series of studies, Trope and Bassok (1982) found, as predicted, that diagnosticity was the major determinant of the information gathering preferences, and little evidence was found for the confirmatory strategy. "In fact improbable evidence was preferred when it was more diagnostic than probable evidence. Thus the confirmatory strategy, whatever appeal it may have had to subjects did not reduce the diagnostic power of the information assembled" (p. 221).

In a set of three further studies, Trope and Bassok (1983) were interested in the information gathering strategies people used as a function whether they were testing the actual hypothesis or its alternative. They argued and demonstrated that when the boundary is at the mid-point of a dimension, hypothesis and alternative questions are equally diagnostic, but at extremes, hypothesis consistent questions become more diagnostic than alternative consistent questions. Furthermore, they were able to show that subjects' judgement about the diagnosticity of questions for discriminating different boundaries parallelled subjects' preferences among these questions. In other words the lay information gatherer does not enquire about features of the hypothesis unless the feature is simultaneously unrelated to the hypothesis and vice versa with the alternative thesis. Lay theorists thus consider not only the implication of the hypothesis, but also the implication of the alternative in the evidence they seek.

More recently, Trope *et al.* (1984) have examined the kind of question that lay interviewers *spontaneously* formulate, as opposed to rating a predetermined set of questions. Subjects were encouraged to formulate questions which were classified as biased *in favour* of the trait, *against* the trait, about *consistent* features, about *inconsistent* features, *bidirectional* and open-ended. As predicted most of their subjects asked open-ended or bidirectional rather than biased questions. Furthermore, they demonstrated in a second experiment, concerned with the diagnosticity of questions formulated by subjects either with or without a hypothesis, a similar result. As a result they believe Snyder's results to be artefactual in the sense that people use biased questions not because of their reliance on the confirmatory strategy, but because the hypothesis they are testing and its alternative are not accurately conveyed to them.

There are, therefore, many doubts about the behavioural confirmation or self-fulfilling prophecy strategy of lay persons engaged in information gathering and hypothesis testing. Snyder has carried out research and collected reports from others to support his case. Yet many have challenged the results or the interpretations of the results of his studies, suggesting that there are many caveats for the rather simplistic model of behavioural confirmation. This is not to suggest that all the results of experiments in the behavioural confirmation are wrong or artefactual, but rather that bias in the process of information gathering and by hypothesis testing is dependent on specific circumstances and not as prevalent as previously suggested.

2.6 Conclusion

This chapter concerned two basic themes. The first section dealt with the issue of common sense and people's views on human nature. Both of these sections focused on the content of lay theories. Studies on common sense have attempted to demonstrate that many psychological findings are indeed counter-intuitive, thus not supporting a common-sense view. Others have pondered on the logic of common sense; what to make of common-sense explanations; the relationship between ordinary language and common sense, etc. Empirical work on common-sense beliefs has done much to reveal both the process of how lay people come to understand their world, and how academics' theories are based very much in lay thinking.

The section on beliefs about human nature attempted to review various attempts to look at the basic dimensions that people agree and disagree on, as to the fundamental nature of man. Various dimensions have been proposed and instruments developed to measure them. It has been suggested that those beliefs function to make the world a more stable, orderly and predictable place and provide a filter or script through or by which to make sense of one's own and others' actions.

The second part of the chapter was more concerned with how to study lay theories of human behaviour. The content approach aimed specifically to describe the major dimensions or categories of belief that people hold. This approach attempts to differentiate and describe in detail the contents of different belief systems about human behaviour. The process approach, on the other hand, is concerned more with how people process information in order to arrive at an explanation. Once again, there are many approaches to this issue, the currently most fashionable of which is attribution theory.

The final section of this chapter reviews briefly the growing research on how lay people test hypotheses and assumptions in general. It looks specifically at the sort of information that people select and reject, and how they use this information to examine or test, various hypotheses that they may wish for or have been asked to verify. Various strategies have been examined though there is some doubt as to whether everybody uses the same strategy on all occasions.

This chapter has been concerned with lay theories and beliefs at a very general level. Subsequent chapters will look at various lay theories within specific contexts.

3

Lay Theories in Psychology

3.1 Introduction

Probably more than any other discipline, there is no generally accepted definition of psychology as an academic enterprise. Definitions vary from the science of mental life to the study of behaviour or, more specifically, the study of cognition, emotion and behaviour. For some the boundaries of the discipline are extremely wide: "Anything that people are, or people do, or people think can be studied by psychologists. Psychologists are concerned with what makes people tick, why they do things and how they do things" (Gale, 1985, p. 1). Others find it easier to define what psychology is not rather than what it is (Colman, 1984).

Another way of describing the scope of psychology is to offer a picture of what is known as the short history of the long past of psychology. Nearly all textbooks set out the major schools in psychology or the approaches of different branches in psychology. These are *not* theories but explicit schools with different assumptions. Roediger *et al.* (1984) set out the various schools — psychobiological, ethological, behavioural, cognitive, psychoanalytic and humanistic.

Academic and professional psychologists may well feel happier classifying themselves in terms of their approach rather than the school that they fall into. In fact, the concept of school is rather old fashioned and some (i.e. structuralists, functionalists and Gestalt psychologists) may hardly exist at all, being replaced by humanistic, existential or cognitive psychology.

However, it may be that the beliefs and values that lead some psychologists to fall into a particular school or adopt a certain approach, similarly influence lay people to take up a certain epistemological stance. That is, there may be lay behaviourists who reject introspection, cognitive or emotional factors in explaining behaviour, preferring the infamous "black box" approach. On the other hand some people might "naturally" gravitate to psychoanalytic thinking, preferring to emphasise the importance of unconscious motivation.

The issue of values or beliefs determining research paradigms of scientists has recently surfaced again. Kimble (1984) has argued that current *academic* psychology has two distinct cultures, labelled scientific and humanistic,

47

TABLE 3.1. *Scales and Subscales of the Epistemic Differential.*

Scale	Related opposing ideas
1. Most important values: scientific vs human	Increasing knowledge vs improving human condition; methodological strength vs relevance; obligation to apply vs no such obligation
2. Degree of lawfulness of behaviour: determinism vs indeterminism	Lawful vs not lawful; understandable vs incomprehensible; predictable vs unpredictable; controllable vs uncontrollable
3. Source of basic knowledge: objectivism vs intuitionism	Sense data vs empathy; observation vs self-report; operational definition vs linguistic analysis; investigation vs common sense
4. Methodological strategy: data vs theory	Investigation vs interpretation; induction vs deduction; evidence vs argument
5. Setting for discovery: laboratory vs field	Experimentation vs survey/case study; manipulation vs naturalistic observation; hypothesis testing vs correlation; control vs realism; precision vs ecological validity
6. Temporal aspects of lawfulness: historical vs ahistorical	Development vs descriptive approach; longitudinal vs cross-sectional study
7. Position on nature/nurture issue: heredity vs environment	Physiology vs situation; biological vs social science
8. Generality of laws: nomothetic vs idiographic	Species general vs species specific; "standard man" vs individual uniqueness; universalism vs contextualism
9. Concreteness of concepts: hypothetical constructs vs intervening variables	Biological reality vs abstract conception
10. Level of analysis: elementism vs holism	Molecular vs molar; part vs whole
11. Factor leading to action: cognition vs affect	Reason vs emotion; thinking vs motivation; intellect vs impulse; rational vs irrational
12. Conception of organisms: reactivity vs creativity	Automaticity vs voluntary control; associationism vs constructivism

which differ on specific explicit values. *Scientific*: "All behaviour is caused by physical, physiological or experiential variables. In principle it is possible to discover exact laws relating every individual's behaviour to these variables. Behaviour is understandable, predictable, controllable." *Humanistic*: "The concept of causality probably does not apply to behaviour, certainly not to individual behaviour. There is nothing lawful about behaviour except perhaps at the level of statistical averages. Even in principle, behaviour must be regarded as incomprehensible, unpredictable and beyond control" (p. 835). This is most clearly seen in his 12-point table which emphasises some of the major differences in the discipline (see Table 3.1). It should be emphasised that these are not lay theoretical approaches but the positions of polarised academic psychologists who are frequently explicit about their assumptions.

Psychologists of a tough-minded natural science approach tend to favour the "scientific" approach, while psychologists in the tender-minded, social science school tend to value the more humanistic approach.

The idea that psychology is not value free but value laden has also been taken up by Krasner and Houts (1984) who also demonstrated the existence of two groups, which they called *behavioural* and *non-behavioural*. They showed that people who endorsed freedom or enquiry as opposed to ethical constraints on research, and who favoured social Darwinism as opposed to social altruism favoured the behavioural over the experimental approach to psychology. Essentially the same point is being made — psychologists as a group tend to polarise on various discipline-specific epistemological assumptions and values. But, as Howard (1985) points out, one must be careful to separate non-epistemic values (attitudinal or emotional responses in certain individuals) from epistemic values (criteria employed by scientists to choose among competing theoretical explanations). It is only on the latter that one might expect psychologists to differ.

Indeed some researchers have suggested that certain psychology textbooks have strong epistemological biases. For instance, Hogan and Schroeder (1981) claim that authors of textbooks introduce the following behaviouristic biases: (a) They ignore traditional topics such as thoughts, feelings, sensations, states of mind; (b) They equate "scientific study" with a search for causal relationships, relationships inferred from the covariation of events; (c) They equate "scientific study" with laboratory experimentation and statistical analysis, implying thereby that non-experimental methodologies are unscientific or worthless.

This finding or claim is disputed by Brown and Brown (1982) whose analysis of texts showed little evidence of glaring behaviourist, environmentalist, or liberal biases in treating the topics of emotion, personality assessment, and instincts.

Therefore, there is, probably always has been, and will be, various major issues — nearly all of them epistomological — on which psychologists differ. Whether these are called schools, approaches, sub-disciplines, values or cultures is immaterial — suffice it to say that they exist. What is unclear however is what leads people who presumably have shared a fairly homogenous education, to adopt different theoretical axioms or stances. That is, what are the aetiological factors in the preference for one or other stance. It may well be that the same factors predetermine how lay people fall along the scientific–humanist continuum.

Harré (1984), however, sees the divide not within academic psychology but between academic psychologists and laymen. He writes:

> Two images of human psychology compete for our attention. Academic psychologists, particularly those who work in the "experimental tradition", make the implicit assumption that men, women and children are high-grade automata, the patterns of whose behaviour are thought to obey something very like natural laws . . . it is assumed that there are programs

which control action and the task pf psychology is to discover the "mechanisms" by which they are implemented. Lay folk, clinical psychologists, lawyers, historians and all those who have to deal in a practical way with human beings tend to think of people as agents struggling to maintain some sort of reasoned order in their lives against a background flux of emotions, inadequate information and the ever-present tides of social pressures.

I shall try to show that the great differences that mark off these ways of thinking about human psychology are not ultimately grounded in a reasoned weighing of the evidence available to any student of human affairs. They turn in the end on unexamined political and moral assumptions. . . .

Although these profoundly different ways of interpreting and explaining human thought and action have their origin in preferred linguistic forms rather than any compelling facts of the matter, they do have profoundly different practical consequences. They carry with them very distinctive stances as to the moral, political and clinical problems with which modern people are beset. (p. 4)

Harré therefore appears to recognise the two cultures of psychology, but presumes that most psychologists favour the "scientific" culture and lay people the "humanistic" culture. He provides no evidence for this assumption, which may be something of a straw man as it is quite likely that many psychologists (not only clinical psychologists) are "humanistic" and many lay people (i.e. non-psychologists) believe they are "scientific". It is not necessarily the fact that one is a trained academic scientist that determines one's values — it could well be other factors, such as conservatism, predict better which epistemological position a person favours.

3.2 Knowledge of Psychological Principles

Many psychology textbook authors, particularly if they are writing a general or social psychology introduction for the layman or beginning student, provide a brief quiz, or short test, at the beginning of their book for the readers to assess the extent of their knowledge of the topic. The aim of the author is usually to persuade the reader how little he or she knows and by implication, how much he/she has to learn. Many of these questions, therefore, have counter-intuitive answers and are designed to impress upon the reader how little he or she knows. The tests have not been validated and may not fulfil appropriate psychometric criterion but are meant to be illustrative of the ignorance of the lay reader of basic psychological principles.

However there has been some research into popular misconceptions about psychology and the knowledge of the layman. Most of this research using the behavioural myths questionnaire has been done on introduction psychology classes at the beginning of their course. (McKeachie, 1960; Vaughn, 1977; Ellis and Richard, 1977; Best, 1982). Nearly all this research has been done in order to assess the effectiveness of an introductory course in dispelling myths about the nature of psychology. For instance, Ellis and Richard (1977) compared a group of students who completed an introductory psychology course with a matched group who had not on a 75-item multiple choice test. The former got about 25% of the answers correct, while the students who completed the course only got 30% correct. Nearly all the findings have been disappointing: although students improved significantly in the studies of McKeachie (1960) and Vaughn (1977) the change was neither substantial nor impressive (6.6 and 5.5% improvement respectively). Other research in this area has been concerned with the image of psychology as a discipline (Smith *et al.* 1969). Recently Kirton *et al.* (1983) found that school children were surprisingly inaccurate in their belief about the course content of typical psychology courses and the nature of psychology as a career, but were moderately well informed about the work psychologists do.

Out of a possible score of 56, sixth formers got mean scores of 30.36, (53% correct). Less than 50% knew that not all psychologists are medically qualified and many confused psychoanalysis and psychology as well as psychology and sociology.

Smith and Casbolt (1984) repeated a study 15 years after the first looking at sixth-formers' (12th grade pupils') knowledge of psychology. They were asked such questions as whether they had any talks/lessons about psychology at school (35% said yes); had they ever met a psychologist personally (87% said yes); they were also asked to list psychologists that they had heard of and psychology books that they had read. Relating their results with a comparable study executed 15 years before, the authors found that the pupils' reported less contact with psychology and that the distinction between psychology and psychiatry was no clearer, but that psychology was seen more as a science subject. Curiously, more pupils believed the government should not spend more money on psychological research, and fewer thought that psychology is very useful for society.

On the other hand, there is a not inconsiderable literature attesting to the surprising amount of knowledge that the lay person actually has of psychological phenomena. For instance Mischel and Mischel (1980) found that both 9- and 11-year-old children were able correctly to predict the outcome of nearly two-thirds of the famous experiments presented to them.

In a recent study, Furnham (1985b) set out to examine sixth-form (12th grade) pupils' knowledge of various aspects of psychology in order to determine how much they know or did not know about specific areas of psychological research and findings. In all, 250 subjects took part in the study. Subjects were given a booklet which contained three questionnaires.

(1) *Misconceptions about Psychology Questionnaire* (Best, 1982)

This is a 23-item true–false questionnaire designed to test common myths about psychology. The questionnaire was based on previous questionnaires of this type (McKeachie, 1960; Vaughn, 1977) and other statements were drawn from items appearing in contemporary textbooks (Braun and Linder, 1979). Best (1982) attempted to assess the validity of the items by asking colleagues to evaluate each item's ambiguity. The correct answer to all items was *false* which renders this an unbalanced questionnaire. Some error variance may occur as a result of the decision to key all the items negatively.

(2) *Common Knowledge* (Baron and Byrne, 1981)

This is a simple 10-item true–false test devised to impress upon the reader of this general social psychology textbook the counter-intuitive nature of many social psychological research findings. All the items are false, and refer to various areas of social psychology such as dissonance theory, altruism, conformity, etc.

(3) *Self-Assessment Quiz* (Colman, 1984)

This is a long 20-item multiple choice test, with the possibility of bonus points. Each question is introduced by a long paragraph which sets the question in context. The questions are drawn from all areas of psychology, psycho-physics, learning theory, social and clinical psychology, etc. The test offers between three and four multiple choices and it is, by and large, a very difficult test. The author believes that a score of 13 and above shows that a person is well-read in psychology.

Curiously there were no age, sex or chosen speciality at school, effects on the subject's knowledge. The results are however interesting.

Misconceptions about Psychology (Best 1982)

Overall, subjects got about 50% of the answers correct to this test (i.e. responded that 50% of items were false).

Table 3.2 shows the percentages of correct responses to each question. The range is fairly substantial (11–93%). Over three-quarters gave the correct response to items 4, 5, 13 and 15. Yet under a quarter gave the correct answer to items 3, 9 and 19. It is possible that the subjects were fairly accurate on items 4 and 5 because they related to their own experience in school, while their superficial reading in psychology may have led them to be able to distinguish between the mentally retarded and the mentally ill (item 13). These results are surprisingly similar to those of Best (1982) who found that first year university students got about 50% of these questions correct both before and after their course.

Common Knowledge

Subjects tended to fare slightly better on this test of social psychological knowledge. The results showed that over three-quarters of the subjects knew the answer to the question on crowding and dissonance (items 5 and 8). On the other hand they had little idea of the research on the risky-shift phenomena (Item 3) and just world beliefs (item 8). On the other questions about half the subjects gave the correct answer.

Self-Assessment Quiz

Predictably subjects did least well at this difficult multiple choice test. On only eight of the 23 items did more than half of the subjects get the correct answers while on two, less than 10% got the answer correct. The best answered questions referred to people's knowledge of cognitive dissonance and how often individuals dream. Overall, subjects found this a very difficult task. There was also a predictably negative correlation (-0.27) between the percentage of people who offered the correct answer and the number of choices available.

TABLE 3.2. *Percentage of Respondents who correctly gave FALSE as responses to each item* (N = 250)

		Percentage correct
1.	The behaviour of most lower animals — insects, reptiles and amphibians, most rodents, and birds — is instinctive and unaffected by learning	56
2.	For the first week of life, a baby sees nothing but a grey blue regardless of what he or she "looks at"	61
3.	A child learns to talk more quickly if the adults around him habitually repeat the word he is trying to say, using proper pronunciation	18
4.	The best way to get a chronically noisy schoolchild to settle down and pay attention is to punish him	93
5.	Slow learners remember more of what they learn than fast learners	86
6.	Highly intelligent people — "genuises" — tend to be physically frail and socially isolated	68
7.	On the average, you cannot predict from a person's grades at school and college whether he or she will do well in a career	29
8.	Most national and ethnic stereotypes are completely false	38
9.	In small amounts alcohol is a stimulant	24
10.	LSD causes chromosome damage	57
11.	The largest drug problem in the United States, in terms of the number of people affected, is marijuana	41
12.	Psychiatry is a subdivision of psychology	69
13.	Most mentally retarded people are also mentally ill	82
14.	A third or more of the people suffering from severe mental disorder are potentially dangerous	63
15.	Electroshock therapy is an outmoded technique rarely used in today's mental hospitals	55
16.	The more severe the disorder, the more intensive the therapy required to cure it, for example: Schizophrenics usually respond best to psychoanalysis	50
17.	Quite a few psychological characteristics of men and women appear to be inborn in all cultures, for example, women are more emotional and sexually less aggressive than men	44
18.	No reputable psychologist "believes in" such irrational phenomena as ESP, hypnosis, or the bizarre mental and physical achievements of Eastern yogis	91
19.	To change people's behaviour toward members of ethnic minority groups, we must first change their attitudes	11
20.	The basis of the baby's love for his mother is the fact that his mother fills his physiological needs for food, etc.	24
21.	The more highly motivated you are, the better you will do at solving a complex problem	31
22.	The best way to ensure that a desired behaviour will persist after training is completed is to reward the behaviour every single time it occurs throughout training (rather than intermittently)	34
23.	A schizophrenic is someone with a split personality	36

The results of this study show that if psychology is common sense, then this population certainly did not appear to have a great deal of it. However, certain objections to the use of these measures may be made, which casts severe doubt over the reliability of these results. The first is that the questions themselves were badly worded or ambiguous. Yet according to Morgan (1961), that is a sufficient reason to reject them as false. A second possible artefact occurred because *all* the items in both the first and second test were false. With most tests there is a balance between true and false being correct and, realising this, subjects may have been tempted to put "true" in instances simply because they were led to expect at least some correctly true answers. That is, there was a response category bias in these questionnaires. A third objection refers to the representativeness of the items. Indeed, Colman (1984) writes:

> The questions do not represent an entirely balanced selection from a typical undergraduate syllabus in psychology. The choice of topics was constrained in a number of ways. In the first place the questions were specifically chosen to trip you up; they were based on ideas and research findings which are on the whole unexpected or about which there is widespread misunderstanding. Finally, the author's personal interests have inevitably played a part in biasing the selection. (p. 71)

These three factors all militate against the subjects getting a good score. However, to off-set this bias it should be borne in mind that the majority of these subjects were above average intelligence with a strong interest and reading in psychology.

Turning to the actual results themselves, they are much the same as those of previous studies (Best, 1982; Smith *et al*., 1969). Common misconceptions still abide: less than half the subjects realised that schizophrenia is not a "split personality", that alcohol is not a stimulant and that fixed interval ratios are not as "addictive" as variable ratio interval ratio schedules of reinforcement. However, over half knew that psychiatry was not a subdivision of psychology and that the mentally retarded are not necessarily mentally ill. Certainly some of these results reveal that there has been an increase in six-formers' knowledge of psychology over the past decade (Smith *et al*., 1969; Plowman and Leytham, 1957). Furthermore, they seemed to have a grasp of some of the more fundamental social psychological principles, but a direct test of their knowledge of the early psychological laws (Weber's, Fechner's) revealed considerable ignorance.

Houston (1983, 1985) has also been interested in what he calls the self-evident and obvious basic principles in psychology. He developed a 21-item multiple choice questionnaire (see Table 3.3) to measure the principles of *learning* and *memory* found in classical experimental psychology. It can be seen that the items are jargon free and generally comprehensible. He found that 71% of the items were correctly answered (more often than by chance) by the 50 introductory psychology students, and that the probability of an item being answered correctly was unrelated either to the familiarity with the names of the phenomena or psychologists' ratings of the importance of the phenomena (Houston, 1983). This study was replicated on 50 volunteer adults recruited in a Los Angeles park on a Sunday afternoon (Houston, 1985). He found 76% of the questions were answered correctly more often than by chance but that the correct answers were correlated with age (education partialled out) and education (age partialled out).

TABLE 3.3. *Sample Questions Embodying, Respectively, Extinction, Subjective Organisation, Memory for Words vs Pictures, Levels of Processing, Partial Reinforcement Effect, Recency in Free Recall, and Secondary Reinforcement*

1. If, over several weeks, a child has been feeding pigeons on her window sill and then suddenly one day stops feeding them altogether the pigeons will:
   (a) immediately start coming to the window much more often than they did when they were fed there.
   (b) gradually increase the frequency with which they come to the window.
   (c) come to the window sill just as often as they did when they were fed there.
   (d) gradually stop coming to the window.
   (e) never come to the window again.

2. Suppose someone reads a list of words to you in a random order and then asks you to recall as many of the words as you can, in any order. Then he reads the same list of words to you again, but this time in a new random order, and asks you to recall them again in any order. You go through this procedure a number of times, each time hearing the same words in a new random order before you attempt to recall them. As you progress you will:
   (a) recall the words in the random order that you just heard.
   (b) begin to recall certain words together even though they are not presented together.
   (c) recall the words in an essentially random order each time you try to recall them.

3. One group of subjects is shown the *words* pencil, dog, cloud, branch, car, ant, shirt, and building. Another group is shown *pictures* of these *same* items. Both groups are tested for recall of these items at a later time. Which of the following is true?
   (a) the group shown the pictures will do best on the retention test.
   (b) the two groups will do about the same on the retention test.
   (c) the group shown the words will do best on the retention test.

4. What should be the best way to think about words if you want to remember them?
   (a) to think about what they sound like (e.g. think about where the accent falls, or whether the word has an ''r'' sound in it).
   (b) to think about what the word looks like (e.g. think about how many syllables the word has, or whether it has any curved letters in it).
   (c) to think about the meaning of the word (e.g. can it fit in your hand, or how pleasant is it).
   (d) all of these ways of thinking about words will lead to equal recall.

5. Suppose a child likes to feed two pigeons that come to two different windows at her house. One pigeon she gives a piece of corn each and every time it lands at its window. The other pigeon she only feeds every fourth time it comes to its window. After a while both pigeons come to their respective windows equally often, but only one of them gets fed every time. Then the girl moves away and the house is empty. Which pigeon will come back to the window more often?
   (a) the pigeon fed every time.
   (b) the pigeon fed every fourth time.
   (c) they will both come back equally often.

6. Someone reads a list of words to you and asks you to recall them in any order
   (a) the first few items in the list will be the easiest to recall.
   (b) the last few items in the list will be the easiest to recall.
   (c) all the words, regardless of their position in the list, will be of equal difficulty.

7. A rat first learns to run down a little hallway to find food in a white compartment at the end of the hallway. Then the rat is put in another little hallway, but this time, when the rat runs down to the end of the hallway, it is faced with a choice. If it turns left it will enter a black compartment. If it turns right it will enter a white compartment. But there isn't any food in either compartment. What will the rat tend to do?
   (a) turn left and right about equally often.
   (b) turn into the white box.
   (c) turn into the black box.
   (d) it will not turn into either compartment unless someone puts food in one of them.

Reprinted with permission of author and publisher from Houston, J. P. Psychology: a closed system of self-evident information? Psychological Reports, 1983, *52*, 203–208. Table 1.

Houston suggests that psychology is a system of self-evident information but does point out that some important principles are not obvious, even when framed in ordinary language, as a quarter of the items were not answered correctly, more than one might expect by chance. He suggests that the fact that lay people can predict many psychological findings (albeit in only one area of psychology) does not invalidate or render pointless the discipline of psychology. Rather, what psychology can and does offer is firstly the *precise measurement* of behavioural phenomena and secondly a good *theoretical explanation* for why they occur. In other words, lay people, through observation and experience, may be able to predict behaviour patterns but have no theory for why they actually occur.

Overall studies tend to show three things: first, that lay people's psychological knowledge is patchy — they tend to know a lot about some aspects of behaviour but very little about others. Second, people are not able to distinguish between the different emphases of the different social sciences or knowledge of to what extent psychologists are medically trained. Third, individual differences, as well as specific educational experiences in psychology, do not make much difference in people's lay knowledge of psychological theories and principles.

3.3 Changes over Time

One argument used by psychologists to refute the "all psychology is common sense" objection is that because psychology is frequently popularised people become more knowledgeable about psychological principles, which in turn are regarded as common sense. One may, therefore, expect psychological knowledge to increase over time.

Various research projects are of relevance here. The first concerns the maintenance of superstition over time. In 1925 Nixon sought to demonstrate that his students arrived at the beginning of his psychology classes with "unsubstantiated beliefs" about human behaviour, but that these changed as a function of teaching. He gave over 350 students the 30-item *True–False* test shown in Table 3.4. Despite the fact that nearly all are false the students rated, on average, between 10 and 12 to be true. Over 50% believed items 11, 22, 29, 18 and 24 to be true yet less than 25% circled 19, 9, 10, 14, 3, 7, 5 and 13 to be true.

Twenty-five years later Levitt (1952) replicated this study on superstitions which he defined as irrational; popularly accepted; usually influencing the behaviour of the holder; may relate to supernatural phenomena; have no sound evidence of personal experience to support it and arises spontaneously and spreads without ever having had the sanction of authority. The same questionnaire was administered to 110 men and the results compared with those of Nixon. There was, overall, a significant change in superstition with the mean true response dropping from 8.31 to 1.76. He categorised the

TABLE 3.4.

---

1. The number of man's senses is five.
2. A child comes into the world with an instinctive knowledge of good and evil. This is his conscience and is born in him.
3. Certain lines in a person's hand foretell his future.
4. If you will stare at a person's back you can make him turn around. This is a form of telepathy.
5. It really is unlucky to have anything to do with the number thirteen.
6. A man's character can be read by noting the size and location of special developments of his head.
7. People with greenish eyes are not as trustworthy as people with blue or black eyes.
8. An expectant mother by fixing her mind on a subject can influence the character of her unborn child.
9. Women are inferior to men in intelligence.
10. People born under the influence of certain planets show the influence in their characters.
11. Intelligence can be increased by training.
12. Long, slender hands indicate an artistic nature.
13. Beginning an undertaking on Friday is almost certain to bring bad luck.
14. If a man but had faith enough he could heal a broken limb instantly.
15. Many eminent men have been feeble-minded as children.
16. Some animals are as intelligent as the average human.
17. No defect of body or mind can hold us back if we have enough will power.
18. Adults sometimes become feeble-minded from overstudy.
19. All men are created equal in capacity for achievement.
20. The marriage of cousins is practically certain to result in children of inferior intelligence.
21. Especially intelligent chidren are likely to be weak and retarded physically.
22. The study of mathematics is valuable because it gives one a logical mind.
23. A square jaw is a sign of will power.
24. You can estimate an individual's intelligence pretty closely by just looking at his face.
25. A high forehead indicates intellectual superiority.
26. Fear is unnatural. It is a bad habit.
27. Women are by nature purer and better than men.
28. A person who does not look you in the eye is likely to be dishonest.
29. Man is superior because his conduct is very largely guided by reason.
30. Any physical or mental disease can be contracted by thinking about it.

Reproduced from Nixon (1925).

superstitions to highlight the point about the drop in numbers. Some superstitions, like those concerning phrenology and physiognomy he believes extinct, while others such as those concerning magic will probably find modern replacements. The author concludes that superstitions (or cognitive distortions) must be important to the individual (otherwise they would not be held), ambiguous (because the true facts are lacking or concealed) and related to certain personality factors (insecure, anxious, neurotically prone).

Over 30 years later Tupper and Williams (1986) replicated the study in Australia and found the level of superstition back up to 21% — compared with Nixon (1925) at 30.4% and Levitt (1952) at 6.5%. These results, categorised, are seen in Table 3.5. Thus instead of seeing a steady decline in superstitious beliefs over time the results are moderately consistent between 1925 and 1983. These results do show a modest decline but not as much as predicted by Nixon (1925) and indeed an increase on Levitt (1952). Of course,

TABLE 3.5. *Prevalence of Superstitions 1925, 1950 and 1983 by Categories.*

Category	Item number	Average percentage 1925	1950	1983*
Phrenology–physiognomy	6, 7, 23, 24, 25	33.40	1.98	7.2
Cheiromancy	3, 12	25.00	4.10	10.7
Numerology	5, 13	1.00	1.35	4.0
Natural phenomena	2, 19, 20, 26, 27	32.20	6.80	13.8
Astrology and magic	4, 8, 10, 14, 17, 28, 30	28.71	7.17	19.6
Intelligence and mental conditions	9, 15, 16, 18, 21, 22	40.17	11.87	25.5

*The 1983 data were gathered in Australia by Tupper and Williams (1986), other data reproduced from Levitt (1952).

it may well be that methodological artefacts account for these results: i.e. Levitt (1952) only had male subjects; Tupper and Williams's (1986) study was done in Australia; subjects from all three groups were not comparable in terms of education, etc.

On the other hand, it may well be that superstitious, non-scientific beliefs regarding human nature have only marginally decreased over time. They believe that although these superstitious beliefs may be culturally relativistic and changeable following fashions, they are unlikely to decline greatly as they fulfil an important psychological function, namely the reduction of anxiety.

In a similar study Warburton (1956) replicated a study by Ralya who gave 141 American pre-medical students a questionnaire in which they were required to note whether they believed or disbelieved the truthfulness of the statments in Table 3.6.

The topics covered astrology, heredity, etc. The results showed that on 13 items (3, 4, 10, 11, 14, 15, 20, 21, 23, 24, 36, 38, 40) over 50% of the subjects responded incorrectly, whereas on 11 items less than 10% got the answers incorrect. Warburton (1956) repeated the study more than 10 years later on 143 British graduate education students, but found no clearly defined differences between the two groups, although on average 3% more of the Manchester sample marked each item correctly. Thus, once again, there is little evidence for the decline in superstition and the increase in psychological knowledge over time.

Thirdly, Gregory (1975) replicated a study by Conklin (1919) on genuine superstitions in college students, such as unlucky symbols (black cats, the number 13, broken mirrors). The results showed that superstitious beliefs and practices have changed rather than declined over time. For instance, carrying a lucky rabbit's foot or avoiding pavement cracks were no longer held, while saving certain coins and finding horse shoes were thought to be even more lucky than was thought in the past.

There are, however, a number of methodological problems with these studies that have investigated change in beliefs over time. First, the results are

TABLE 3.6.

No.	Statement	Key*	Percentage of subjects incorrect All students 141
1.	The position of the stars at the time of a man's birth determines, in part, his character	D	18
2.	The ancient Greeks were born with better intellects than people are endowed with today	D	21
3.	Man is biologically descended from a species of existing apes	D	61
4.	Apes have been known to solve problems that the average 3-year-old child could not solve	B	52
5.	Some of the higher apes are as intelligent as the average man	D	11
6.	Animals depend to a greater extent on inherited ways of doing things than does man	B	10
7.	The conscience is part of man's natural equipment at birth	D	36
8.	Mothers instinctively know the best ways of caring for their children	D	46
9.	Most children are born bad	D	19
10.	Most children are born good	D	68
11.	Human nature cannot be changed since it is based upon instincts	D	55
12.	All people reach physical maturity by the age of 18	D	10
14.	All traits present in a child at birth are inherited traits	D	66
15.	All traits appearing in a child after birth are the result of environmental influence	D	54
16.	With the exception of identical twins, it is extremely unlikely that any two people have exactly the same heredity	B	29
17.	Voodoism is in the blood of the negro	D	32
18.	An English speaking person with German ancestors finds it easier to learn German than an English speaking person with French ancestors	D	32
19.	If the tails are cut off of generation after generation of rats, there will eventually be born rats without tails	D	42
20.	An average child of the cave-man of 10,000 years ago, if brought up in an American home of today, would in all probability become an ordinary American adult	B	65
21.	Human progress is due to increased native intelligence from age to age	D	74
22.	All men are born with equal powers	D	9
23.	The average white man is born superior, intellectually, to the average man of any other race	D	65
24.	Primitive people are born with keener senses than the more highly civilised	D	51
25.	Men are, on the average, born superior intellectually to women	D	37
26.	People cannot be sharply differentiated into blondes and brunettes in many cases	B	11
27.	If we knew all about a person's heredity we could predict his success in the world	D	22
28.	Any child, if carefully trained from birth, could be made into a successful doctor, lawyer, engineer or journalist	D	30
29.	Geniuses are always successful, whatever the handicaps of their environment	D	21
30.	Most great men have been born of poor but honest parents	D	43

31.	On the average the strongest men physically are the weakest mentally	D	18
32.	Homely women are born with more intelligence than beautiful women	D	7
33.	Brilliant children are more subject to brain fever than children of average or sub-normal intelligence	D	49
34.	No defect of body or mind can hold us back if we have will-power enough	D	32
35.	Faith alone can heal a broken leg	D	6
36.	Intelligence plays a larger role in human happiness than does emotion	D	55
37.	We are more likely to become fatigued from work that does not interest us than from work that does interest us	B	3
38.	A person who is fatigued invariably does poorer work than the same person fully rested	D	92
39.	Two individuals of the same intelligence will give almost identical testimony concerning an accident which they have both witnessed	D	26
40.	All of man's actions are determined by his desire to seek pleasure and avoid pain	D	52
41.	A man's character can be read by noting the size and location of certain developments on his head	D	18
42.	Certain lines on a person's hand are indicative of his future	D	20
43.	People with long fingers are likely to be artistic	D	47
45.	Red-headed people are likely to be temperamental	D	40
46.	Large-mouthed people are likely to be generous	D	28
47.	Green-eyed people are likely to be more jealous than blue-eyed people	D	16
48.	Brunettes are more trustworthy than blondes	D	21
49.	Cold hands are a sign of a warm heart	D	8
50.	A person who holds his thumbs in his hands is a coward	D	7
51.	A person may be a coward in one situation and not in another	B	6
52.	Illegible handwriting is a sign of superior intelligence in the educated adult	D	7
53.	If your ears burn it is a sign that someone is talking about you	D	4
54.	It is unlucky to have anything to do with the number 13	D	1
55.	Beginning an undertaking on Friday is almost sure to bring bad luck	D	4

*Key to attitudes which the writer takes as correct: B — Belief; D — Disbelief.
Reproduced with permission from Warburton, F. (1956), published in the *British Journal of Educational Psychology*.

not necessarily comparable, as different groups have been used. Thus, one might attribute the findings to sex, age, educational or national differences just as much as differences over time. Second, the samples have nearly always been university students, who are not at all representative of the population as a whole and hence might give very misleading results. Third, nearly all of these studies have concerned non-factual superstitions rather than psychological facts and it may well be that the two do not change similarly. Yet, despite these shortcomings, it seems that beliefs about behaviour do not alter as much over time as some people might expect.

3.4 Personality and Individual Differences

The use of the term "personality" by the lay person (she has no personality; he has a strong personality) is very different from that of the academic psychologist who uses it in a technical sense. This does not suggest however that there is an agreed upon definition of personality. Compare:

(a) *Sullivan* (1947, p. 10) "Personality is the relatively enduring pattern of recurrent interpersonal situations which characterise a human life . . . A personality can never be isolated from the complex of interpersonal relationships in which the person lives."

(b) *Child* (1968, p. 80) "Personality is . . . the more or less stable internal factors that make one person's behaviour consistent from one time to another, and different from the behaviour other people would manifest in comparable situations."

(c) *Maddi* (1976, p. 9) "Personality is the stable set of characteristics and tendencies that determine those commonalities and differences in the psychological behaviour of people that have continuity in time and that may or may not be easily understood in terms of the social and biological pressures of the immediate situation alone."

(d) *Pervin* (1984, p. 6) "Personality represents those characteristics of the person or of people generally that account for consistent patterns of response to situations."

Although it could be argued that these definitions were not dramatically different it is still true that no one accepted definition exists. Furthermore, there are numerous, very different theories of personality in academic psychology. Reviewers and propagandists of these theories appear to fall into three groups: benevolent ecclectics, partisan zealots and taxonomic enthusiasts.

Benevolent ecclectics are happy to list and describe the theories of the most famous personality theorists: Adler, Cattell, Eysenck, Freud, Rogers, etc. Although limitations of each theorist are mentioned they are usually impartially compared and contrasted with no good–bad, correct–incorrect, valid–invalid judgement made. For instance Hall and Lindzey (1957) in their celebrated textbook compared 17 personality theorists on 18 dimensions including unconscious determinants, organismic emphasis and multiplicity of motives. Similarly, Phares (1984) who reviews personality theorists from various approaches, argues that they can be compared on six dimensions. Systematic vs unsystematic; operational vs non-operational; content vs process; experience vs heredity; generality vs specificity; internal vs situational. A major problem with this approach is that there is no explicit criterion for inclusion or exclusion of any theory or theorists. One cannot afford to be benevolent with theories that may have historical interest but precious little empirical support.

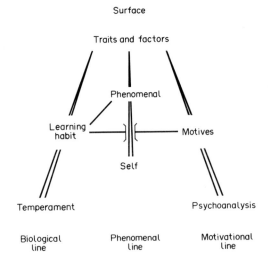

FIG. 3.1. The "Surface" of Personality and Three "Lines" Travelling Beneath it. Reprinted with permission from Cook, M. (1984). Levels of Personality. London: Holt, Ruehart and Winston.

Partisan zealots on the other hand tend to ignore all theories except one, denying the relevance, significance or validity of all theories except the one. Thus, Cattell (1965) rejects psychoanalytic and phenomenological theories of personality arguing for a multivariate experimental methods being used to define and measure the underlying traits. Similarly followers of Kelly's (1955) personal construct theory frequently choose to ignore all other theories of personality in favour of their chosen approach. The main danger of this zealous defence of one theory is the potential blindness to contradictory evidence that may result. Everybody recognises the complexity of personality and individual differences and it seems unlikely that any one narrow-band theory would be sufficiently powerful to predict and describe all human behaviour.

Taxonomic enthusiasts on the other hand have attempted to classify all personality theories into groups. This may be done historically in terms of schools, empirically in terms of methods or epistemologically in terms of the sort of data admitted in support of the theory. Although there are numerous and dramatic differences between the resultant taxonomies of reviewers there does tend to be some agreement. For instance, Cook (1984) describes four types of personality theory — those on the surface (the description of traits and factors) and those below the surface biological, phenomenal and motivation. This is set out diagrammatically in Fig. 3.1.

Of course one could split each one of these approaches (schools, lines) into further groups. Thus, for instance, trait theorists may be split into single trait theorists who emphasise just one major dimension (e.g. field independence-dependence; A/B type behaviour patterns; locus of control) or those who favour multi-trait theories (Cattell has 16, Eysenck has three).

But as Hampson (1982) points out there are three quite different perspectives on personality: the *personality theorists'* perspective which involves studying other people and deriving coherent theories; the *lay* perspective, which are everyday theories derived from experience, general knowledge, language, etc.; and the *self*-perspective which concerns our knowledge of, and theories about, ourselves.

The lay perspective has been investigated extensively by psychologists who have usually referred to it as *implicit personality theory*. For instance, the boxer Mohammed Ali has made explicit his theory of personality which is based on fruit. The theory depends on the hardness/softness of the inside and outside of fruit. This allows for four types of fruit thus:

		Outside	
		Hard	Soft
Inside	Hard	Pomegranate	Prune
	Soft	Walnut	Grape

The boxer confessed to being a "Grape" (in his view the most desirable of the various fruit) but usually letting the public see only his "Walnut" personality.

Perhaps one of the areas where lay theories are best observed is at work. Managers frequently hold strong beliefs based on taxonomic theories. As a result many "theories" in occupational psychology reflect this bias. McGregor (1960) has in fact argued that managers have two basic theories (called X and Y) about the personality of employees which lead him or her to exercise high levels of control (if a follower of theory X and less control if a follower of theory Y).

In essence, theory X assumes human beings inherently dislike work and will, if possible, avoid it; most people must be controlled and threatened with punishment if they are to work towards organisational goals; the average person actually wants to be directed, thereby avoiding responsibility. Security is more desirable than achievement.

Theory Y proceeds from a different set of assumptions. These are that work is recognised by people as a natural activity; human beings need not be controlled and threatened, they will exercise self-control and self-direction in the pursuit of organisational goals to which they are committed; commitment is associated with rewards for achievement; people learn, under the right conditions, to seek as well as accept responsibility; many people in society have creative potential, not just a few gifted individuals; under most organisational conditions the intellectual potential of people is only partially utilised.

The plethora and diversifications of these idiosyncratic lay theories have led cynics to argue that there are basically two types of people in this world — those that believe that there are two types and those that do not.

Psychological research on implicit personality theory has been concerned with the ways in which people organise or systematise judgements of other people into "naive, implicit theories of personality" (Bruner and Taguiri, 1954). There is a rich literature on people's unstated assumptions about which personality traits are associated with each other; the range, meaning and relationships between trait descriptions; the differences between central and peripheral traits; the nature of prototypes, etc. (Cook, 1979).

Strictly speaking, this literature is not about personality theory so much as a postulate or inference system of rules by which people process information about others. It is not about the development or structure of a coherent systematised working model or theory of personality functioning which may explain when, how and why people behave as they do.

Essentially, studies on implicit personality theory can be divided into two areas. The first is concerned with the usage and structure of personality traits. Thus Rosenberg and Sedlak (1972) found students used the terms intelligent, friendly, self-centred, ambitious and lazy most frequently when describing people that they knew. Others have attempted to describe the structure or dimensions underlying these traits. Perhaps the best known is that of Osgood (1962): evaluation (good–bad), activity (active–passive) and potency (hard–soft). Norman (1963), on the other hand, found five factors which have been widely replicated: extraversion, agreeableness, conscientiousness, emotional stability and culture. Still others have attempted to describe centrality power or preference for various traits (Asch, 1946).

The second area of research has been on what Sharteau and Nagy (1984) call information integration theory. This has been concerned with how individuals process trait information about others in order to derive an impression or picture. There is extensive research on how people acquire these implicit theories but most concern the integration and inference from material presented. Terms like cognitive algebra have been replaced by schema theory, and psychologists from various traditions (cognitive, linguistic, personality) have all attempted to look at this process. Despite different (and often rather sterile) methodologies lacking in external validity there is considerable agreement as to why and how people process information about others (Hampson, 1982).

What is less clear and of course probably more important, is how accurate these perceptions are. Different investigators have focused on different types of personality ratings to attempt to access what they measure. Some have argued that the personality ratings (or trait words) reflect neither actual nor believed co-occurrence likelihood of traits, but reveal semantic similarity between the trait terms (D'Andrade, 1974). Further, it has been concluded from research that ratings of behaviour made from memory are all subject to systematic distortion, caused by the rater confusing the similarity in meaning between the terms with the memory of whether the two categories did (or did not) actually co-occur in the stimulus person that they rated (D'Andrade, 1974). Others have adopted a constructionist position which argues that just as trait theorists categorise (through factor analysis) social behaviour into a small number of higher order factors, so lay people implicitly derive their own coding or categorising scheme.

Psychoanalytic theories of personality are generally not well understood by lay-people (Kline, 1972). While lay people probably know of the distinction between conscious and unconscious, most do not understand the concept of preconscious. Furthermore, the three-fold structure of id, ego and superego, as well as defence mechanisms, instinctual processes, etc., are not well known. The odd concepts like phallic symbol and penis envy have become part of lay language (albeit bawdy rather than serious) few lay people know or understand the frequently counter-intuitive psychoanalytic theories of personality (Pervin, 1984).

3.5 Intelligence

The way in which one defines, measures and perceives the "causes" of intelligence has long been a source of considerable interest to lay people, no doubt because of its obvious policy implications (Furnham *et al.*, 1985). Many lay people appear to believe that intelligence is either some sort of problem solving ability (thinking) or acquired knowledge, or preferably both. Many of the passionate debates that academics have had concerning such things as the genetic basis, definition and measurement of intelligence have been of equal interest to lay people. One example of this was the considerable correspondence to *The Times* (of London) concerning the Burt scandal — the idea that Sir Cyril Burt had "faked" his data concerning the heritability of intelligence in twins. Over 50 letters were published over a period of a month (26 October–29 November, 1975). Letters were received from prominent academics as well as lay people. Some were frivolous and trivial, and others genuinely naive. They give, in their own way, a fascinating account about lay theories of the origins of intelligence (Furnham, 1986b). Consider for example the following:

(a) *C.M. Johnson*, 11 November
"Can some expert explain why equally loved children, with identical home backgrounds and equal educational opportunities, should vary so greatly in their ability and achievements? I have a *horridly* right-wing suspicion that the answer lies in the genes."
(b) *B. Barnadiston*, 15 November
"Does it matter whether intelligence is inherited or not? Common sense, integrity and the will to serve the community are far more important."

There were many puzzled lay people asking supposedly straightforward questions:

(c) *J.A.G. Miller*, 15 November

"I am one of two sons born to middle-class parents. At the age of 68 I look back on an undistinguished career befitting a person of quite average intelligence. My late brother, on the other hand, was a man of outstanding intelligence, a distinguished engineer, research scientist who held for many years a high position in industry. Am I average and was he brilliant because he inherited superior genes, or did my different IQ arise from 'social institutions and structures'? If the latter, how did this arise? We lived in the same house, went to the same grammar school and both received the same devoted and impartial love and care from our parents."

(d) *M. Tracy*, 15 November

"Would experts debating the question of whether intelligence is inherited please say why the intelligence of children of the same parents can differ so much when their intellectual environment is usually so similar. Surely the explanation is genetic?"

(e) *M. Baglow*, 17 November

"Although only a parent, not an expert, I think I can answer Mrs Tracy's query. Different children in one family have different environments in at least two respects: one, that the parents who coped with the first child, learned from doing so and will probably handle their next child differently (over anxious with the first, perhaps, more relaxed with the second); two, that each child in a family is in its own place in relation to the others: Mary has a different environment from Jimmy in that she is his sister, and he has his own, because he is her brother. A third consideration is that one child may be born with curly hair and engaging ways (heredity!) and another may be ugly and less apparently lovable; this will produce different reactions from the people who form his world, and these are an important part of the individual's environment. Having said that, I would like to add that no matter who has experienced the vivid and varied personalities of her brand new infants can possibly doubt the importance of heredity, and that it is also important to remember that when experts talk about 'intelligence' they only mean 'the ability to do well in intelligence tests'. "

It has been suggested that academic researchers too are not value-free (or value fair) in their conception of intelligence. Several commentators on science believe that modern bourgeois ideology is responsible for the acceptance of ideas of biological determinism which attempts to justify human inequality on a social-Darwinian view of human nature (Albee, 1982; Lewontin *et al.*, 1982). Eysenck (1982) has recently offered current and historical evidence to justify his position that the "alleged conformity of political ideology and scientific stance is, in fact, completely erroneous and historically untenable" (p. 1288). In a reply, Albee (1983) has claimed that biological determinism is a major ideological weapon against Marxism although he omitted the inverse implication that environmental determinism is a major ideological weapon against bourgeois ideology and social-Darwinism. Yet a study by Pastore (1949) which investigated the relationship between an individual's views about the nature–nurture controversy and his/her attitudes to social, political, economic questions, found upon examining the works of famous scientists (Galton, Rutherford) that there was a strong correlation between beliefs in the influence of heredity and the degree of conservatism in the sociopolitical attitudes.

Certainly more work has gone into the *determinants* and *measurement* of intelligence, than has gone into its operationalisation. There are considerable problems and debates as to what constitutes intelligence. Various attempts were made in the 1920s to come to an agreed definition but none such were found. Some argued that it was the ability to carry on abstract thinking; while others thought adjustment to the environment a better definition. Just as there is no agreement on the definition of intelligence among psychologists, so there is no agreement about the nature of intelligence (whether there is one primary or more than one factor) or indeed the best way to measure intelligence. In many ways these debates are not different from lay conversations about intelligence, though there are numerous technical terms which have to be mastered (e.g. fluid vs crystallised intelligence; culture-free vs culture-fair tests, etc.). Sternberg is one of the few people who has done systematic research on lay theories of intelligence (Sternberg *et al.*, 1981; Sternberg, 1982) though others have worked in this area (e.g. Neisser, 1979). Sternberg argued that ordinary lay people have definite ideas as to what intelligence actually is, and how to measure it, and that, equally, academic, scientific researchers' ideas are also firmly based in the real world.

In a fairly large study Sternberg and colleagues asked nearly 500 lay people and about 150 psychologists specialising in intelligence to list behaviours they thought characteristic of "intelligence", "academic intelligence", "everyday intelligence" and "unintelligence". They found such characteristics as reasons logically, widely read, open minded, and displays common sense, were quoted but that there was a great diversity of often idiosyncratic responses. These characteristics were then rated on a 7-point scale and factor analysed. For both groups three quite clear factors emerged, and though they were similar, they were not exactly the same (see Table 3.7).

Sternberg (1982) notes:

> On the whole, the informal theories of intelligence that laymen carry around in their heads — without ever realising that their ideas constitute theories — conform fairly closely to the most widely accepted formal theories of intelligence that scientists have constructed. That is, what psychologists study as intelligence seems to correspond, in general, to what people untrained in psychology mean by intelligence. On the other hand, what psychologists study corresponds to only *part* of what people mean by intelligence in our society, which includes a lot more than IQ tests measure. (p. 35)

In a second series of studies Sternberg (1985) looked at implicit or lay theories of intelligence, creativity and wisdom. When rating attributes of all

TABLE 3.7. Laypersons' vs Experts' Ratings of Intelligence

(a) Laypersons' Rating Characteristic in Ideal Person

Factor	Factor loading
I. Practical problem-solving ability	
Reasons logically and well	0.77
Identifies connections among ideas	0.77
Sees all aspects of a problem	0.76
Keeps an open mind	0.73
Responds thoughtfully to others' ideas	0.70
Sizes up situations well	0.69
Gets to the heart of problems	0.66
Interprets information accurately	0.65
Makes good decisions	0.64
Goes to original sources for basic information	0.62
Poses problems in an optimal way	0.62
Is a good source of ideas	0.62
Perceives implied assumptions and conclusions	0.61
Listens to all sides of an argument	0.61
Deals with problems resourcefully	0.61
II. Verbal ability	
Speaks clearly and articulately	0.83
Is verbally fluent	0.82
Converses well	0.76
Is knowledgeable about a particular field of knowledge	0.74
Studies hard	0.70
Reads with high comprehension	0.70
Reads widely	0.69
Deals effectively with people	0.68
Writes without difficulty	0.65
Sets aside time for reading	0.64
Displays a good vocabulary	0.61
Accepts social norms	0.60
III. Social competence	
Accepts others for what they are	0.88
Admits mistakes	0.74
Displays interest in the world at large	0.72
Is on time for appointments	0.71
Has social conscience	0.70
Thinks before speaking and doing	0.70
Displays curiosity	0.68
Does not make snap judgements	0.68
Makes fair judgements	0.66
Assesses well the relevance of information to a problem at hand	0.66
Is sensitive to other people's needs and desires	0.65
Is frank and honest with self and others	0.64
Displays interest in the immediate environment	0.64

(b) Experts' Rating Characteristicness of Important Behaviours in Ideal Person

Factor	Factor loading
I. Verbal intelligence	
Displays a good vocabulary	0.74
Reads with high comprehension	0.74
Displays curiosity	0.74
Is intellectually curious	0.68
Sees all aspects of a problem	0.66
Learns rapidly	0.66
Appreciates knowledge for its own sake	0.65
Is verbally fluent	0.65
Listens to all sides of an argument before deciding	0.65
Displays alertness	0.64
Thinks deeply	0.64
Shows creativity	0.64
Converses easily on a variety of subjects	0.64
Reads widely	0.63
Likes to read	0.62
Identifies connections among ideas	0.60
II. Problem solving ability	
Able to apply knowledge to problems at hand	0.74
Makes good decisions	0.73
Poses problems in an optimal way	0.73
Displays common sense	0.66
Displays objectivity	0.66
Solves problems well	0.64
Plans ahead	0.62
Has good intuitions	0.62
Gets to the heart of problems	0.62
Appreciates truth	0.61
Considers the end result of actions	0.61
Approaches problems thoughtfully	0.60
III. Practical intelligence	
Sizes up situations well	0.84
Determines how to achieve goals	0.83
Displays awareness to world around him or her	0.69
Displays interest in the world at large	0.63

three qualities he found that both academic *and* lay people believe intelligence and wisdom most similar, and creativity and wisdom to be the least similar of the three possible pairs of attributes. A short analysis yielded various bi-polar dimensional solutions to the ratings of each quality, i.e.:

Intelligence	1. Practical problem-solving ability vs verbal ability
	2. Intellectual balance and integration vs goal orientation and attainment
	3 Contextual intelligence vs fluid thought
Creativity	1. Non entrenchment vs integration and intellectuality
	2. Aesthetic taste and imagination vs decision skill and flexibility
	3. Perspicacity vs drive for accomplishment and recognition
	4. Inquisitiveness vs intuition
Wisdom	1. Reasoning ability vs sagacity
	2. Learning from ideas and environment vs judgement
	3. Expeditious use of information vs perspicacity.

Sternberg argues that lay people's theories of intelligence overlap with, but also go beyond, skills measured by tests. That is, the intelligent person is believed to solve problems well, reason clearly, think logically, have a good store of information but also able to balance information, and show one's intelligence in wordly, as well as academic contexts. Lay theories of creativity overlap with those of intelligence, but tend to down play analytic abilities stressing rather unconventional ways of thinking and acting. Also, aesthetic taste, imagination, inquisitiveness and intuitiveness are part of lay theories most of which go way beyond conventional psychological tests of creativity. Lay theories of wisdom stress sagacity and making clear, sensible and fair judgements that take account of long and short-term issues, as well as learning from experience and being flexible.

Sternberg (1985) believes that while lay theories are precursors to academic theories they are worth studying in their own right. In fact he lists four reasons why the study of lay theories of intelligence, creativity and wisdom are worth pursuing:

(a) the terms — intelligence, creativity, wisdom — are frequently used in everyday discourse as well as in psychological discourse with no or minimal definition, and it is useful to know what people mean when they use these terms; (b) people evaluate the intelligence, creativity, and wisdom of themselves and others with some regularity, and it is worthwhile to know the psychological bases on which these evaluations are made; (c) as people make these judgements, it is helpful to know to what extent they correlate with measures derived from explicit theories, such as psychometric tests; and (d) the implicit theories may eventually help us broaden and change our explicit theories, as we come to realise those aspects of cognition or affect that the current explicit theories of intelligence, creativity, and wisdom do not encompass, but possibly, should encompass. Thus, the study of implicit theories is not merely an easy substitute for the formation and study of explicit theories of psychological constructs. Implicit theories deserve to be studied in their own right, and such study is complementary to the study of explicit theories. (p. 625)

However, Sternberg does note that the test of a lay theory is quite different from an explicit academic theory. The former is tested by whether any account is an accurate, comprehensive account of what people "have in their heads", while the latter are tested through classic empirical methods. These lay theories change over time with fashion (see Chapter 2), as well as develop and change in people. Furthermore, they are learnt and hence culture bound. This, of course, suggests more work in this important field!

Both lay people and expert/scientific people were asked to rate academic intelligence, everyday intelligence and general intelligence. They both felt them to be highly correlated but there were two main differences between the groups. Experts, more than lay people, stressed the importance of motivation (dedication, persistence), while lay people stressed social competence more than the experts. Lay people consistently stressed *inter*-personal competence in a *social* context (getting on with others) while experts stressed *intra*-personal competence in an *individual* context (learns quickly, solves problems fast).

Although lay theories of intelligence may have many similarities to expert theories they are more often descriptive than explanatory. That is, scientific theories must ask what it *means* to reason logically, solve problems or get on with others; scientists must also devise ways of *measuring* these concepts; more importantly, they must explain individual *variation* in the concepts. Despite the fact that lay theories are descriptive, they are functional in that people use them to assess the ability and competence of others. Most people believe that they are very good at this, though Sternberg has shown that they are only modestly good at assessing or predicting their own personality. They are, however, much better at self-descriptions, or checklists, of their own ability which relate more closely to their actual IQ test derived scores.

It may be naive to suppose that there are individual group, sub-cultural, or even cultural differences in lay people's understanding of the nature of intelligence (Berry, 1984; Valsiner, 1984). Studies by anthropologists and psychologists have shown remarkable cultural differences in the meaning of the term intelligence. For instance the *Shona* of Zimbabwe regard intelligence as being cautious and prudent, particularly in social relationships (Irvine, 1969) while even within Uganda two tribes had rather different views (Wober, 1969). The *Baganda* associated intelligence with mental order, while the *Batoro* with turmoil. Other studies in Africa (Serpell, 1974; Pulman and Kilbride, 1980; Super, 1982), Latin America (Klein *et al.*, 1973) and Asia (Gill and Keats, 1982) have all pointed to subtle cultural differences in the understanding and definition of intelligence. Many reflect a distinction between cognitive and social skills, while in many cultures alertness and wisdom are stressed.

Berry (1984) has set out a possible framework for exploring both local and universal features of different groups' conceptions of intelligence, though at this stage it has not been tested. However, as many have pointed out, a culture's definition of intelligence (like intelligence itself) changes, particularly with the introduction of schooling. Valsiner (1984) has argued:

> The major difference between cultures in conceptualising intelligence seems to be in the inclusion of *social-interactive characteristics* ("friendly", "honourable", "correct", "happy", "public" — in the African and Asian cases, which were not paralleled in the Australian groups under study) together with cognitive "skills". On the other hand, it should not be taken for granted that in non-European cultures, all skills that would be labelled "cognitive" or "intellectual" in European cultures, share the same category assignment. . . .
>
> In the systems of meanings in different cultures, "intelligence" and other terms related to it, can cover different areas of the space of meanings, and can be associated with different other concepts. Therefore, building a scientific conception of intelligence on the common-sense meaning of the term "intelligence" within a given culture, would not help us to arrive at a universal conceptualisation of intelligence, equally applicable to all human beings, in the particular structure of their cultures and habitat.
>
> The cross-cultural differences in the meaning of "intelligence" and related terms seem to fit the notion of *correspondence* between the characteristics of "intelligence" and the causal texture or demand-character structure of the modes of human activities in the given cultures. In cultures where technological advancement is in the centre of the cultural demand-character structure, the application of the terms of intelligence tends to exclude social, moral, or emotional aspects of human action. More specifically, it may prescribe additional implicit criteria — e.g. speed and numerosity of responses, or taxonomic classification of objects — to characterise intelligence. If, however, the demand-character structure of a culture is more complex, including different central units at the same time (e.g. both technological advancement *and* retainment of traditional values), then characteristic features of intelligence can include corresponding qualities (e.g. "reasoning logically", "having a storehouse of knowledge" together with "correctness", "social orientation" as in the case of the Chinese). If, in a particular culture, individuals (rather than social groups) are expected to control their environments, then the characteristics of individuals' actions that have the goal of controlling the environment may dominate the meaning of "intelligence". If, however, the control over the environment is conceptualised as the task for social groups (family, clan, collective), the meaning of "intelligence" is very likely to include the characteristics of social relationships and social (moral) norms."

3.6 Conclusion

This chapter focused on people's lay knowledge and beliefs about psychology and psychological topics. Psychology as a discipline is itself divided into different schools or approaches, often with different epistemological assumptions and it is quite possible that lay people tend to believe in, or support, the axioms of one school (e.g. psychoanalysis) vs another (e.g. behaviourism). More recently, research has suggested that a more simple dimension of scientific vs humanistic or behavioural vs non-behavioural may be sufficient to divide people into different "believer" groups.

Studies of lay people's actual knowledge of psychological principles are difficult to compare because they have used different material presented in rather different (simple vs complex; true/false vs multiple choice) ways. Some results tend to indicate that many lay people, even with fairly advanced education, hold many misconceptions about psychology and have only limited knowledge about psychological principles. On the other hand, there appears to be evidence for the fact that if presented in clear, simple jargon-free language many people, even comparatively young children, have a good knowledge of principles and theories in cognitive, biological and social psychology. Some evidence suggests, however, that these beliefs may change over time, some superstitions being forgotten, others remaining relatively unchanged and still new ones arising.

The chapter focused on two topics that are of interest to the academic psychologists and layman alike. The first concerned personality and individual differences. There are a great number of personality theories in psychology, some with much more support than others, and attempts have been made to taxonomise or categorise them. Although lay people do hold lay theories about personality their implicit personality theories are more frequently ways of processing information about others. The language people use to describe others is a very useful beginning to get at this process.

Similarly, lay people hold theories about human intelligence. Once again, there are numerous academic theories about the exact nature of human intelligence and studies done on lay theories suggests a close similarity between lay thinking and academic research.

It is, of course, no surprise that lay people have a fairly good grasp of psychological principles. Indeed it would be strange if they did not. Yet there are areas where lay people are simply incorrect about human behaviour. Interestingly lay theories of psychological phenomena seem to fall into schools of thought much the same as those found in academic textbooks.

One area, not extensively discussed in this chapter that is a psychological theory of the non-common sense kind is psychoanalysis. A great many of the theories and models in psychoanalysis are counter-intuitive and paradoxical, such as the idea that people gamble to lose, not to win. On the other hand, many Freudian insights, such as the relationship between money and faeces, are not part of common sense. Indeed, one reason why some people reject psychoanalysis and others find it a particularly interesting, insightful and powerful theory is precisely because many of the theories and ideas are not commonsensical!

4
Lay Theories in Psychiatry

4.1 Introduction

A very large number of lay people are ignorant of the differences between the academic disciplines of psychology and psychiatry. This may be perfectly understandable because although the training of a psychologist may be very different from that of a psychiatrist there may be considerable overlap in their theories, methods and interests. Of course, a cognitive psychologist interested in visual illusions may have very little in common with a psychiatrist interested in alcohol dependence, nevertheless, there is frequently a fair degree of overlap between the two disciplines.

Lay people's knowledge (or ignorance) of psychiatry may be observed in the numerous jokes about psychiatrists. Many of the jokes are reflected in the remark attributed to Sam Goldwyn, who said that "Anyone who goes to a psychiatrist ought to have his head examined". A common belief is that psychiatrists are themselves rather odd, and possibly dangerous because of their perspicacity. Essentially, psychiatry may be defined as that speciality in medicine concerned with the diagnosis, treatment and prevention of mental disorders associated with disturbances of emotion, thought, perception and behaviour (Kisker, 1964).

There are probably as many myths about psychiatry as there are about mental illness. For instance, it is frequently erroneously believed that *all* psychiatrists advocate the disease or medical model of mental illness which asserts: Mental illnesses are of organic origin with specific etiology, course and outcome; an underlying physical state affects surface psychological symptoms, and hence changing the symptoms will not cure the disease; people frequently get these mental illnesses through no fault of their own; cure depends primarily on professional intervention by medically trained people; mental illness may have small culturally distinct manifestations but the process is essentially universal and not culturally specific.

Psychiatry is, and must be, concerned with a wide range of disorders, at the one extreme identifiable in terms of physical malfunctioning, and hence amenable to conventional medical treatments and at the other extreme behaviour patterns that are compared with social norms and where management focuses on counselling or legal measures. However, because of the

TABLE 4.1. *Some of the Questions used in Nunnally's (1981) Study*

1. The mentally ill pay little attention to their personal appearance
2. People who keep themselves occupied with pleasant thoughts seldom become mentally ill
3. Few people who enter mental hospitals ever leave
4. Older people have fewer emotional problems than younger people
5. People cannot maintain good mental health without the support of strong persons in their environment
6. Will power alone will not cure mental disorders
7. Women have no more emotional problems than men do
8. X-rays of the head will not tell whether a person is likely to become insane
9. Emotional problems do little damage to the individual
10. Psychiatrists try to teach mental patients to hold in their strong emotions
11. Mental illness can usually be helped by a vacation or change of scene
12. Disappointments affect children as much as they do adults
13. The main job of the psychiatrist is to recommend hobbies and other ways for the mental patient to occupy his mind
14. The insane laugh more than normal people
15. Psychiatrists try to show the mental patient where his ideas are incorrect
16. Mental disorder is not a hopeless condition
17. Mental health is one of the most important problems
18. Mental disorder is usually brought on by physical causes
19. It is easier for women to get over emotional problems than it is for men
20. A change of climate seldom helps an emotional disorder
21. The best way to mental health is by avoiding morbid thoughts
22. There is not much that can be done for a person who develops a mental disorder
23. Mental disorder is one of the most damaging illnesses that a person can have
24. Children sometimes have mental breakdowns as severe as those of adults
25. Nervous breakdowns seldom have a physical origin

diversity and ambiguity inherent in the discipline there has, and continues to be, considerable controversy and dissent.

4.2 Attitudes to, and Concepts of, Mental Health

There are many historical accounts of how people at various periods in time — the classical period, the middle ages, the age of reason — perceived and treated the mentally ill. However, it was not until the 1940s that systematic studies were done on public attitudes towards mental illness (Ramsey and Seipp, 1948).

Perhaps the most important study conducted was that of Nunnally (1961) which was a 6-year study on what the general public knew and felt about mental illness and its treatment. A nationally representative sample completed a number of questionnaires, an example of which is set in Table 4.1.

This scale was factor analysed and 10 interpretable factors resulted, these were labelled: look and act different; will power; sex distinction; avoidance of morbid thoughts; guidance and support; hopelessness; external cause vs personality; non-seriousness; age function; organic causes. Attempts have been make to replicate the factor structure with lack of success (Ahmed and Viswarathan, 1984). But the exercise should not be seen as purely an example of descriptive research, as it set out to test a number of propositions. Public information is not highly structured; the public do not make connotative distinctions among the subprofessions in the mental health field; public attitudes are different toward neurotic and psychotic disorders, etc. Proposition 2.3 read: "The average man is not grossly misinformed" and Nunnally was forced to conclude "Regardless of which way comparisons are made the same conclusion is reached: Mean responses for the public are not markedly different in most cases from mean responses for experts" (p. 22). However there were issues on which the two disagreed:

1. Books on "peace of mind" prevent many persons from developing nervous breakdowns. (Experts repudiate, public agrees.)
2. If a person concentrates on happy memories, he will not be bothered by unpleasant things in the present. (Experts repudiate, public agrees.)
3. The main job of the psychiatrist is to explain to the patient the origin of his troubles. (Experts repudiate, public agrees.)
4. Good emotional habits *cannot* be taught to children in school as easily as spelling can. (Experts support, public disagrees.)
5. When a person is recovering from a mental illness, it is best not to discuss the treatment he has had. (Experts repudiate, public agrees.)
6. A person *cannot* rid himself of unpleasant memories by trying hard to forget them. (Experts support, public disagrees.)

Summarising the results it seemed that "as is commonly suspected, the mentally ill are regarded with fear, distrust and dislike. The stigma associated with mental illness was found to be very general, both across all social groups and across attitude measures, with relatively little between people from different demographic groups such as age and education. Old people and young people, highly educated people with little formal training — all tend to regard the mentally ill as dangerous, dirty, unpredictable and worthless. A strong negative halo surrounds all the mentally ill, and considered, unselectively, as being all things bad." (p. 186) However, these negative attitudes were not held because of *existing* information or even *mis*information about mental illness by the public but, rather, because of *lack* of information. While marked differences were found as a function of age and education regarding kinds of *information* held, *differences in attitudes* were small. The younger, better educated, held slightly less derogatory attitudes, but their attitudes were still markedly negative. That is, whatever their knowledge of mental illness, the respondents seemed universally negative to the mentally ill. Another study by Whatley (1958) focused on social distance and found that people tend to keep a distance between themselves and former mental patients which tends to create for the patients the problem of social isolation which usually serves only to exacerbate their problem.

All the early studies found that mental patients were feared, stigmatised and shunned. In her review of findings since 1960 Rabkin (1974), however, divided the studies she reviewed into the optimistic findings, the pessimistic findings, and equivocal findings. Despite certain methodological problems and limitations (definitions, ratings scales, etc.) some studies (Lemkau and Crocetti, 1962; Bentz and Edgerton, 1970) seemed to suggest an increase in the public's acceptance of mental illness and less extreme rejection of those labelled mentally ill. Other studies, however, demonstrated that the dislike, fear and aversion traditionally associated with the mentally ill continued, probably because they are unpredictable (Bord, 1971). There were, however, also some equivocal findings which did not clearly indicate greater or lesser rejection. Rabkin (1974) notes that people are better informed about mental illness but that although various moral issues remain, social and medical considerations have become, for most people, more significant. Furthermore, people believe that mental illness is like any other illness.

The characteristics of patients that influence the degree of public acceptance include: the degree of unpredictability and loss of accountability; the personal characteristics of persons manifesting the behaviour; the particular symptoms and diagnostic category involved, the visibility of the disturbed behaviour and the extent to which violence is an issue. Similarly, the research has indicated that the characteristics of the public that influence the degree of acceptance of mental illness include age, education, occupation, race, ethnicity, social class, and predictably, actual experience with mental patients. The results of these studies may be expected: the older the person, the more intolerant, unsympathetic and rejecting are his/her attitudes to the mentally ill; the lower the social-economic class the more rejecting they are of the relative of a mental patient; the lower the class the greater feelings of fear and resentment, while the higher the class the greater the feelings of shame and guilt. Race or ethnicity is nearly always confounded with income, class and status and by itself does not relate to either positive or negative attitudes. Similarly, mere contact with the mentally ill is not a sufficient condition for attitude change.

Because different communities have different levels of familiarity with mental health professionals and services, different expectations regarding ease of access to treatment, and different perceptions of how common or unusual it is to be a mental patient, there are various contextual features as well that predict beliefs about mental illness and mental patients.

Rabkin (1974) concludes her review thus:

The gross inhumanity of involuntary psychiatric hospitalisation, its immense financial cost, the emergence of psychotropic drugs, and the development of alternative styles of treatment have, together, impressed many mental health professionals and legislators with the undesirability of inpatient care for mental illness, and with the consequent need for identification of populations at risk in the community to facilitate early intervention and treatment. Once such an epidemiological framework is adopted in the search for precipitating factors, attention becomes addressed to stressful aspects of everyday living, such as poverty, over-crowding, unemployment, and social isolation. At this point it no longer seems helpful to regard mental illness as an illness like any other that can strike anyone at any time, as a germ or a virus might do; alternative formulations of a psychosocial nature offer greater explanatory value. Concepts developed within this latter framework today seem more important to communicate to the public, but prevailing educational efforts still follow the older, traditional format. (p. 29)

More recent studies in different countries, with different populations, looking at different aspects of mental illness tend to show the same pattern of results. Thus Furnham and Pendred (1983) found people being more favourably disposed towards the physically, rather than the mentally handicapped. Similarly Nieradzik and Cochrane (1985) confirmed the following hypotheses in a recent study: public attitudes towards mental illness are more rejecting than accepting; social rejection increases with increasing severity of disturbance in behaviour, and attitudes of the general population towards the mentally ill will be influenced by the label of mental illness as well as by behaviour indicative of mental illness.

Studies on attitudes to mental illness have traditionally focused on different features of the problem: for instance sex differences in mental disorders. Thus Farina (1981) found from an extensive review of the literature that men and women express similar beliefs about the mentally ill but behave in quite different ways towards them: females are kinder and more sympathetic than men towards the mentally ill; women who are or have been mental patients are treated more benignly and favourably than men. The reason for the fact that female patients are treated better than males is probably that they are less aggressive and adventurous but also because their "deviant" behaviour is less inconsistent with traditional sex role norms (Rosenfield, 1982).

Others have focused on children's attitudes towards mental illness. In a developmental study Weiss (1985) showed that as children got older (between 7 and 14) they saw the mentally ill as more similar (less inferior) to themselves; they were less likely to distinguish between mental illness and other afflictions; they thought the mentally ill less of a threat to society and the family system, and thought that mental illness was less likely to be attributable to inadequate, deprived or inter-personal experiences. Yet in a later study (Weiss, 1986) she found attitudes to deviant groups were evidenced by kindergarten (a 6-year old) and did not change appreciably with age and that "crazy people" are regarded with the same fear, disgust, and aversion by children and adults alike. However, according to Roberts et al;. (1981) children (aged 9–13) can differentiate between medical and psychological disorders in their peers in terms of diagnosis, aetiology, prognosis, effective treatment strategies and desirability. Yet the children did not consistently respond on the severity dimension, and in fact saw more serious psychological problems (hallucinations) as less severe than less serious problems (acting out).

There is also evidence of ethnic differences in reactions to mental illness and consequent help-seeking. For instance, Tucker (1979) found a majority of American blacks held concepts of mental illness inconsistent with the standard (explicit, white) conceptions formulated by mental health professionals, and that they (the blacks) had less need because they had better coping strategems. Hall and Tucker (1985) similarly found significant differences between blacks' and whites' conceptions of mental illness in that blacks' responses were more stereotyped than whites. They believed, for instance, more than whites, that the mentally ill look and act differently from normals, that women are more likely to suffer from mental illness than men, and that mental illness can be controlled by the avoidance of morbid thoughts. Thus it is argued that attitudes to the mentally ill, as well as help-seeking beliefs and strategies are culturally specific.

It seems, then, that attitudes to the mentally ill are learnt from parents, teachers and the media. Hence, there have been studies which have focused on the way the media presents mental illness and how these presentations affect attitudes (Matas et al., 1985). One may suppose that as mental illnesses are portrayed more frequently in films and on the television that people would become more familiar with, and less hostile towards, them. However, television drama may in fact have the opposite effect and misinform as much about psychiatric problems as it informs.

Certainly, the results from many studies in different countries leads one to believe that many lay people remain ignorant as to the aetiology, prognosis and most effective cures of a wide range of psychiatric illnesses.

4.3 Attributions for Addiction

Most people are very familiar with the concept of addiction, be it to alcohol or drugs, food or nicotine, stimulants or depressants. Many admit to being addicted to some substance or at least know others who are. As a consequence they often hold strong, complex beliefs about both the causes of, and the cures for, these addictions.

Within the social sciences, explicit theories of addiction fall roughly into three main categories. Biological models or theories often tend to emphasise the pharmacological properties of the addictive substance (alcohol, nicotine, LSD, etc.) and its effect on the central nervous system. This approach tends to see the addict as someone who is biologically predisposed to developing physiological dependence. Psychological theories on the other hand tend to assume that addicts share personality traits, beliefs and values, and/or maladaptively learned behaviour patterns which make them particularly vulnerable or predisposed to develop addiction. Thirdly sociocultural or structural models point to class, regional or other macro-sociological differences in addition and tend to explain addiction as a means of coping with structurally induced stress or inequality. Clare (1979) has subdivided these approaches yet further. *Biological* causes include ideas concerned with metabolic defects, neurotransmitter alterations and genetic factors; while *psychological* causes include approaches from psychoanalysis (the alcoholic is dependent), personality theorists (identifying alcoholic traits) and behavioural (learning history) theories; as well as *sociocultural* theories which may emphasise occupational factors, ethnic factors, familial factors, or more simply the availability of alcohol. However, progressively fewer researchers and reviewers are zealously partisan regarding one or other approach, preferring to be more benevolently ecclectic.

Considerably less work has gone into implicit lay theories of addiction, yet a surprising amount of highly varied material exists. This section will concentrate on lay theories of two of the most common forms of addiction: alcoholism and addictive smoking.

It should be pointed out that lay theories about addiction may be held by at least three groups: non-addicted lay people, addicts themselves, and professionals who have not received any specific theoretical training. Others include ex-addicts and those specialists trained to deal with addictions.

(1) Alcoholism

As the drinking of alcohol in nearly all societies is, and has been, a frequent occurrence, people are very familar with the consequences of alcoholism. However, they remain surprisingly ignorant about the effects of alcohol and the causes of, or cures for, alcoholism.

Table 4.2 shows 17 common misconceptions about alcohol. A surprising number of people would endorse these items as true despite the fact that all are demonstrably false. If their knowledge is so patchy, if not downright wrong, it is perhaps, therefore, not surprising that their explanations of, or theories for, alcoholism are simple or misguided.

Research in lay theories of alcoholism originated from studies investigating the attitudes of various professional and non-professional populations such as doctors, nurses, psychiatrists and alcoholic counsellors towards alcoholism and alcoholics. Furthermore, much of this research is based on the implicit assumption that a person's belief about the causes of alcoholism influences their attitudes towards the alcoholic person. However, this research into public attitudes usually assumed a simple moralistic (they were bad) vs medical (they were sick) dichotomy, revealing evidence for an increasing acceptance of the disease concept of alcoholism, which views the alcoholic as someone who is medically unable to tolerate the effects of alcohol (Mulford and Miller, 1961, 1964; Linsky, 1972; Hey, 1977; McHugh *et al.*, 1980). A problem with this approach, however, is that beliefs about the causes of alcoholism do not fit into neat bidimensional categories, and endorsement of one view does not necessarily imply rejection of another.

Many studies have shown people to be ambivalent, endorsing both moralistic *and* medical models (Mulford and Miller, 1961). Furthermore, this is to assume that there are only two models — thus people may support a psychological or sociocultural model in addition to the above two. Mulford and Miller (1961) found an almost equal preference for moralistic and

TABLE 4.2. *Some Common Misconceptions About Alcohol and Alcoholism*

---

 1. Alcohol is a stimulant
 2. Alcohol is essential to the treatment of certain diseases
 3. You can always detect alcohol on the breath of a person who has been drinking
 4. One ounce of 86 proof liquor contains more alcohol than a 12-ounce can of beer
 5. Body size has little or nothing to do with how much liquor a person can hold
 6. Drinking several cups of coffee can counteract the effects of alcohol and enable the drinker to "sober up"
 7. Alcohol can help a person sleep more soundly
 8. Impaired judgement does not occur before there are obvious signs of intoxication
 9. The individual will get more intoxicated by "mixing" liquors than by taking comparable amounts of one kind — e.g. bourbon, Scotch or vodka
10. Exercise or a cold shower helps speed up the metabolism of alcohol
11. People with "strong wills" need not be concerned about becoming alcoholics
12. Alcohol cannot produce a true addiction in the same sense that heroin does
13. One cannot become an alcoholic by drinking just beer
14. Alcohol is far less dangerous than marijuana
15. In a heavy drinker, damage to the liver shows up long before brain damage appears
16. The physiological withdrawal reaction from heroin is more dangerous than is withdrawal from alcohol
17. Most alcoholics who have successfully completed treatment can safely resume social drinking

---

From *Abnormal psychology and modern life*, by James, C. Coleman, James N. Butcher, and Robert C. Carson. Copyright © 1980, 1976 by Scott, Foresman and Company. Reprinted by permission.

medical models in an initial survey of public attitudes. Yet, in a subsequent study that enabled subjects to endorse both views, nearly half of the subjects endorsed both models, suggesting the complexity of lay views. Orcutt (1976) obtained similar results, indicating that a more flexible methodology was required for assessing lay beliefs about alcoholism. The simple dichotomy not only excludes the wide range of alternative theories available, but it also prevents researchers from investigating the possibility of multivariate explanations. Several researchers, such as Tolor and Tamerin (1975), Robinson (1976) and Beckman (1979), attempted to overcome this problem by using questionnaires which included items representing several different models, which the subjects rated on a scale indicating their degree of support. However, as Furnham (1983b) observed, studies of this kind assumed a direct correspondence between explicit academic theories and the causal beliefs of the lay person, restricting the subject to those particular explanations expressed in the questionnaire.

   An alternative approach is to ask subjects to give free responses to open-ended questions about the causes of alcoholism. Use of a free-response measure enables one to explore the degree of congruence between formal models and lay explanations, whilst avoiding constraints imposed by the experimenter (McHugh, 1979; Antaki, 1981). It has the additional advantage of allowing for the possible discovery of previously unrecognised lay theories of alcoholism.

A free-response technique was utilised by Linsky (1972), who asked a sample of adult subjects what they believed to be the causes of alcoholism. The responses were divided into five categories, which suggested a strong resemblance to formal models. The majority of subjects viewed alcoholism as a psychological illness rather than a biological illness, and very few of the subjects expressed a moralistic view of alcoholism. Twenty-seven per cent believed alcoholism to be caused by "disorders of the personality system" while a similar number believed it to be due to "psychological reactions to structional problems" while only 9% attributed it to the "moral character of the alcoholic".

In a similar study, McHugh (1979) asked both alcoholics and non-alcoholics why the alcoholics drank. Nine categories of attributions made by the subjects were generated, under general headings including "dissatisfaction", "boredom", "personal characteristics", "illness" and "escape", almost all of which reflect elements of formal aetiological models. Only 1.8% of responses referred to the medical or disease model of alcoholism, and there were no attributions referring to a moralistic view of alcoholism. External factors such as not enough money, job pressures and children's behaviour accounted for nearly a fifth of the responses while 12.3% rather tautologically gave the explanation that they were addicted. Curiously, nearly 10% of the respondents cited boredom as a factor which may be related to sociocultural ideas of deprivation or individual measures of arousal.

Similarly, Robinson (1976) asked members of the general population to explain why they thought people drank "in a way that causes them problems". Anxiety, depression and worry were the commonest explanations, and other common responses were because of loneliness, boredom, life problems, to escape problems or from habit.

Interesting though these content analysis-type studies are, they must be considered as preliminary, particularly as they do not take into account any demographic (age, sex, class) features of their subjects, with the exception of their occupation/profession, or the amount of drinking that they report. Freize (1979), however, found that females used the same basic categories to explain alcoholism in women, but they attributed female alcoholism more to factors relating to "dissatisfaction" and "escape", and less to "addiction" and "liking to drink".

Methodological problems have beset this research, however, primarily because researchers have ignored individual *determinants* (demographic, psychographic) of lay theories or else the structure of the lay theories has been treated non-empirically. Hence, Furnham and Lowick (1984a) did a study aimed to look specifically at the *determinants* — sex, age, education, employment status, amount drunk etc. — and *structure* derived empirically of lay people's theories of the causes of alcoholism. Over 250 people completed a questionnaire in which they rated 30 explanations for the importance in explaining the causes of alcoholism. They showed a number of significant sex differences, with females believing more than males that alcoholics were socially inadequate, with feelings of aggression, inferiority and anxiety. They also believed that there was too much pressure for, and not enough prohibitions against, drinking. There were also various age, educational, employment and drink-consumption related differences.

Overall, subjects preferred explanations which referred to social stresses, psychological traits and cultural or social norms, as opposed to biological, genetic and moralistic explanations. These results confirm the shift away from a moralistic model and towards a psychological model, which previous studies of lay beliefs about alcoholism have revealed.

Table 4.3 shows the mean scores. Overall the subjects thought the three most important explanations were 14 "They have found that alcohol helps them reduce their anxiety", 23 "They find drink is the only way to cope with frequent depression" and 24 "They suffer from considerable stress at work". The explanations thought least important were "Alcohol is far too cheap", "Religious prohibitions against drinking are not so often heard" and "They have genetically inherited alcoholism from their parents".

Table 4.3 also shows the results of the factor analysis. The factor analysis revealed six clear explanation types for alcoholism, some of which strikingly resembled formal models: for example, several items referring to inadequate development and unresolved conflicts were grouped together. These closely resemble a psychoanalytical model of alcoholism, which views alcohol as the means of providing relief from psychic anxiety, and addiction as the defensive mechanism which suppresses unresolved childhood conflicts. Furthermore, the fourth factor can clearly be compared to a sociocultural model of alcoholism which emphasises cultural beliefs, attitudes and practices, and the role of social learning. As revealed in previous studies on lay beliefs and confirmed in this study, boredom seems to be an important lay explanation for alcoholism, and yet it has not been incorporated into any of the formal explicit models or received much attention from researchers. The explanations referring to biological or genetic causes were not regarded as being very important by the respondents in this study, as was found in previous studies (Frieze, 1979; McHugh, 1979). However, these aetiological factors have received much attention from theorists and researchers alike.

In a second related study, Furnham and Lowick (1984b) focused specifically on actor–observer differences between those who were non-, light, medium and heavy drinkers. The results showed similar findings to studies on smoking. Indeed, there have been quite a number of studies on alcoholics' (or problem drinkers') beliefs about alcoholism and much is made of actor–observer differences which suggest that non-alcoholics would tend to make dispositional (individual pathology) attributions while alcoholics would tend to make situational attributions or appeal to uncontrollable factors (Richard and Burley, 1978; McCartney and O'Dowd, 1981). Both McHugh (1979) and

TABLE 4.3. *Factor Analytic (Varimax) Results for the 30 Explanations for Alcoholism over the Total Sample (N = 265)*

Factors/items		Mean	Loading	Eigenvalue	Variance (%)
Psychological					
10	They cannot cope with their financial problems	3.50	0.48		
14	They have found that alcohol helps them reduce their anxiety	2.36	0.74		
16	They have feelings of inferiority that alcohol alleviates	3.13	0.64		
19	Drinking helps them cope with the boredom of their lives	2.83	0.68		
20	They have found drink the cheapest and quickest way to relax	3.32	0.53	7.14	23.8
22	They are confronted with frustrated ambition which alcohol relieves	3.68	0.59		
23	They find drink is the only way to cope with frequent depression	2.66	0.74		
24	They suffer from considerable stress at work	2.91	0.59		
30	They are socially inadequate and cannot make friends	3.83	0.44		
Personal and social					
2	They have experienced considerable marital discord	3.15	0.80		
4	They have experienced job insecurity and instability	3.41	0.67	2.93	9.8
10	They cannot cope with their financial problems	3.50	0.58		
11	They often have sexual problems	3.83	0.64		
"Freudian"					
6	They are immature, self-indulgent people	4.57	0.47		
7	They feel alienated from their own society	4.01	0.52		
16	They have feelings of inferiority that alcohol relieves	3.13	0.42	1.87	6.2
17	They have self-destructive urges	4.40	0.67		
26	They often rebel against a puritanical repressive upbringing	4.24	0.59		
29	They are unable to express aggression towards others	4.93	0.62		
Sociocultural					
1	There is so much social pressure put on people to drink	3.34	0.48		
5	There is too much socialising in pubs and clubs	3.82	0.69		
18	They grew up in a culture where everybody drinks to excess	3.67	0.55	1.46	4.9
25	They have never been taught to use alcohol sensibly	3.87	0.42		
27	They enjoy the company of other heavy drinkers	3.70	0.68		
Biological					
9	They have a biological need for a drink	4.83	0.63		
13	They are often physically ill and feel there is no hope	4.36	0.63	1.27	4.2

15	They have genetically inherited alcoholism from their parents	5.33	0.70		
Social desirability					
1	There is so much social pressure put on people to drink	3.34	0.51		
8	There is too much emphasis on boozy business lunches	4.37	0.66	1.16	3.9
12	Advertising encourages people to drink too much	4.62	0.72		
21	Religious prohibitions against drinking are not so often heard	5.48	0.49		

Means on scale: Important 1 2 3 4 5 6 7 Unimportant.
Reproduced with permission from Furnham, A. and Lowick, V. (1984a). Lay theories of the causes of alcoholism. *British Journal of Medical Psychology*, 57, 319–332. Published by the British Psychological Society.

Beckman (1981) attempted to test this theory but found little support for it, suggesting that there is a consensual view about the causes of alcoholism that is independent of actual drinking. In fact, a study by Robinson (1976) showed that distressing events or environmental stresses (early home life, failed marriages, job stress) were rated by alcoholics as *less* important in causing one's own (severe) drinking problem than in causing most drinking problems. In fact, alcoholics seem to accept a large amount of personal responsibility for their drinking problem.

In a study comparing the beliefs of hospital staff, other personnel and alcoholics, Hey (1977) found a high amount of agreement and concluded that there may be a "very general stereotype of alcoholism consistent with a personality disorder concept which is implicitly held even in the face of nominal acceptance of other concepts" (p. 227).

These results carry additional implications concerning people attempting to help alcoholics and those designing treatment programmes. As suggested by Furnham (1982a), the success or failure of strategies of social change partly depends on the extent to which the innovators have taken into consideration the cognitive structure of those being changed. Hence it may be beneficial to investigate alcoholics' explanations for alcoholism. Different treatment programmes are related to different theoretical beliefs about the causes of alcoholism, and their effectiveness may be improved if the relationship between alcoholics' concepts of causation and the relevant theoretical concepts is examined and substantiated. A treatment programme based on theoretical concepts which are strongly associated with those of the patients would be expected to produce successful results. Conversely, a treatment derived from aetiological models which are incongruent with the alcoholic's implicit theories would be much less effective in overcoming the problem of alcohol addiction.

As McHugh *et al.* (1980) have noted:

causal beliefs about alcoholism have several important implications. First, the internality (and possibly the intentionality) of the causal attribution is seen as mediating affective reactions to the alcoholic individual, including the degree of derogation, and the willingness to endorse treatment as opposed to punishment. And, based on several attributional perspectives, a tendency to attribute alcoholism to internal factors is predicted. Second, beliefs about the causes of alcoholism are related to the type of treatment an individual advocates or endorses. Third, the stability of the causal attributions given for alcoholism is seen as mediating an individual's expectations concerning the prognosis of the alcoholic. More intensive efforts are directed towards the alcoholic when he is perceived as curable — that is, when the causal factors are perceived as modifiable. (p. 174)

It seems, then, that lay people tend to support psychological, rather than biological or sociocultural theories for the causes of alcoholism. However, there are systematic individual differences which relate to which particular theoretical position a lay person might adhere.

(2) Nicotine

Although the smoking of tobacco does not have as long a history as that of alcohol consumption (at least in the West) it has been known and consumed by Europeans for nearly 500 years. In the early 1970s nearly 130,000,000 cigarettes were consumed annually in Great Britain, though this number is gradually reducing (Elkind, 1982).

A range of factors determine smoking behaviour: psychological (personality, image); pharmacological (amount/effects of nicotine); sociological (demography, family); medical (anti-smoking advice); commercial (price, advertising) and political/legal (anti-smoking legislation, taxation). Research into smoking has focused on each of these factors with psychologists focusing on smoking as a psychological tool to increase psychological comfort by increasing arousal (and hence vigilance and performance) as well as controller of stress. Psychologists have also looked at personality differences between smokers and non-smokers as well as different typologies of smokers. Sociologists have focused on social attitudes towards smoking, social class and family determinants of smoking behaviour and the development of the habit in young people. Pharmacologists have predictably focused on the effect of nicotine — specifically the absorption into, and distribution of nicotine in the body as well as its biphasic effects on the central nervous system.

Scientists as well as lay people have speculated for a long time on why people begin and continue to smoke. In an early paper published in *Science* Finnegan *et al.* (1945) wrote:

optical perception of the smoke; fire worship; agreeable smell and taste; mechanical manipulation somewhat resembling the influence of the nipple on the infant; pleasurable irritation of the laryngeal and tracheal sensory branches of the pneumogastric nerve; relief of tension; stimulation; sociability; gives people something to do; permits one to do nothing, gracefully; produces a rise in blood sugar; satisfies a desire or craving; . . . combating hunger and thirst, joy and pain, heat and cold; irritation and languidness. (p. 94)

Others have attempted to categorise popular theories for smoking. Ashton and Stepney (1982) list the following:

(a) *Displacement activity* — the various activities involved in smoking (a pipe in particular) can give the impression of pleasure rather than the real reason which is anxiety.

(b) *Taste, smell and irritation* — smoke excites various sense organs including the lips, mouth and throat causing sensations of touch, taste, heat and irritation, but unlike eating does not accumulate in the body.

(c) *Sex* — smoking is substitute suckling or a sort of oral eroticism that may take many forms.

(d) *Absorption of nicotine into the body* — smoking is a way of ingesting into the body a powerful drug.

(e) *The control of arousal* — smoking facilitates arousal control such that smoking can decrease arousal (and hence alternate stress) or increase arousal (and maintain vigilance or increase selective attention).

Along with beliefs as to why people smoke, or what type of gratification they derive from this activity there is a wealth of interesting and important studies on individual and social attitudes towards smoking and smokers. For a long time psychologists have been interested in the attitudes of smokers vs non-smokers and the denial of the former regarding the consequences of smoking.

Eiser *et al.* (1977) addressed this topic directly in a series of studies. They observed that many smokers recognise the well-publicised health risks which they incur by smoking, and yet persist in the habit. Eiser *et al.* (1977) set out to investigate whether, and to what extent, smokers overcome the attributional dilemma posed by the health factor, by labelling themselves as "addicts". Attribution theory would lead one to expect that individuals who hold a very negative view of smoking (usually non-smokers) would be more likely to regard smokers as addicts than smokers themselves. It was predicted that non-smokers would be more willing to apply the unattractive label of "addict" to the habit of smoking (which they disapprove of), than smokers would be willing to apply to themselves. It was hypothesised that those smokers who *do* apply the label of "addict" to themselves make this attribution to absolve themselves from the personal responsibility of continuing a potentially dangerous habit.

A questionnaire investigating the differences between smokers, and non-smokers' views of addiction supported the former prediction: about four-fifths of non-smokers regard smokers as addicts, whereas approximately half of the smokers saw themselves as addicts. Non-smokers underestimated the amount of pleasure obtained by smokers, viewing the typical (addicted) smoker as someone who would find it difficult to give up smoking but who does not particularly want to give up, even though smoking is not especially pleasurable. In contrast, among smokers, the self-attribution of addiction was associated with wanting to give up, deriving more pleasure from cigarettes and smoking more heavily, as well as the estimated difficulty of giving up. Furthermore, those smokers who wanted to give up but were not trying to do so tended to say they were more addicted, derived more pleasure from smoking and would experience more difficulty in giving up.

These findings support the explanatory function of attributions such as "addiction". These attributions enable smokers to rationalise their behaviour whilst acknowledging the health hazards of smoking and claiming that they would like to give up. Non-smokers seem to use the label of addiction as a more *internal* attribution to explain why smokers continue an unhealthy habit even though it is not perceived to be particularly pleasurable.

In a second study, Eiser *et al.* (1978a) found non-smokers underestimated the amount of pleasure obtained and the degree to which smokers are frightened about the health risks. Subjects were also asked to estimate the amount of influence various factors have in "starting people off smoking". People who have never smoked tended to attribute more influence to seeing advertisements about smoking and seeing actors and personalities smoking on TV than did smokers. Thus, non-smokers seem to regard smokers as being more susceptible to the influence of the media. That is, compared with smokers, non-smokers seem to attribute smoking more to *internal*, dispositional characteristics of smokers, such as their greater persuasibility, ignorance, or disregard of the health hazards, and less to external factors, such as the pleasure derived from smoking itself.

However, Eiser and Van der Pligt (1983), who investigated the influence of evaluative factors upon preference for situational and dispositional attributions relating to smoking, found that actor–observer differences in attribution are related to evaluative factors in accordance with a "positive bias". Thus, although the actor–observer distinction seems to apply to smokers' and non-smokers' attributions, one should not assume a *general* self–other difference without taking into account the attributor's evaluations of the actor or situation.

As Eiser *et al.*'s (1978) study revealed, many smokers are concerned about, or at least they recognise, the personal risks of smoking. McKennell and Thomas (1967) distinguished between "consonant" smokers, who hold fairly positive attitudes about smoking and do not wish to give-up, and 'dissonant' smokers, who wish to stop but have greater difficulty in doing so and thus seem more "addicted". According to Festinger's (1957) theory of cognitive dissonance, dissonant smokers experience inconsistency between the cognitions that they smoke and that smoking is bad for their health. The nicotine in tobacco does produce physiological dependence, inability to give up experienced by the majority of smokers obviously involves other social and cognitive factors. Bem's (1967) theory of self-attribution states that individuals may make self-attributions on the basis of observations of their own behaviour, in order to account for previous behaviour and to predict their behaviour in the future. The self-attribution of addiction may be one way in which dissonant smokers resolve the problem of counter-attitudinal behaviour. The belief that one is addicted accounts for past failures at giving-up and it also predicts that one will fail in future attempts at giving-up. The dissonance aroused in the dissonant smoker can be resolved by regarding smoking as beyond voluntary control, or, more specifically, by labelling the behaviour as an addicted behaviour. Thus, self-attribution provides a justification for smoking whilst enabling the dissonant smoker to admit the potential health hazards. The contrasting implication is that the consonant smoker who smokes from choice is less motivated to see him(her) self as an "addict" and less likely to acknowledge the potential health risks.

Both of these predictions were substantiated in Eiser *et al.*'s (1978b) study of the relationship between the self-attribution of addiction, "consonant" and dissonant" smokers, and the smoker's perception of personal risk. Over two-thirds of the subjects were dissonant smokers (i.e. they would like to give up smoking if they could do so easily) and they were more likely to say they were addicted, to acknowledge the potential health hazard, and to say that they had tried to give-up smoking. The health factor seemed to be important in encouraging the wish to give up smoking, and it was also an important predictor of trying to stop or reduce smoking. However, it did not affect success or failure. Loker (1982) has confirmed that the health hazards are not the most important determinants of trying to give up smoking: smokers are generally aware of the harmful effects of smoking, although they do not evaluate them as negatively as non-smokers do. The difference in beliefs about smoking held by non-smokers, light smokers and heavy smokers were generally found to be unrelated to the health hazards of smoking. This substantiates Eiser *et al.*'s assertion that anti-smoking campaigns which focus exclusively on health are not effective in discouraging smokers from smoking, particularly if they associate smoking with addiction.

Although often overlooked by anti-smoking campaigners, the amount of pleasure derived from smoking was found to be an important variable (Eiser *et al.* 1977, 1978). More "real pleasure" was associated with not wanting to give up, with perceiving oneself as addicted and unable to give up easily. The number of cigarettes smoked per day was *not* associated with whether subjects attempted to give up smoking, nor was it associated with the success of their attempts. However, it was correlated with the self-attribution of addiction, suggesting that this cognitive factor plays an important role in maintaining and predicting the course of the behaviour, in addition to pharmacological factors.

More recent studies have confirmed Eiser's results on attribution for smoking among smokers and ex-smokers (Kleinke *et al.* 1983; Sadava and

Weithe 1985). As a result researchers and practitioners involved in helping smokers stop the habit stress cognitive therapies (cognitive restructuring, change in self-definition). In other words these lay "theories" of smokers are dysfunctional in that they help to maintain the habit that many smokers are trying to give up.

The particular interesting feature of this research on lay attributions for smoking is not so much the structure of the theories that people hold but rather the function of those theories.

4.4 Explanations for Depression

Although not always recognised under this term, the phenomenon of depression (also called melancholia), has been recognised by lay thinkers for literally thousands of years. Kant (1798) in his Anthropologie described the characteristics of melancholia thus:

> *The Melancholic Temperament.* People tending towards melancholia attribute great importance to everything that concerns them. They discover everywhere cause for anxiety, and notice first of all the difficulties in a situation, in contradistinction to the sanguine person. They do not make promises easily, because they insist on keeping their word, and have to consider whether they will be able to do so. All this is so not because of moral considerations, but because interaction with others makes them worried, suspicious and thoughtful; it is for this reason that happiness escapes them.

As is the case with many psychological and psychiatric conditions there have been many attempts to classify different types of depression: i.e. neurotic vs psychotic; exogenous vs endogenous; unipolar vs bipolar; primary vs secondary. One of the reasons for these different, often overlapping classifications is that they have looked at the different types of depression at different levels and stages, some concentrating on aetiology, others on symptom presentation and still others on treatment response.

There exist a number of different theories for depression. Gilbert (1984) has described three major approaches:

(a) *The psychoanalytic approach*: Though there are numerous subtle differences between various neo-psychoanalytic thinkers (Jung, Bowlby) an underlying theme is that of loss (of object or self-esteem). This approach has also attempted to understand the role of inherited psychobiological predisposition and the function of depression.

(b) *The behavioural approach*: Once again there are various different theories under this rubric but all are united in attempting to understand depression in terms of a person's specific learning histories, environmental responses and stimuli that maintain maladaptive behaviours. That is, a person learns a particular behaviour pattern which may cause and/or maintain depressive reactions.

(c) *The cognitive approach*: These theories argue that maladaptive cognitive processes translate external events into meaningful internal representations which are the pathogenic agents (not the events themselves). It is in the organisation, storage and retrieval of this information that maintains depression. The concept of learned helplessness is perhaps the best known of this approach.

There are, however, other academic approaches to depression, including psycho-neurochemical and psycho-evolutionary. Yet, predictably there is no common agreement as to the primary causes and cures of depression.

However, unlike many other areas of mental illness, there have been a number of studies on lay theories of depression. This has been dominated by Rippere (1977, 1979, 1980a,b,c) who has described her work as "exploratory, tentative, heuristic and descriptive" (Rippere 1981a, p. 169). Amongst other things, she has demonstrated that, perhaps unsurprisingly, people (who may or may not be depressed) have clear ideas about: how often they and others say they feel depressed; how often they try to do something about it; whether their "treatment" works; the extent or depth to which they feel depressed; how long their depression lasts; the most appropriate thing to do under these circumstances; how helpful various theories are; how much consensus there is about lay theories of depression; and what sort of things people say, makes them worse.

A theme running through her work is that ordinary people have extensive knowledge of depression and how people manage it which they bring to, amongst other things, psychological studies. Also, people are prepared for the experience of depression through socialisation, though what is unclear is "what people learn, from whom, how, where, and how, having learnt, they apply their knowledge in their daily lives" (Rippere, 1977, p. 62).

Rippere (1980a) has been particularly impressed by the degree of consensus that she has found in lay people's knowledge of depression and anti-depressive behaviour. This is seen to be descriptive and normatively functional in that they (the consensually held cognitives) enable individuals to estimate their own and others' depressive state, and do something about it.

To give some idea of the sort of findings that Rippere (1981b) has found, Table 4.4 illustrates the 10 pairs of historical prepositions (and their anti-theses) in order of their degree of consensus. The asterisk represents beliefs consistent with historical beliefs (8 out of 10).

Rippere has also attempted to replicate her work cross-culturally (Caro *et al.*, 1983; Miralles *et al.*, 1983). She compared British and Spanish answers to the question "What's the thing to do when you're feeling depressed?" The British showed a higher ratio of consensual to non-consensual items, but overall there were fewer differences than similarities suggesting a corpus of Western common-sense ideas on dealing with depression. In fact Caro *et al.* (1983) drew up a list of 12 consensually and cross-culturally held solutions for depression.

TABLE 4.4. *Observed Percentage of People (N = 64) Endorsing Statements*

Statement	Observed (%)	Consensus with historical view
*1a Some types of people are more likely than others to become depressed	89.06	+
b The chances of becoming depressed are pretty much the same for everyone	10.94	
2a The way people live is not an important factor in whether or not they get depressed	12.50	
* b The way people live can be an important factor in whether or not they get depressed	87.50	+
5a A person's diet is probably unrelated to whether or not he gets depressed	18.75	
* b An improper diet can help bring on a depression and a proper diet can help protect people from it	81.25	+
*8a Keeping one's bowels regular is important in preventing depression	18.75	
b Keeping one's bowels regular has little to do with preventing depression	81.25	—
*3a The weather and climate can affect people's liability to depression	76.69	+
b People's liability to depression is generally unaffected by weather and climate	20.31	
9a A philosophical outlook isn't really much use when things go wrong in one's life	23.44	
* b A philosophical outlook may help a person when things go wrong in his life	76.56	+
4a The amount of sleep a person gets is probably unrelated to whether or not he gets depressed	26.56	
* b Loss of sleep can help bring on a depression and obtaining adequate sleep can help prevent it	73.44	+
*7a An active person is less likely to get depressed than one who is idle	71.88	+
b A person's amount of activity is unlikely to contribute much to whether or not he gets depressed	28.12	
6a The amount of exercise a person gets is probably unrelated to whether or not he gets depressed	37.50	
* b Insufficient exercise can help bring on a depression and sufficient exercise can help prevent it	62.50	+
*10a Keeping a check on one's emotions may be helpful in preventing depression	50.00	=
b Keeping a check on one's emotions is not much use in preventing depression	50.00	

*Indicates the "correct" answer.
Reproduced with permission from Rippere, (1981c). The survival of traditional medicine in lay medical man: An empirical approach to the history of medicine. *Medical History*, *25*, 411–414.

1. Attributing the depression to a cause.
2. Attempting to rectify the problems considered responsible for evoking the feeling of depression.
3. Finding social and moral support.
4. Engaging in diverting and distracting recreations.
5. Keeping busy and working.

6. Focusing one's attention elsewhere than on the depressing problem or feelings.
7. Restructuring one's cognitions so as to minimise the significance of the depressing events.
8. Engaging in self-care and self-maintenance activities.
9. Venting one's emotions.
10. Taking prescribed medication and self-medicating.
11. Finding compensations and boosting feelings of self-esteem or self-efficacy through useful, purposive activity.
12. Taking comfort in one's religion.

In another study using the same populations, Miralles *et al.* (1983) asked "When you're feeling depressed, what sort of things can make you feel worse?". Again the English speaking groups produced a large variety of items and showed a higher degree of consensus in their responses. However, the authors were able to come up with eight generally held beliefs about what makes depressed people feel worse such as: feeling isolated and depressed; being reminded of the depressing problem or the fact of being depressed; encountering further problems or an exacerbation of the original problem; feeling overworked or unable to cope; having to do things one doesn't want to do; contact with other people, etc. By-and-large these are "correct", though it is difficult to generalise to all cases.

The authors noted the paradoxical nature of the findings:

Feeling depressed appears to be a paradoxical state in which certain opposites can have similar effects: rejection and sympathy, isolation and social contact, reminders of the problem and distractions from it. Another paradox is that so many of the situations mentioned as making people feel worse when they are feeling depressed are variants of the same situations which subjects of the previous studies mentioned as being "the thing to do when you're feeling depressed": seeking social support and sympathy, crawling away on one's own, scrutinising and analysing the reasons for one's depression, working hard, forcing oneself to keep going, wallowing in one's feeling of depression, going to a cheerful social event, having a meal with people, having a drink, talking about something other than the problem. (Miralles *et al.*, 1983, p. 490)

It is no doubt that, because depression of all sorts is such a wide-spread phenomenon, there is such high consensus as to its causes and cure. The work above has, however, not attempted to see if there is an underlying structure to lay people's theories of depression, nor has it been considered that certain lay theories of the causes of depression may themselves be partly responsible for the aetiology and maintenance of that depression. The rise in interest in cognitive explanations for depression point to the fact that attributional styles may be, alone as well as in addition to other factors, a major cause of depression and it is indeed these styles that relate to lay theories of depression.

4.5 Explanations for Neuroticism

The concept of neuroticism is used widely by lay persons and frequently occurs in everyday conversation, popular writing and literature. Though the term is most often used pejoratively, some people have suggested that there may be benefits to neurosis. For instance *Proust* is said to have remarked: "Everything great in the world is done by neurotics, they alone founded our religions and created our masterpieces". The idea that unhappiness and/or neurosis is related to artistic creativity is relatively widespread among lay people but has little or no empirical support.

Etymologically the term means "weakness of the nerves" and is derived from the Greek work for nerves. In fact, until the 19th century all forms of mental illness were included in the class *neurotica*, so much that the diagnosis was abandoned as too general until the end of the 19th century (Kisker, 1964). Beard (1880) introduced the term *neurasthenia*, whose symptoms included lack of energy, fatigue, physical complaints and general disability. Kraepelin (1915), however, distinguished between neurasthenia, psychasthenia and hysteria, which remained the basis for the description of the neurotic conditions from the 1890s until the appearance of the American Psychiatric Association's publication of their *Diagnostic and Statistical Manual* in 1952. However, the latest edition (1980) has no reference to neurosis at all.

Most textbooks have difficulty in arriving at a clear definition of neuroticism, though most are agreed on categorising neurotic symptoms into various groups — anxiety, phobic, obsessive–compulsive, conversion, dissociative and depressive reactions (Buss, 1966; Kisker, 1964). Although he admits a number of ambiguities in the concept of neurosis, Eysenck (1978) offered a simple definition for his lay readers:

> Neurosis is a term we often use for behaviour which is associated with strong emotion, which is maladaptive, and which the person giving rise to it realises is nonsensical, absurd or irrelevant, but which he is powerless to change. (p. 15)

Similarly in their EPQ Manual, Eysenck and Eysenck (1975) define a typical neurotic as a person being:

> an anxious, worrying individual, moody and frequently depressed. He is likely to sleep badly, and to suffer from various psychosomatic disorders. He is overly emotional, reacting too strongly to all sorts of stimuli, and finds it difficult to get back on an even keel after each emotionally arousing experience. His strong emotional reactions interfere with his proper adjustment, making him react in irrational, sometimes rigid ways . . . If the highly neurotic individual has to be described in one word, one might say that he was a *worrier*; his main characteristic is a constant preoccupation with things that might go wrong, and a strong emotional reaction of anxiety to these thoughts. (pp. 9–10)

Psychologists have been fascinated by the *neurotic paradox* — the self-defeating strategies of neurotics whereby they continue behaviour or thought patterns that are maladaptive and bring distress and unhappiness.

Predictably there exist a number of theories which cover the aetiology and cure of neurosis: *dynamic* theories, which suggest that neurotic behaviour is an external manifestation of an underlying disturbance; *learning* theories, which see neurotic behaviour as the product of an inappropriate contingency of behaviour learning or conditioning; and *cognitive* theories, which suggest that the neurotic condition is characterised by particular patterns of selective information processing (Young and Martin, 1981). There are, however, other academic theories of neurosis. For instance followers of *Personal Construct Theory* have argued that neurotics have tight inflexible construct systems, an anxiety occurs because so many daily occurrences are unable to be interpreted within the construct system. Rogerian *phenomenologists*, on the other hand, believe the tension and anxiety in neurosis is caused by people's realisation that there is lack of congruity between their experiences and their self-concept because they falsify their own experiences to percieve them only in terms of the values of others (Mackay, 1975).

However, very few theories attempt to explain neurosis in general preferring to divide neurotics into various categories. For instance Mackay (1975) mentions six and offers a brief definition of each: *Anxiety neurosis* — this neurosis is characterised by anxious over-concern extending to panic and frequently associated with somatic symptoms; *Phobias* — a phobia is a persistent fear of a specific object or situation for which there is no rational basis; *Obsessive-compulsive neurosis* — the patient with obsessive–compulsive neurosis experiences persistent thought patterns which he tries to prevent (obsession) and repetitive tendencies to behave in a way which he does not wish to (compulsions); *Neurotic depression* — in the case of reactive depression the individual's symptoms of extreme dejection are seen to be a response to some stressful event or series of upsets; *hysterical conversion-type neurosis* — traditionally the diagnosis of conversion hysteria is used with those conditions where the symptoms of some physical illness appear in the absence of any organic pathology; *Hysterical dissociative-type neurosis* — As the name might suggest, it is used in those cases where the patient attempts to escape from stress by cutting his/herself off in some way or other.

To some extent researchers have advocated slightly different forms of treatment depending on the precise type of neurosis that they are considering: desensitisation, modelling, psychotherapy, electro-convulsive therapy, etc. Suffice it to say that most researchers are agreed that neurosis takes different forms but they are not agreed on either the cause or cure of these different types of neuroses.

A number of issues concerning lay theories of neurosis are important. First, *to what extent can people predict their neuroticism* score derived from valid measures? A number of studies have looked at normal people's ability to predict their score derived from the Eysenck (EPI or EPQ) measures. Correlations have been modest, positive and significant between the subjects' estimate, and the actual score. Harrison and McLaughlin (1969) 0.56; Gray (1972) 0.21; Furnham and Henderson (1983) 0.47; and Furnham (1984b) 0.40. While the actual/estimated correlations are significant, the data do not provide very strong support for the convergence of ordinary people's estimates and standardised test scores.

Another way of looking at people's conception is to get them to *fake neurotic*. Thus, Salas (1968) administered the EPI twice to soldiers — once under normal conditions, and then they were asked to respond "in a manner you would expect of a neurotic, badly adjusted soldier" (p. 56). As predicted under the latter conditions, their scores rose significantly. There are many other studies which support this conclusion, namely that when asked to fake bad (or mad), neuroticism scores go up, while when asked to fake good, neuroticism scores go down (Farley and Goh, 1976; Michaelis and Eysenck 1971; Power and MacRae, 1977; Furnham and Henderson 1983a). Though the scores change they do not do so perfectly! In other words, though subjects know which direction to move on a neuroticism score from high to low, they do not (or cannot) move to the extremes.

Interestingly, the evidence suggests that it is not only "normal" non-neurotic people who can simulate or fake neurotic, but neurotics can fake normal (Gendreau *et al.*, 1973). MacCarthy and Furnham (1986) asked two groups of psychiatric patients — anxiety state and depressed — and a normal group to fill in two questionnaires twice: first responding honestly and then as they believed a "normal person" might. The results showed that "normal" people tend to see other normals as well-adjusted as themselves, if not slightly less well-adjusted, whereas patients see themselves as less well-adjusted than the ordinary person. The controls were not significantly more able to predict the normal response to these measures than the patient groups were. However, the depressed and anxious groups differed in the accuracy of their estimates and in their conceptions of normal functioning. The two patient groups did differ in their levels of accuracy, the depressed patients were generally fairly accurate in their estimate, although holding a somewhat negative view of ordinary adjustment. The anxious patients estimates were always further from the scale norms than those of the depressed patients and they substantially overestimated the adjustment of the ordinary personality and underestimated the adjustment of ordinary social behaviour. Overall, the anxious patients' estimates deviated from scale norms in the same direction as the controls' but this deviation was usually more *extreme*.

Thus, it seems that it is not possible to generalise about abnormal groups' perceptions of normality: psychiatrically disturbed patients are *not necessarily* less able than undisturbed normal people to perceive normality accurately. It is anxiety but not depression that appears to impair this ability.

It appears, then, that both normal and neurotic people have some idea of what normality and neuroses are, even though this is by no means perfect. One reason for them not being able to fake perfectly is that they may not realise the various dimensions of neuroticism. That is, they may recognise that, say, anxiety and obessionality are neurotic but not phobic or hysteria responses.

TABLE 4.5. *The Percentage of Ss Correctly Identifying the Items in the EPQ which Supposedly Measure Neuroticism*

Items from the EPQ	%
3. Does your mood often go up and down?	45.8
7. Do you ever feel "just miserable" for no reason?	41.6
12. Do you often worry about things you should not have done or said?	87.5
15. Are you an irritable person?	25.0
19. Are your feelings easily hurt?	41.6
23. Do you often feel "fed-up"?	25.0
27. Are you often troubled about feelings of guilt?	75.0
31. Would you call yourself a nervous person?	58.3
34. Are you a worrier?	62.5
38. Do you worry about awful things that might happen?	91.6
41. Would you call yourself tense or "highly strung"?	79.1
47. Do you worry about your health?	79.1
54. Do you suffer from sleeplessness?	66.6
58. Have you often felt listless and tired for no reason?	16.6
62. Do you often feel life is very dull?	8.3
66. Do you worry a lot about your looks?	54.1
68. Have you ever wished that you were dead?	33.3
72. Do you worry too long after an embarrassing experience?	79.1
75. Do you suffer from nerves?	54.1
77. Do you often feel lonely?	20.8
80. Are you sometimes bubbling over with energy and sometimes very sluggish?	54.1
84. Are you easily hurt when people find fault with you or the work you do?	4.1
88. Are you touchy about some things?	37.5
Mean %	53.9
SD	28.1

The second important case for investigating lay theories of neuroticism is to attempt to identify *lay people's understanding of the dimensions of neuroticism.* One way of going about this is to see which items in a neuroticism inventory people can identify. Furnham (1984b) gave subjects the 90 item EPQ and told them that 23 items measured neuroticism. Their task was to identify those 23. Table 4.5 shows the results.

The mean number of items selected by the subjects was 21.3 (SD = 3.41), and correct identification for the 23 "neurotic" items ranged from under 10% to over 90%, the mean correct identifications being 53.9%. Six items (12, 27, 38, 41, 47, 72) were identified by over 70% and they related primarily to worrying, while six items (15, 23, 58, 62, 77, 84) were identified by less than 30% of the lay people and they related primarily to feeling bored and listless.

They seemed best able to detect items concerning anxiety, but less sensitive to items about depression. This finding was confirmed when another group of lay people were asked to rate 100 characteristics of people for how characteristic each was of neuroticism. The three most highly characteristic were "tends often to be very anxious", "tends to be highly strung", and "finds it hard to relax". When these ratings were factor analysed four quite clear factors emerged. These were labelled *communication problems* (shy, anti-social, erratic), *unstable* (emotionally labile, unable to concentrate), *obsessional* (ritualised, superstitious) and *phobic* (panics, repetitive). Although people may not be able to taxonomise types of neuroticism or even recognise items from all categories, their rating of traits tends to show a clear underlying structure. Once again, therefore, people are moderately good at perceiving the different types of neuroticism.

Thirdly, there is the issue of beliefs about the *occurrence of neurotic traits* in others as opposed to self. Furnham (1984b), and others, have demonstrated that people have a tendency to believe themselves to be significantly less neurotic, disturbed, depressed and generally "mad" and more happy and stable than the average person. This appears to be a common adaptive feature of "normal" people that is not found in psychiatric patients which may help to account for their problems.

There remains a great deal of work to be done on lay theories of neurosis. Researchers have concentrated far more on the perceived characteristics of neuroticism than its cause, occurrence or cure. Furthermore, little is known about the perceptions of people differing in neurotic symptoms about neurosis itself (MacCarthy and Furnham, 1986). In view of the current research it would appear as if neurotics have a different view of the level and extent of their own neurosis as well as that of non-neurotic people. Furthermore the manifestations of neurosis may be culture and time specific, in that in certain cultures at specific times it may be more or less acceptable to display forms of neurotic behaviour. Indeed these trends may themselves be a function of the dominant lay theories prevailing at the time.

4.6 The Attribution of Cure

People have beliefs and theories not only about the *cause* and *occurrence* of psychological problems in the community but also how these problems are best cured.

Despite considerable research interest in the perception of the causes of problems, comparatively little attention has been paid to the perception or attribution of the *cure* of these problems. It might be argued that the type of explanation/attribution people offer for a phenomenon implies the sort of remedy that is necessary to cure or eradicate it. Thus, if one believes that the primary cause of delinquency is inadequate discipline and neglect of moral education in schools, it is logical to attempt to change educational practices in order to discourage delinquency. On the other hand, if one believes that delinquency is primarily due to societal factors such as high unemployment or inadequate leisure and recreational facilities, attempts to prevent delinquency would involve such things as government expenditure on job creation schemes and/or more recreational facilities. Similarly, if one believes the causes of addictions (smoking or drinking) to be pharmacological, presumably one would advocate some sort of drug therapy, whereas if one perceived the cause to be psychological one might advocate some sort of psychological therapy (psychotherapy, behaviour modification). It is more difficult, however, to predict which curative measures would be advocated where the cause is perceived to be genetic or socio-cultural — other, perhaps, than the detection of specific types of individuals (and preventing them having children), or in the case of the latter explanation, a radical change in the structure of society.

It appears, therefore, that beliefs about "cause" and "cure" may be closely linked, but it cannot be as certain that the one (cause) necessarily precedes the other (cure). That is, it may be that beliefs in the most effective way to eradicate delinquency or cure alcoholism imply the cause of delinquency or alcoholism rather than the other way round. More importantly it may not even be the case that people's beliefs about cause and cure are consistent or indeed logical. That is, their beliefs about effective cure may be unrelated to, or even contradictory to their beliefs about cause.

There is also an extensive literature on "coping behaviours", which could be viewed as a sort of application of cure attributions. That is, the coping behaviours that people adopt might reflect their beliefs about the efficacy of these various strategies. As Pearlin and Schooler (1978) have pointed out, little is known about the nature and substance of general coping repertoires, and even less about their relative effectiveness. However, in a recent study, Parker and Brown (1982) found six structural dimensions (coping styles) that mediate between major life events and depression. These were recklessness (break things, take alcohol), socialisation (spend time with friends, socialise), distraction (busy yourself in work), problem solving (think through the problem, pray), passivity (read, ignore the problem), and self-consolation (spend money on yourself).

Yet there are a number of reasons why the examination of coping styles and strategies do not necessarily reflect lay beliefs. For instance, people may not be able to indulge in the strategy they believe most effective or appropriate because of various restraints, such as cost (of psychotherapy). Also, people may not be able to fulfil their preferred coping strategy (seek out social support) because others reject them. Further, people may believe in a sequential pattern of coping strategies or completely different strategies for different problems and hence an examination of strategies pursued by a person for one particular problem at one point in time might not reveal the true complexity of people's beliefs.

On the other hand, there may be conservatively held beliefs about cure in society at large, which may or may not be accurate.

Rippere (1979, 1980, 1981a,b) has argued, on the basis of her own extensive work on lay beliefs concerning the treatment of depression, that "well cultivated adults" in our society possess a rich and complex store of knowledge about the causes and cures of psychological illnesses in themselves and others. But Rippere's work does not suggest why certain people hold different views from others, and how effective these various treatments actually are (see Chapter 4).

In one of the few investigations specifically concerned with the attribution of effective cure and overcoming personal problems, Knapp and Delprato (1980) asked subjects the extent to which they believed will power to be necessary for overcoming 24 "problem behaviours" such as smoking, gambling, shoplifting, stuttering and bedwetting. The results showed large differences, will power being rated as more necessary for overcoming "self-indulgence" problems (e.g. alcoholism, smoking) and certain "non-self-indulgent" problems (e.g. shyness, fear of flying) than for overcoming "psychopathological" problems (e.g. nervous breakdown, hallucinations) and "ability deficits" (e.g. inability to swim, poor mathematical ability). Judgements of the importance of will power were unrelated to years of education, number of psychology classes completed, whether or not the respondent ever attended a college, and particular college attended. That is, education however measured is not necessarily a predictor of lay beliefs about cure.

In a later study, Knapp and Karabenick (1985) examined the perceived importance of will power and various other contributors towards overcoming six problems: smoking, stuttering, nightmares, excessive fear of dogs, hearing voices and overeating. Factor analysis yielded four factors thought to be variously useful in the solution of these problems, namely social consequence, inner control, understanding and positive outlook. "Will power" was seen as extremely important in overcoming smoking and overeating problems, less so for stuttering and dog phobia, and relatively unimportant for nightmares and hearing voices. "Inner control" contributors (self control, effort) were seen as most important for overcoming smoking and overeating, while "positive outlook" ("the instrumental approach") was seen to be most important for curing stuttering and fear of dogs. The authors point out that factor analysis differentiated between two somewhat different forms of internal control — inner control, referring to self-reliance or self-help implying little external intervention, and positive outlook, referring to the possibility of helping oneself by surrendering self-reliance and getting help. They suggest that these scores should relate to general locus of control beliefs, but did not themselves look at any individual difference variable in the perception of overcoming personal problems.

Following this work Henley and Furnham (1988) set out to examine lay beliefs about important contributors towards overcoming some relatively common *social* psychological problems — specifically, alcoholism, depression, sexual dysfunctions and shyness — to examine the underlying factors or dimensions of coping, and whether or not the factor structure differed according to the problem being considered. In doing so they asked

TABLE 4.8.

1. How hard a person tries
2. How much willpower (inner strength) a person has
3. How lucky a person is
4. Whether a person gets professional help
5. A person's general ability to overcome problems
6. How much information a person has about the problem
7. Whether the problem is a symptom of some other deep-rooted problem
8. Whether the person believes it is possible to eliminate the problem
9. How embarrassed the person feels about having the problem
10. How damaging the problem is to the person's feelings of self-worth or self-esteem
11. How much eliminating the problem would please others
12. How much a person stays away from situations that make the problem worse
13. How much a person understands about the underlying reasons for the problem
14. How much self-control the person has
15. Whether the person gets help from other people (friends and loved ones)
16. How intelligent the person is
17. How much a person believes in God
18. How much the person stays away from others with similar problems
19. Whether there is something wrong with the person's brain or nervous system
20. Whether the person's mother and/or father have a similar problem
21. Whether the person seeks out trained medical/psychological professionals
22. How much the person really wants to get better
23. Whether the person joins other self help groups for this problem
24. How much courage a person has to change his/her lifestyle

their subjects to rate the effectiveness of the 24 strategies shown in Table 4.8.

Factor analysis yielded seven interpretable factors, the first four, which accounted for nearly 50% of the variance, were almost identical to those found by Knapp and Karabenick (1985). This replication is all the more impressive given (a) that all five factor analyses yielded the same structure and (b) that the responses were to four rather different problems. Indeed, these four factors are not unlike those found in studies of actual coping (Parker and Brown, 1982).

Overall, understanding was thought of as the most important contributor, particularly for overcoming sex problems. As Knapp and Karabenick (1985) suggest, this "may reflect the belief on the part of respondents that these problems are symptomatic of something else that needs to and can be addressed, but not through personal effort alone" (p. 351). In fact, understanding was seen to be most important for all four problems, though least so for shyness. Social consequences (embarrassment, stigmatisation) were seen to be less important in relation to alcoholism and depression, but moderately so for sex problems and shyness. Subjects believed that a physical or genetic basis to the problem was most important in depression, but of limited importance in relation to the other problems. The idea of isolating oneself from people or situations that aggravate the problem yielded a highly significant difference, primarily due to the fact that this was perceived as relatively important in overcoming alcoholism.

This is not inconsistent with the idea that will power or effort is perhaps the

TABLE 4.9. *Mean Scores for the Perceived Efficacy of the Seven Factors for the Four Psychological Problems. The Higher the Score the More the Factor is Thought Effective in Curing the Problem*

Factor	Alcoholism	Depression	Sex problem	Shyness	F level
1. Inner control	6.98^a	5.94^b	5.29^c	6.38^d	25.62***
2. Receives help	6.77^a	6.50^{ab}	6.27^{bc}	6.05^c	5.42***
3. Understanding	6.51^a	6.48^a	6.97^b	6.17^a	6.45***
4. Social consequence	5.07^a	4.30^b	5.93^c	5.53^{ac}	16.92***
5. Physical base	4.10^a	4.46^a	3.38^a	4.16^a	6.92***
6. Isolation	5.11^a	4.74^a	3.03^b	3.73^c	24.75***
7. Fate	2.30^{ab}	2.83^a	2.09^b	2.35^{ab}	2.84*

*** $p < 0.001$.
** $p < 0.01$.
* $p < 0.05$
Means with common super scripts (a, b or c) *do not* differ significantly one from another.
Numbers are means on the scale 0 = Not at all effective; 9 = Very effective.

most important factor in overcoming alcoholism in that it takes a certain strength of character to cut oneself off from friends and familiar situations that contribute to one's addiction. Finally, fate (luck) was seen to be largely irrelevant, particularly for sex problems, but less so for depression.

Interestingly, the first two factors, which suggest the importance of self-help and help from a variety of others (family, friends, professionals), respectively, and which together accounted for a third of the variance, appear, on the face of it, to be contradictory, though they are both thought to be equally important. As Knapp and Karabenick (1985) point out, these may be mutually exclusive in that over-self-reliance may reduce or preclude seeking assistance, while stressing help from others may increase the abdication or personal responsibility. On the other hand, it is quite possible that these two approaches to solving personal problems are entirely complementary. Thus, one may consult professional or sympathetic helpers for advice or insight into an appropriate and effective curative strategy, yet require considerable will power and effort to undertake it. Indeed, the fact that both factors were rated comparatively highly in importance in relation to all four problems suggests that the subjects perceived them to be complementary.

In a second study using the same 24 item questionnaire, Furnham and Henley (1988) looked at lay people's beliefs about the effective cures for four rather different problems. Agoraphobia, anorexia nervosa, compulsive gambling and schizophrenia. As before, they did a factor analysis and found five factors similar to those that had been found before. Table 4.10 shows the results.

As in previous studies, *inner control*, or *will power*, was perceived by lay people as a very important contributor towards overcoming psychological problems — in fact the *most* important for three of the four problems under

TABLE 4.10. *Mean Scores for the Perceived Efficacy of the Seven Factors for the Four Psychological Problems. The Higher the Score the More the Factor is Thought Effective in Curing the Problem*

	Agoraphobia	Anorexia nervosa	Compulsive gambling	Schizo-phrenia	F F level
1. Inner control	7.97[a]	8.03[a]	8.74	5.65	80.91***
2. Understanding/help	6.33[ab]	6.93[a]	6.54[bc]	6.40[c]	6.13***
3. Avoidance	5.70[a]	6.50[a]	9.16	5.71[a]	60.55***
4. Physical basis	5.02[a]	4.87[a]	4.84[a]	7.07	39.94***
5. Fate	1.85[a]	1.84[a]	2.47	1.77[a]	4.97***

*** $p < 0.001$.
** $p < 0.01$.
Means with a common superscript (a, b or c) *do not* differ significantly one from another.
0 = Not at all effective; 9 = Very effective.

consideration. Interestingly, factors perceived as major contributors to cure did not discriminate between agoraphobia and anorexia nervosa. In both instances people believed *inner control* to be most effective, followed closely by *understanding* and *help*; *avoidance* of situations likely to exacerbate the problem was seen as third most important, followed by *physical basis* and finally *fate*. This suggests that, although the symptoms of these disorders may be very different, the perceived "cure" — and hence, possibly, the perceived cause — of these problems was much the same. Furthermore, if inner control is perceived as the most important contributor towards overcoming agoraphobia and anorexia, it is quite possible that its converse, lack of inner control or "inner weakness", is perceived by lay people as a causal factor in these disorders. However, the fact that two factors — one internal (inner control) and the other external (understanding/help) — were rated nearly equal in importance as contributors towards overcoming agoraphobic and anorexia suggests that these may be perceived as the sort of psychological handicaps that are partly caused or exacerbated by personal weakness but which can be overcome only by a combination of personal determination and help from others.

Studying the beliefs about the efficacy of various "cures" or "therapies" is of considerable interest. Theories or practices of self cure, or advice to others about cure, may be valuable indicators of theories of cause. That is, if one believes inner control is the best cure, presumably inner weakness is believed to be the major cause. On the other hand, if understanding the problem is seen as the most effective cure, lack of insight is probably seen as the most common cause. Secondly, studying the attribution of cure of either patients or lay people may give one valuable insights into the actual cognitive or behavioural strategies people use when experiencing a problem. These may be highly effective or totally inappropriate depending on the problem and the person. Certainly self-reliance and inner control are important constituents of most cures, but would need to be supplemented by various other strategies in the case of numerous problems.

Finally, comparing cure attributions of patients, ordinary lay people, and mental health professionals may yield interesting and important differences. If a person goes to a friend or professional for help for a specific problem and is recommended a "cure" that the patient does not "believe in", it may well be that he or she either fails to follow the cure or ensures that it is not effective. Thus, attempts to help people must take into consideration the cognitions of those helping as well as those being helped. Explaining to a patient the rationale for a particular coping strategy (i.e. increasing under-standing) may be one way of ensuring that he/she utilises it.

4.7 Conclusion

The academic discipline of psychiatry, like that of psychology, may be divided into various schools or approaches, some radically different from others. Lay theories about psychiatric problems revolve essentially around conceptions of mental health and illness (cause, consequence, manifestation, cure) and the efficacy of psychiatrist or general psychiatric treatment to help the mentally disturbed.

Although conclusions from studies are equivocal concerning the extent to which lay people are different from experts in their theories of psychiatric illness it seems to be the case that there remain numerous very negative stereotypes about the mentally ill. Systematic features of lay people (their education, class, experience of mental illness) and of particular patients with specific illnesses are related to those attitudes and beliefs, but there still remains a good deal of ignorance rather than correct information about psychiatric disturbances.

This chapter focused on lay theories of addiction to alcohol and nicotine and two interesting results emerge from the studies reviewed. First, that the structure of lay theories (that is the range and relationship between them) seems to be essentially similar to those of experts though lay people tend to prefer psychological rather than biological or sociological theories. Secondly, there are clearly important differences between various groups in the theories that they hold and there appears to be evidence that the theories held serve specific ego-defensive functions.

Studies on lay theories of depression have revealed a fairly high consensus in lay people's knowledge of the causes of, and cures for, depression, no doubt because it is such a common problem. Cognitive psychologists have pointed out that certain attributional styles, which are closely related to lay theories, may account for the aetiology and maintenance of depression. Hence, lay theories may have self-fulfilling prophesies with respect to depression and other psychological illnesses.

Studies on lay theories of neurosis raised further interesting issues. To what extent do people know that they are neurotic? The answer appears to be moderately well, though "normals" believe themselves to be marginally less neurotic than the average person and neurotics far more neurotic than they actually are. To what extent are people aware of the different kinds of neurosis? Overall lay people realise that different symptoms (obsessionality and phobia) cluster together and are associated with different psychological problems.

Not all lay theories are about cause — many are about coping strategies and cure. There appears to be a fairly robust structure to the factors lay people believe important in curing psychological problems like alcoholism or anorexia, such as inner control (will power), receiving professional help, and the amount of understanding that they receive from lay people. Predictably, lay people assume different cures are appropriate for different problems — thus, will power is seen as most relevant for alcoholism and sympathetic understanding for sex problems. No doubt people's theories about cure may, in part, determine where they seek help and how they respond to therapy of various sorts (Furnham, 1986c).

5

Lay Theories in Medicine

5.1 Introduction

Perhaps the area where lay theories have most important consequences is that of medicine. Nearly all people have theories as to the cause and most effective cure of both minor, frequently occurring, ailments (coughs, colds, etc.) but also important and relatively rare complaints. Based on their theories, lay people frequently self-medicate and give advice to family and friends. There are both appalling and amazing stories of what people do to themselves when ill. Heart attack victims have been known to take indigestion tablets or even go for a brisk walk while experiencing the attack, while others take "medicines" which are actual poisons and the cause, not the cure of, the symptoms they are seeking to prevent. These lay theories also dictate who people turn to for advice, help and information when faced with illness. According to Helman (1984):

> There are certain individuals, though, who tend to act as a source of health advice more often than others. These include: (1) those with long experience of a particular illness, or type of treatment, (2) those with extensive experience of certain life events, such as women who have raised several children; (3) the paramedical professions (such as nurses, pharmacists, physiotherapists or doctor's receptionists) who are consulted informally about health problems; (4) doctors' wives or husbands, who share some of their spouses' experience if not training; (5) individuals such as chiropodists, hairdressers, or even bank managers who interact frequently with the public, and sometimes act as lay confessors or psychotherapists; (6) the organisers of self-help groups; and (7) the members or officiants of certain healing cults or churches. All of these people may be considered resources of advice and assistance on health matters, by their friends or families. Their credentials are mainly their own *experience* rather than education, social status or special occult powers. A woman who has had several pregnancies, for example, can give informal advice to a newly pregnant younger woman, telling her what symptoms to expect and how to deal with them. Similarly, a person with long experience of a particular medication may "lend" some to a friend with similar symptoms (pp. 44-45).

It is not unusual to find that households possess an encyclopaedia or guide to family health. These weighty tomes which are frequently out-of-date, with possibly misleading information, are used by people who attempt some sort of diagnosis before or instead of consulting trained help. Older books tend to be like dictionaries giving a definition of various sicknesses, their more common symptoms and cures. More modern books offer self-diagnosis charts to help people decide whether they can rely on self-treatment or

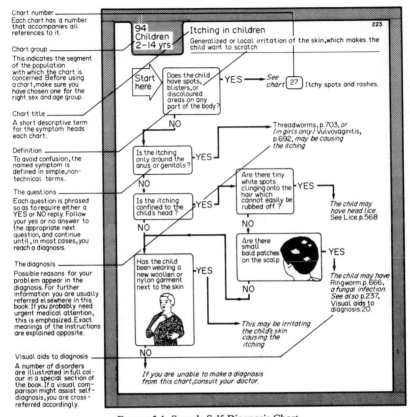

FIGURE 5.1. Sample Self-Diagnosis Chart.
Reprinted with permission from Smith, T. (1982) *The Macmillan Guide to Family Health*,
London: Macmillan.

whether they need to consult a specialist. Smith (1982) offers nearly 100 of these charts in his medical guide which deal with topics as varied as crying in infants to abnormal looking urine. A sample chart is shown in Fig. 5.1.

The aim of such books is to enable people to make a reasonably good diagnosis of their own illness so that they can decide on some form of treatment, or whether they should consult specialist advice. The flow chart format is presumably to enable people to simulate the step-wise diagnostic process of experts.

Others have written single books, pamphlets or notes on various aspects of medicine: special diseases; addictions; how to ensure a good consultation. In doing so they are frequently aware of the sort of questions that lay people ask. For instance, King *et al.* (1985) set out a typical scenario of a lay person attempting to understand, diagnose and treat his problem:

Imagine a forty-five-year-old man — Mr Setback — who wakes up one morning with chest pains. He has never had this kind of pain before. It is not something he recognises and it seems to have appeared quite out of the blue. What goes through his mind?

1. What has happened? Is it indigestion? a chest infection? some kind of heart attack?
2. Why has it happened? Was it last night's heavy meal? that game of squash? problems at work? (stress pains?)
3. Why has this happened to him? Is there something odd about him? Or could it have happened to anyone? Is it because his father died of a heart attack — could the same thing be happening to him?
4. Why now? Is it his age? the time of year — there are a lot of germs about? is it just one of those things that could have happened at any time?
5. What would happen if nothing were done about it? Will it clear up on its own? will it get worse? will it be dangerous? could it happen again?
6. What should he do about it? Rest for a few days and see if it goes? take a couple of aspirin? do nothing at all unless it happens again? talk to his wife about it and see what she says? go to the doctor?

What Mr Setback thinks about his pains will help him to decide what to do next. He probably won't go to the doctor straight away unless the pains get worse. Instead (as many people do), he may talk to a friend or relative or buy an over-the-counter remedy from the chemist.

But none of these seems to help. What's more, although Mr Setback hates to admit it, he's anxious that it may be something serious, especially as there is heart trouble in his family. So he thinks that if he goes to the doctor he'll find out what the chest pains are. He also hopes that the doctor will give him some tablets to clear up the problem. (pp. 25–26)

They then go on to describe a good consultation where the GP takes into account the patient's (Mr Setback) lay beliefs and a bad consultation where he does not.

In fact diagnosing oneself as being ill may involve a number of subjective experiences including: perceived changes in outward bodily appearance (change of weight, changes in skin texture); changes in regular bodily functions (urinary frequency, and short menstrual periods, irregular heart beats); unusual bodily emissions (blood in the urine, discharge from nose or genitalia); malfunctions of limbs (paralysis, or tremor in hands and legs); changes in one of the major senses (deafness, blindness, lack of smell, loss of taste sensation); unpleasant perpetuating physical symptoms (headaches abdominal pain, changes in temperature); extreme or unusual emotional states (anxiety, depression or mania); behavioural changes in relation to others (particularly negative behaviour towards other family or work colleagues).

Perhaps the areas of research that have most greatly contributed to our knowledge of lay theories in medicine, are medical anthropology and the social psychology of health beliefs. The former is concerned with cultural and sub-cultural determinants of lay explanations for the causes of illness and health; the types of treatment that people have trust in; and to whom they turn when they or their kin get ill. This approach is content oriented. The latter approach is concerned with the cognitive processes that individuals go through in understanding their health and illness problems and how they act upon these cognitive processes. This approach is therefore process oriented.

5.2 Cultural Determinants of Health Beliefs

A central feature of any culture is the beliefs and practices relating to ill-health and other misfortunes such as conflicts, national disasters and accidents. In every culture consensually held health and illness beliefs mean that people "know" how to present their illness to others and recognise it in them, and how to attribute the cause. Further, every culture has ways of selecting, training and monitoring their healers and doctors.

There have been a number of extremely interesting medical anthropological studies of health and illness (Helman, 1984; Herzlich, 1973). They have all been concerned with cultural definitions and beliefs concerning different issues such as the following.

(1) Anatomy and Physiology

People from different groups share rather different beliefs about the ideal shape and size of the body in both sexes; beliefs about the structure of the body; and beliefs about how it functions in illness and in health.

For instance, whereas some cultures value thinness in the female body, others prefer fatness (Furnham and Alibhai, 1983). Studies have also shown that people are remarkably ignorant about what lies inside the body and where. Thus, Boyle (1970) found half the lay people he interviewed believed the kidneys to be low down in the groin and the liver as lying in the lower abdomen, just above the pelvis. The functioning of the body is perhaps even more important. Helman (1984) has considered various aspects of lay theories of physiology such as the idea of balance and inbalance or hot vs cold theories of disease. He points to two different "models" of the body held by lay people — the *plumbing* model of pipes, tubes, chambers full of fluids and the *machine* model which stresses fuel and energy. Hence "blow one's top" and "let off steam" belong to the plumbing model and "re-charge one's batteries" to the machine model. Pregnancy and menstruation are also particularly associated with unusual culturally determined lay beliefs.

(2) Food, Diet and Nutrition

One of the most common sources of illness as well as means of self-medication is through various foods. Different cultural, ethnic and religious groups have different definitions of what constitutes a food and also a medicine. Like all the lay theories those beliefs are not fixed, but may change with economic circumstances, travel and so forth. Of course foods take on a religious and social significance. Food taboos are common in all religions, while other foods become sacred or invested with purity (Farb and Armelagos, 1980). It is not surprising that various foods are thought — rightly or wrongly — to have medicinal value. This may mean that these lay beliefs may lead to malnutrition by the deliberate exclusion of important vitamins and proteins or overnutrition by the over consumption of particular foods.

(3) Pain and Discomfort

Cultures differ in the extent to which they encourage or discourage people from actually publicly displaying genuine pain. Cultures differ in the virtue they place on stoicism and in their expectations of pain. Both the form of, and the response to, pain behaviour differ widely from one society to another. Thus, some cultural groups tend to underexaggerate the extent and character of their pain and withdraw from society when experiencing it, while others will through graphic verbal and non-verbal responses, overexaggerate the duration, location and suffering caused by the pain.

(4) Pharmacology

Although imperfectly understood, the considerable research on the placebo suggests that although they may be very effective in one culture they may not be in another. The success of a placebo depends on a number of features, such as the colour, size and type (pill, fluid) of the "medicine"; the attributes of the patient; and the characteristics of the healer.

Most actual drugs are taken to change mood — usually induce euphoria or lessen tension. Drugs that are used extensively in a culture (e.g. alcohol, tobacco) are normalised and seen to be good because they facilitate "normal" behaviour (self-controlled, sociable, assertion) and reduce "abnormal" behaviour (nervousness, depression). Thus, for instance, with alcoholic drinks, cultural rules, moves and sanctions determine the amount and type of alcohol consumed, when, where and by whom, cultures may be abstinent, ambivalent or permissive. Other chemical comforters like tea, coffee and nicotine function similarly.

Lay medical beliefs then are highly culture specific. The methodology of medical anthropology particularly ethnography are particularly suitable at revealing lay theories of illness and health.

Fitzpatrick (1984) has also stressed the importance of cultural determinants on lay concepts of illness, particularly as they demonstrate the survival of forms of explanations of illness quite different from those found in Western medicine. Furthermore, these form part of the more general system of beliefs that provide a "coherent philosophy of misfortune". Cultural factors influence the perception, labelling and explanation of illness. People in the West apparently seek out explanation for illnesses, such as disease, environmental factors, stress and so forth, much more than people in non-Western societies.

Various analogies (metaphors, models) may be used by people in different cultures or sub-cultures to describe and "explain" illnesses: *Time running out* or degeneration, where illness is attributed to the wearing out of the body; *Mechanical faults* or damage, where illness is attributed to broken or faulty body mechanisms; *Imbalance* or lack of harmony, either between various parts of the body or between the individual and his/her environment; *Invasion* or penetration of the body by germs or other foreign bodies causing illness.

These metaphors or analogies are the ways in which lay people think about illness but they often contrast dramatically with those found in Western medical science. Though these lay beliefs are complex they are frequently illogical and inconsistent. Indeed, patients may feel self-conscious about the relatively unsophisticated, foolish or even superstitious nature of their beliefs about illness when confronted by a doctor and may therefore be loath to disclose them. These beliefs are often highly idiosyncratic being derived and adapted from a wide variety of sources. They are also highly flexible and changeable in particular circumstances. Yet these beliefs form a "system", in the sense that they are interconnected to other non-illness related beliefs, but also because they are connected to the beliefs of other people in the community.

Many lay beliefs about illness are associated with other images and ideas. For instance, Herzlich (1973) found French informants believed in the toxic influences of city life which cause physical and mental fatigue and render the dweller vulnerable to illness, while the rural environment was perceived as more natural and harmonious.

Fitzpatrick (1984) has cautioned against overemphasising the gulf between lay and medical concepts. First, he argues that one should not forget the difference between textbook medicine and actual clinical practice, the former with complex and technical terms and the latter with much simpler ideas based on selected facts. Many practising physicians retain lay assumptions and metaphors, which they use along with more scientific principles. Secondly, it may be that patients influence doctors as much as the other way around and that doctors use the categories, terms and prescriptions that are important to patients. Thus, they may prescribe medicines which the evidence suggests are ineffective but which make sense in terms of the folk metaphor. Thirdly, many patients have a reasonably correct understanding of many minor and major illnesses — their aetiology and prognosis.

Thus it may be unwise to overemphasise the "unbridgeable" gap between the medical belief worlds of the lay novice and trained "experts" in Western medicine. Furthermore, it may be unwise to assume that all lay theories of illness are incorrect — many contain (like stereotypes) a kernel of truth. Indeed, from a social Darwinian perspect one would imagine that only correct theories would survive in the sub-culture.

5.3 Health Beliefs

Social and medical psychologists, as well as medical sociologists, have developed a model of mainly Western lay-people's health beliefs. It has been suggested that these health beliefs are better predictors of a person's health behaviour than personality or individual difference variables favoured by

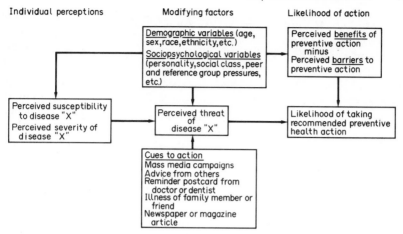

Individual perceptions   Modifying factors   Likelihood of action

FIGURE 5.2. The original health belief model (after Becker and Maiman, 1975).
Reprinted with permission from Pendleton, D. and Hasler, J. (Eds.) (1983) *Doctor–Patient Communication,* London: Academic Press.

psychologists or demographic variables favoured by sociologists. These health beliefs may be better called *health understanding* as they concern knowledge, attitudes, values and beliefs (Pendleton, 1983).

The health belief model, developed and tested extensively in the 1970s, is set out in Fig. 5.2 (Becker, 1974; Rosenstock, 1974). According to King (1983) the model has five major points all of which stress that it is the person's subjective perceptions of health and illness rather than the actual or objective medical facts that are of course open to bias and misjudgement but that actually determine health behaviour.

King (1983) argues that the model contains the following main elements:

(a) *Health motivation:* an individual's degree of interest in, and concern about health matters.

(b) *Perceived susceptibility:* perceived vulnerability (or susceptibility) to the particular illnesses, including acceptance of the diagnosis of others.

(c) *Perceived severity:* perceptions concerning the probable seriousness of the consequences (organic and social) of contracting the illness or leaving it untreated.

(d) *Benefits and costs:* the individual's estimate of the benefits of taking recommended, possibly unpleasant, health action, weighed against the costs or barriers involved. Costs might include financial expense, physical and emotional discomfort, or possible side effects, while benefits of course mean a release from symptoms.

(e) *Cue to actions* something must occur to "trigger" these perceptions and lead to the appropriate health behaviour. These stimuli may be either internal (such as symptoms), or external (such as magazine articles, a reminder from the doctor, or illness in the family).

Each of these features has attracted a good deal of research. For instance, psychologists have been interested in general health locus of control beliefs. For example, it has been shown that internals were more likely to take part in physical exercise activities (Strickland, 1978), are better at losing weight (Balch and Ross, 1975) and are better at avoiding alcoholism (Nowicki and Hopper, 1974). Indeed, there are a number of *health* locus of control scales including the Lau–Ware Health Locus of Control Scale (Lau, 1982); the Multidimensional Health Locus of Control Scale, (Wallston *et al.*, 1978), the Weight Locus of Control Scale (Saltzer, 1982), Children's Health Locus of Control (Parcel and Meyer, 1978) and Mental Health Locus of Control (Calhoun *et al.*, 1973 Wood and Letak, 1982). The scale has also been used in studies of dental health (Ludenia and Denham, 1983). These health scales and studies have been well documented and reviewed (Wallston and Wallston, 1981) in "state-of-the-art" reviews. Though the literature is equivocal there seems to be sufficient evidence that beliefs about who controls one's health are powerful and motivating factors in determining health-related behaviours.

Studies on patients' perceived susceptibility and vulnerability (and re-susceptibility) have shown that these perceptions are strongly related to the patients' compliance with medical advice, be it as serious as cancer or as common as dental problems. Studies on the effects of the patients' perceptions of severity of the illness have not demonstrated such conclusive results, in that not all studies have shown a positive association between perceived severity and compliance, probably because both high and low levels of perceived threat are associated with a low likelihood of taking preventive action. Moderate levels of perceived severity seem best predictors of health-related behaviours. The cost–benefit analysis too, may be related to health behaviours, however these costs may be psychological as well as monetary. Finally, something must cause a patient to do something about his or her action.

The health belief model has inspired a considerable amount of research in all areas of health. The model has proved to be a good predictor for participation in programmes for the early detection of breast cancer (Calnan, 1984); initial drug therapy defaulting (Fincham and Wertheimer, 1985); compliance with alcoholism treatment (Rees, 1985), etc. Not all studies have found health beliefs significant predictors of health behaviour, but it is probably fair to say that most have. However, it should be pointed out that these health beliefs although significant predictors usually only account for a small percentage (well under a third) of the variance. Thus, whereas health beliefs may be important predictors they are not the only factors leading to health behaviour and probably interact with many other variables.

As one might expect, the health belief model has been criticised, extended and even abandoned by some. For instance, various *omissions* in the model have been noted which include: the patient's social environment, which therefore omits lay referral (e.g. by friends and relations) and social support networks, which may help or hinder health and health related behaviour; the doctor-patient interaction, which does not operate in a vacuum but in specific settings and perceptions of symptoms and lay constructions of illness and the sick role.

King (1983) has pointed to various *limitations* of the model. She argues that for the Health Belief Model to be useful, all its factors need to be considered simultaneously, as it is often only the *interaction* between these that can predict health behaviour. She also laments the fact that there has been no research on the *stability* of the model's major variables over time (over the individual's life span, at different times certain illnesses are more likely than others). Also, there has been no research into the conditions under which the health beliefs were *acquired*:

> What are the determinants of these patient health beliefs? Why does one patient see himself as more vulnerable than another, to a particular illness? How does the patient come to see himself or herself as susceptible in the first place? How does a person come to believe a specific action is preventive? What governs the desire for a particular level of health? (King, 1983, p. 120)

Others have *extended* the model. Jaspars *et al.* (1983) have devised an attributional health belief model. The model stresses first the determinants of causal explanations, which are used in predicting when a person attributes an event (illness) to themselves rather than to the environment. It is argued that a person believes the risk of catching an illness is dependent on consistency beliefs (how often that person has had the illness before), consensus beliefs (whether or not it is a common illness which affects many other people) and distinctive beliefs (whether the illness has a specific cause or several probable causes). These explanations determine the perceived cause of illness being grouped on three dimensions: internal, stable and controllable. In turn these perceived causes lead to various individual perceptions and through modifying and enabling factors to behaviour itself (see Fig. 5.3).

This model has received a certain amount of empirical support though it probably requires further refinement and development.

The models of health beliefs are attempts to understand how lay people process information about their health, which leads them to act, or not act, to do something about their illnesses. The models attempt to describe which are the salient factors/dimensions of relevance and then to explore possible causal chains or "routes" through these variables from beliefs/perceptions to behaviour.

5.4 Doctor-Patient Communication

Perhaps the area that has been most extensively studied by social scientists of all backgrounds, with regard to lay medical theories, is the communication

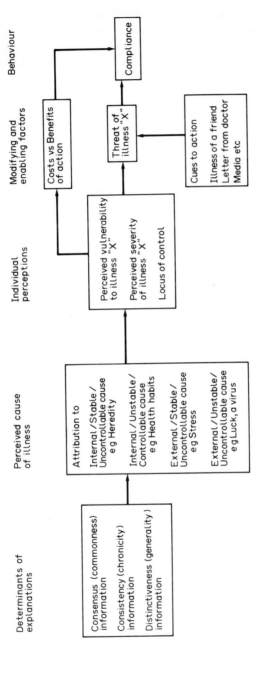

FIGURE 5.3. Proposed attribution — health belief model.
Reprinted with permission from Pendleton, D. and Hasler, J. (Eds.) (1983) *Doctor–Patient Communication*. London: Academic Press.

(or miscommunication) between doctors and their patients. A number of models or processes have been put forward to understand this issue.

Helman (1984) argues that the best way to look at this process is to examine the sorts of questions that people ask themselves, once they "diagnose" themselves as being ill. He lists six:

These are: *What has happened?* (which includes organising the symptoms and signs into a recognisable pattern, and giving it a name or identity), (2) *Why has it happened?* (explaining its aetiology of the condition), (3) *Why has it happened to me?* (Trying to relate the illness to aspects of the patient, such as behaviour, diet, body-build, personality or heredity), (4) *Why now?* (the timing of the illness and its mode of onset, sudden or slow), (5) *What would happen if nothing were done about it?* (Its likely course, outcome, prognosis and dangers), and (6) *What should I do about it?* (strategies for treating the condition, including self-medication, consultation with friends or family, or going to see a doctor). (p. 72)

He goes on to argue that lay theories of illness causation place the aetiology of ill-health in one of four regions or worlds: the patient, the natural world, the social world and the supernatural world; though he does recognise that illness may be ascribed to a combination of causes or the interaction of these worlds: *The patient* — here the patient ascribes responsibility to him or herself — poor diet, inadequate hygiene, unhealthy lifestyle, vulnerability because of heredity or occupation, personal weakness or nervous system inbalance; *The natural world* — here the animate and inanimate environment such as climate, astrological signs, infective germs, are natural man-made irritants such as pollen or poisons are seen to be the cause; *The social world* — in non-Western societies witchcraft, sorcery and the "evil eye" may be seen as social phenomena causing illness, whereas in Western societies occupational, familiar or relational stress are often seen as primary social explanations for health; *The supernatural world* — these may include gods, spirits or ancestral factors which may be personalistic or naturalistic are seen to cause illness.

People as individuals, as well as members of certain racial, ethnic or religious groups, may be more prone to one type or sphere of explanation than another. Thus, depressives from all groups may have a preference for personal attributions; while Protestants may prefer social and Catholics supernatural explanations. Clearly the most important empirical issue to explore is what psychological and sociological factors lead people to choose one type of explanation over another, and when and why these change over time and particular symptoms.

Of course, these beliefs determine the reasons for consulting and not consulting a patient, the presentation of the illness and most probably the outcome of the consultation.

Pendleton (1983) has provided a rather different social-psychological model of the consultation set out in Fig. 5.4

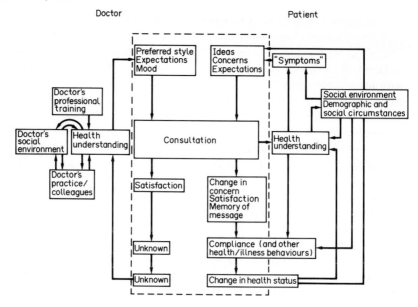

FIGURE 5.4. A Social-Psychological Model of the Consultation.
Reproduced with permission from Pendleton, D. and Hasler, J. (Eds.) (1983) *Doctor-Patient Communication*. London: Academic Press.

The consultation is seen as a social influence process with two phases: an *input* phase which leads to the diagnosis (patient informs the doctor about health problems, interviewing, examining, etc.) and an *output* phase (immediate, intermediate and long-term) which leads to the management of the problem (prescribed treatment, patient's reactions and compliance). The patient's medical knowledge, beliefs and explanations are relevant at both stages, particularly the latter.

Pendleton has argued convincingly that the effectiveness of doctor-patient interaction related directly to numerous outcome variables, like patient compliance and recovery. Perhaps more importantly he argues that because the doctor-patient interaction is dynamic and reciprocal it is important to examine how the beliefs of the doctor are communicated to the patient and vice versa. That is, patients' health beliefs and theories are modified, informed, distorted and changed in communication with doctors and any other person with whom they are discussed. Health beliefs are most often exposed in, and modified by, consultation with doctors. Hence, in order to facilitate better doctor-patient communication King *et al.* (1985) encourage patients who are about to see their doctor to make lists of: What has been happening to them and how it has affected their daily routine; What they think might be wrong with them; What they are most afraid of; What they would like the doctor to do; What they want to know about their problem; What they have already tried to do about the problem.

5.5 Specific Beliefs

(1) Health Locus of Control

There is a vast literature that has consistently demonstrated that people with internal as opposed to external expectations (locus of control beliefs) have greater adaptive functioning. Internals, as opposed to externals, tend to assume more responsibility for their health, guard against accidents and disease, seek more information about health maintenance, and learn more about illnesses and diseases that they contract. Externals believe physical disabilities to be more debilitating than internals, who anticipated less handicaps. Internals also appeared to be more sensitive to internal states, alert to biofeedback cures, and motivated to attempt self-control of bodily functions. Naturally, internals prefer treatments that do not inhibit their freedom or control. Thus, congruence in views of patient and health care professionals appears to enhance behaviour change.

The idea of individualising patient treatment based on locus of control beliefs has received support. Imagine, for instance, that one can classify dental patients as preventive vs restorative and that these types reflect dental locus of control beliefs: preventive patients are internal, believing that as their dental health is in their control preventive measures are best; while restorative patients are external, believing that their dental health is beyond their control. As these two groups appear to have different beliefs that no doubt effect their dental health and visits to dentists, it may be that health education and advice should be quite different for each of the two groups.

Some idea of the concept can be got from the following items, which are the first 10 items from the Lau–Ware (1981) scale: Staying well has little or nothing to do with chance; Seeing a doctor for regular check-ups is a key factor in staying healthy; Doctors can rarely do very much for people who are sick; Anyone can learn a few basis health principles that can go a long way in preventing illness; People's health results from their own carelessness; Doctors relieve or cure only a few of the medical problems their patients have; There is little one can do to prevent illness; No matter what anybody does, there are many diseases that can just wipe you out; Whether or not people get well is often a matter of chance; People who never get sick are just plain lucky.

Although there has been an increasing number of studies using the health locus of control concept and associated scales they have not all provided confirmatory evidence of the hypotheses (Dielman *et al.*, 1984; Furnham, 1983c; Wurtele *et al.*, 1985). Certainly the tendency has been to develop "more and more specific" measures of health control beliefs as more general scales tend not to discriminate or predict health behaviour (Slenker *et al.*, 1985).

Wallston and Wallston (1981) have suggested that even more specific health locus of control scales are developed and that they are used in a clinical as well as a health context. It may be that the scales are better at predicting sick-role behaviour than health related behaviour.

Pill and Stott (1982) have argued and demonstrated that a person's readiness to accept responsibility for his or her health depends partly on views held about the aetiology of illness. In a sample of working-class mothers they found that they attributed illness causation primarily to germs, followed by "lifestyle", heredity and stress. Nearly half of the sample held fatalistic views on the cause of these and, hence, they believed that they were rarely morally accountable. In this sense they did not act as responsible individuals by availing themselves of appropriate preventive and screening measures and leading healthy lives. By attributing illness to germs which are external and random in who they affect, the victim becomes blameless. Better-educated women, however, recognised or admitted that individual behaviour had some part to play in illness and, thus, felt they were morally accountable if they neglected themselves and thereby reduced the level of resistance to change.

In a later paper Pill and Stott (1985) presented a salience of lifestyle index based on answers to the five questions below:

1. What do you think are the main reasons for people falling ill? Can you tell me a little bit more about how X makes people ill?
2. Do you think some people are more likely to fall ill than others? What sort of people are they?
3. Do you think that people can ever be to blame if they fall ill?
4. Everyone becomes ill in the course of their lives but some people do seem to get things worse than others: I wonder what you think about that?
5. Do you think some types of illness are more easily prevented than others? What? How?

Once again they confirmed that "fatalists" accepted less responsibility for their health than "lifestylists" who are committed to the idea that day-to-day habits of diet and exercise have implications for present and future health.

Just as in many other spheres of behaviour, the locus of control concept seems to be very important in predicting lay people's health beliefs and behaviours. Just as in other research, it has been demonstrated that internal locus of control beliefs are more adaptive than external beliefs, so the vast bulk of the literature in this area appears to indicate that health educators need to attempt to encourage "externals" to become more "internal" and take some responsibility for their health and illness.

(2) Just World Beliefs and Victims of Illness

People who believe that the world is a place in which people get what they deserve (and deserve what they get) frequently blame victims for this misfortune by "discovering" facts that caused the person to bring misfortune upon themselves. It is clearly a self-protective belief system which stresses the lawful rather than random relatedness among actions.

Various writers have shown how this process applies to medical issues. For instance, Gruman and Sloan (1983) found that ill people are derogated significantly more than healthy people and that this derogation was related to the severity of the illness. An exception was cancer — victims of stomach cancer were derogated less than victims of pneumonia despite the fact that pneumonia was perceived as less severe. In a second study Sloan and Gruman (1983) got subjects to read two stimulus stories — one depicting a victim of cancer, the other a victim of a heart attack. As predicted, and contrary to the just world hypothesis, victims of less preventable and less well understood diseases received less derogation than victims of preventable ones. This suggests a defensive attribution on the part of the subjects.

This research suggests that there may, therefore, be important caveats to the general just world hypothesis. It may be expected, then, that these people (possibly a majority in the west) who hold just world beliefs, tend to be unsympathetic and even derogatory to illnesses whose aetiology is known and whose treatment is effective. On the other hand, where the disease is perceived as unpreventable or untreatable, victims receive less derogation. Presumably this pattern applies equally to oneself and others and hence may effect self-medication and recovery.

5.6 Lay Theories of Specific Illnesses

Various studies have been done examining lay theories and knowledge of various illnesses and complaints. It is not always clear why some medical problems are isolated for research and others are not. The prevalance of a medical problem (obesity, cancer) may be one reason for the existence of pressure groups who encourage or sponsor research on a particular problem. Suffice it to say that the research is very patchy and only a few topics will be touched on here. Not unnaturally, most researchers have been concerned with the knowledge and attitudes of disease victims, their relations and caretakers rather than of the public in general.

(1) Obesity

Obesity like so many "medical conditions" is a complex multidimensional condition, not particularly easy to treat: what constitutes obesity is, however, culturally and sub-culturally defined. Thus, in developed, rich Western society there is an inverse relationship between high socioeconomic status and low body weight, whereas the inverse is true of less developed non-Western societies (Furnham and Alibhai, 1983). Preference for obese vs anorexic body shapes also changes over time. Theories on the causes of obesity such as problems with the hypothalamic satiety centre or increased external responsiveness have been dismissed as too simplistic.

It has been frequently observed by lay people that there is an actor-observer difference in the explanation of obesity. Obese people blame their glands or metabolism (uncontrollable) whereas non-obese people blame the obese for gluttony and sloth (controllable). More recently, research programmes have actually looked at age, ethnicity, sex and weight determinants of lay beliefs about obesity. Harris and Smith (1982) asked 447 people from various ethnicity and age groups "Why are some people fat?" The most frequent was "Eating behaviours" given by 45% of the 422 subjects responding, followed by "It varies" (15%), "Don't know" (12%), "Physical/medical" (8%), "Eating wrong food" (6%), "They just are" (5%), "No will power" (3%), "Caloric imbalance" (2), "Emotional/ psychological" (2%), "Other people or society" (1%), "Lack of exercise" (0.5%) and "God" (0.2%). Because there were small frequencies in a number of these categories, they were reclassified into four more general categories: Physical/medical (8%), Eating habits (54%), Emotional/psychological including lack of will power (6%) and Other (33%).

Males tended to stress eating habits more than females who placed more stress on physical/medical and emotional reasons. Comparing over the four age groups it appeared that older people placed more stress on physical/ medical and emotional/psychological and less stress on eating habits than younger people. But there were no significant differences as a function of a person's ethnicity or weight.

Subjects were also asked "Whose fault is it that someone is fat?" Whereas 55% said it was the fat person's own fault, 15% said it was nobody's, while the remaining subjects blamed various others, such as parents, God, etc. Adults were significantly less likely to say it was the person's own fault compared with children: Adults 32%; fifth graders (age 11) 66%; first graders (6) 62% and nursery school children 58%. More females than males, and older more than younger subjects admitted to knowing somebody who was fat. The authors conclude "As has been suggested elsewhere widespread education about the complex nature of obesity may be necessary to reduce incorrect beliefs and the negative attitudes towards obesity which frequently accompany them" (p. 1054). Clearly, it is quite possible that lay theories as to the causes of obesity are important in the aetiology and cure of the condition.

(2) Diabetes

Like various other medical afflictions, diabetes is fairly prevalent and imperfectly understood. Although the medical aspects of the problem are complicated they are fairly well understood compared with the psychological factors which have long been recognised.

Patient knowledge about diabetes is clearly very important, as much of the complicated management of the disease must be done by patients themselves. However, studies have shown that patients frequently have inadequate and insufficient knowledge about their own disease. In fact Johnson (1984) has noted knowledge of, and skill in, treating some aspects of diabetes do not necessarily generalise to all areas of the illness. Mothers are generally more knowledgeable than fathers about the illness in their children, no doubt because they usually take more responsibility in the management of the disease.

Johnson (1984) has reviewed studies on patient and non-patient attitudes towards diabetes, particularly with regard to children. These attitudes were shown to be related to adjustment, compliance and health in general, however, the author is aware of inferring cause from mere correlational evidence:

> Patients' knowledge, attitudes and behaviours may be the result of the patients' health status. Poor health may lead to feelings of helplessness; the patient may "give-up" behaving in a highly compliant manner or develop negative attitudes towards the disease. Clearly, the effect of psychological variables on the patients' health as well as the impact of health or illness on the patients' knowledge, feelings and behaviour must be considered. (p. 520)

Finally this research suggests that measures of knowledge, attitudes and diabetic behaviour must be highly specific, as global or general measures are far from useful in predicting how people with the disease behave.

Certainly this is an important area of research, as many diabetics manifest symptoms for years before actually consulting their doctor. Perhaps future research in this area could also be directed to the knowledge and attitudes of members of the public (i.e. non-sufferers) at large.

(3) Alzheimer's Disease

This is a type of dementia that is a progressive disorder of middle to later years, characterised by abnormalities of memory, cognition and behaviour. Because of press and other media coverage both health professionals and lay people have begun to report it as a major health problem, and as dreaded a complaint as cancer.

Price *et al.* (1986) actually set about measuring elderly persons' perceptions and knowledge of Alzheimer's by testing 148 subjects with a mean age of 70 years, about a third of whom had a relative or friend with the disease. The results that they obtained are set out in Table 5.1 and show that only eight items were correctly answered by more than half of the respondents.

Overall, better educated people and those with friends or relatives with the disease tended to know more about the disease. The respondents identified sources from which they had received information about the disease: television (68%); articles (59%); friends (32%); talks (23%), but physicians and family were identified by less than 5% of the subjects. This has, of course

TABLE 5.1. *Per Cent Correct of Knowledge Items on Alzheimer's Disease*

Item (Answer)	%
Demographic Characteristics	
Men are much more likely to develop Alzheimer's than are women (F)	22
Alzheimer's disease is the most common mental health problem of the elderly (F)	25
If one lives long enough all people will eventually develop Alzheimer's disease (F)	61
Blacks do not develop Alzheimer's disease (F)	21
Aetiology	
Alzheimer's disease runs in families (inherited) (F)	20
Alzheimer's disease is a type of cancer of the brain (F)	34
Alzheimer's disease can be caused by poor diet (F)	37
Hardening of the arteries is a common cause of Alzheimer's disease (F)	22
One should be careful around individuals with Alzheimer's disease since one may develop the disease from regular contact with such people (F)	77
Symptoms	
Progressive withdrawal from social activities is common to all people with Alzheimer's disease (T)	55
Fatigue is a common problem for people with Alzheimer's disease (T)	22
People with Alzheimer's disease can no longer learn new skills (T)	23
People with Alzheimer's disease are very agreeable, co-operative and easy to live with (F)	59
Severe memory loss is always caused by disease and is not a common problem in the elderly (T)	22
Diagnosis /treatment and care	
Alzheimer's disease is not curable (T)	55
The younger one is when the first symptoms of Alzheimer's disease occur, the more severe the disease will become (T)	20
It is best if families make arrangements for nursing home placement as soon as diagnosis of Alzheimer's disease is made (F)	53
Eventually the person with Alzheimer's disease will need 24-hour supervision (T)	66
Medicare covers all costs for the care and treatment of individuals with Alzheimer's disease (F)	34
Only a psychiatrist can diagnose Alzheimer's disease (F)	52

T = True; F = False
Reprinted with permission of authors and publisher from: Price, J. A., Price, J. H., Shanahar, P. M.. and Desmond, S. M. Elderly persons' perceptions and knowledge of Alzheimer's disease. *Psychological Reports*, (1986), *58*, 419–424, Table 1.

important implications for the education of lay people about this and many other diseases.

(4) Lung Cancer

The association between smoking and lung cancer is well established. Indeed it may be precisely because this fact is well known that some lay beliefs are open to distortion such as ignoring base-rate data, and assigning greater weight to causal vs diagnostic data.

Kristiansen *et al.* (1983) set about examining lay beliefs about the relationship between smoking and cancer.

Each of the 470 subjects made one judgement which, depending on the condition, consisted of either: (a) a rating of the likelihood that a hypothetical target person had or had not been a smoker, given that he had died of lung cancer, heart disease, alcoholism, a road accident or suicide; or (b) a rating of the likelihood that a hypothetical target person, described alternatively as a smoker or a non-smoker, would die of lung cancer.

In the first set of conditions, subjects were given information concerning the percentage of smokers in the population, and in the second set of conditions, the percentage of deaths from lung cancer. The base rate of information.

They found that the target person was seen as significantly more likely to have been a smoker than a non-smoker, if he had died from lung cancer, heart disease or alcoholism, but not if he had died in a road accident or had committed suicide; also the target person was seen as significantly more likely to die from lung cancer if he was a smoker than if he was a non-smoker, and subjects who were themselves smokers did not differ significantly in their ratings from non-smoking subjects. Thus, people over-estimate the dangers of smoking and perceive it as causing a variety of diseases. In a sense this attests to the success of health education material but it may mean that other equally important health risks are understressed.

5.7 Conclusion

Perhaps more than any other area, ordinary lay people's ideas, beliefs and theories about their own and others' physical health have important consequences for diagnosis, medication and the advice that they give to others. Indeed, these beliefs may be important predictors of who they consult in a time of illness — recognised doctor, medical textbook, neighbour or even priest.

One of the most interesting and important questions in this area is how people diagnose illness — that is, what signs do they look for and how do they interpret them. Given that they recognise a problem the next question concerns how they go about "treating" the problem. Anthropologists have demonstrated that different cultures have "prescribed" ways of presenting their illness to others; the language and models they use to describe illness; how to attribute the causes of illness; and the selection, training and monitoring of recognised healers. The medical treatment given in one culture (e.g. placebos) may therefore have quite different effects in a second culture.

Social psychologists have been most interested in the "health belief model" which is a model of lay theories of health and illness which concerns such things as lay perceptions of susceptibility, and severity of various common or rare illnesses. Various attempts have been made to improve the model so that it is more useful in predicting behaviour. Indeed, there is no reason why an economic belief model (see Chapter 7) or an educational belief model (see Chapter 9) may not be developed along these lines, as model building for lay theories has been sadly lacking.

One dimension underlying much of the work on health beliefs is that of locus on control, which is concerned with the extent to which people believe that they control their own health. The concept has been applied to specific areas of health, as well as more general health practices, and has been shown to be a useful predictor of health related behaviours.

To a large extent all health education is about the eliciting and modifying of the health beliefs of the lay public. The sudden increase in certain diseases (e.g. AIDS) or the formation of pressure groups means that people are exposed to health-related information on a very select and haphazard basis. No wonder, then, that lay theories about health and illness are so patchy and frequently wrong.

Fitzpatrick (1984) has nicely summarised the importance of this area thus:

> The evidence . . . suggests that patients' interpretations of their symptoms are governed by concepts and ideas of considerable complexity and variety. . . . There are firm grounds for arguing that attention to patients' interpretations of their health problems has been shown to be clinically fruitful and can be successfully incorporated into the practice of health care. (p. 31)

Whatever lay people's beliefs about specific illnesses these beliefs may be very relevant to cure. Fitzpatrick (1984) has identified five issues of therapeutic significance regarding lay beliefs:

1. *Identifying the problem*: Because patients present problems rather than diseases and select which aspects, particularly physical, they report, the way they personally define, categorise and link factors concerning the illness are crucially important in diagnosis.
2. *Monitoring the impact of diagnostic information*: Patients assign meaning to the diagnosis that they receive, some of which are highly inappropriate. That is, because of their incorrect understanding of the disease label they have been given, lay people react and even medicate inappropriately. Hence, it becomes important to address the meanings that patients assign to professional diagnoses.
3. *Reassurance in relation to "non-disease"*: Many patients need careful and sensitive assurance that apparent symptoms are normal and not worth worrying about. Patients feel more reassured if they are convinced that doctors have understood their perspectives on the illness.
4. *Obtaining co-operation with long-term treatment*: Patients appear to be more compliant with their prescribed long-term treatment of chronic illness when their health beliefs have been elicited and, where appropriate, modified.
5. *Supporting the patient*: Patients perceive their doctor to be more supportive if his/her behaviour expresses their concerns in their own terms. Studies have shown that patients who were more satisfied that their specialist consultations had been appropriate to their personal concerns showed less severe negative symptoms a year later than those who found the consultation superficial or inappropriate.

6

Lay Theories in Economics

6.1 Introduction

Like most of the social sciences, economic thinkers fall into various schools of thought, e.g. Keynesian, Monetarist, etc. Furthermore, within each area of economics there may be competing or overlapping theories which focus on different economic features, such as in theories of the business cycle.

Some economic theories are more popularly debated than others. Consider different ideas with regard to the demand for money. Put simply, three economic "theories" exist which may, in historic terms, be seen as a sort of thesis–antithesis–synthesis pattern. Thus *classical* theory viewed the relationship between the total amount of money available and prices as direct. The theory would suggest that the total amount of money available in the economy has a great effect on prices but little or no effect on the quantity of goods and services the economy produced. *Keynesian* theorists argue that not all available money would be used for the purchase of goods and services and may be used to purchase securities, which would in turn affect the interest rate. They also argue that in deep depressions, the amount of money may not even affect interest rates as additional money may just be held. *Monetarists* believe that money is not merely a facilitator of exchange but a valuable good in its own right. When money is held it is an item of wealth, like stocks and shares — property and other services are given up when money is held. Money is a good, with a price like any other, and performs a service only when it is used.

Many, indeed most, economic theories (e.g. the theory of wages; the theory of rent; the theory of interest; the theory of profit) are neither known nor understood by the layman. They are rarely debated in popular circles, though political implications of them may be aired, frequently with more heat than light. However, occasionally, economic ideas and theories do get discussed by lay people, usually after they have been exposed to them through the popular press. For instance, in the early 1980s when unemployment rose rapidly in Britain, people became aware of the Phillips curve which suggests that there must be a trade-off between inflation and unemployment. Though frequently imperfectly understood, this controversial hypothesis was to be found in the popular, as well as more serious, papers.

Mosley (1983) has done a content analysis of economic issues discussed by the British popular press from 1960 to 1980. He found that pro-Labour newspapers give more detail on unemployment while pro-Conservative newspapers give more details on inflation and the balance of payments. As Mosley noted, the influence of the media on conditioning people's attitudes towards the economy is not confined to the information that they provide but also involves the assertion of the existence of the relationship between economic variables. Also, the press prescribed particular solutions for economic crises in the 1960s and offered a consensus view of macro-economic problems: unemployment could be eradicated by a sufficient *boost* to aggregate demand; balance of payment deficits and inflation could be eradicated by a sufficiently large reduction in aggregate demand. In the 1970s people were being offered a very different picture of how the economy functions: the popular press suggested that the reduction of inflation was a precondition for the reduction of unemployment. Mosley, however, found no evidence in the press for the belief, so common among academic macro-economists, that full employment could be bought at the cost of higher inflation.

Politicians naturally attempt to persuade people to adopt their particular view of how the economy works and which economic issues are relevant. Good examples of this are the economy analogies used by two main political parties in Great Britain. In order to explain her monetarist policies the British Prime Minister frequently uses the *housekeeping* analogy. The economy is to be perceived as a large household and the Government as the housekeeper. Virtues such as thrift are encouraged and it is stressed that it is extremely unwise to borrow money or spend that which one does not have. On the other hand the Labour opposition party uses the analogy of the *body*. The economy is seen as a whole with every part influencing every other. When parts of the body are ill (economy is weak/faltering) they should receive extra help or care as they effect the general health of the body. In other words monetarist market-forces concepts may be best illustrated to lay people by reference to the economy of the household, while socialist, state controlled economic concepts may be better illustrated to lay people by reference to the health of the body.

There are, of course, no shortage of books and pamphlets to explain economies in general, and particular economic thinkers, (Keynes, Marx, Smith) to the layman. Some begin, like psychology textbooks, with some counter-intuitive findings:

> Even when economists find themselves in agreement, their conclusions frequently seem to have been arrived at with mirrors. We discover, for example, then when robber barons burn money at lavish, ostentatious dinner parties to show off their wealth, they are making a gift to the rest of us; and that high interest rates follow easy, not tight, money-supply policy. We discover that while as individuals, the best way to prepare for unemployment is to increase

savings, for the nation as a whole, savings should be decreased; and we discover that poor harvests can make farmers richer. These conclusions, as well as others more in line with common sense, need deciphering. (Levi, 1981, p. 13)

In his book entitled *Economics Deciphered*, Levi (1981) sets out to explain economics in a question-and-answer format. Questions include: "What is the retail price index?"; "Will a recession cool inflation?"; "How do supply and demand determine market prices?"; "Are flexible and fluctuating exchange rates the same thing?". Though this approach may provide useful information it is clearly informed by various theories held by the author, many of which are not explicitly stated.

Another approach to educating the layman is to attempt to explain what economics is all about. Thus, Williams (1978) writes:

Need we be poor? Are we producing as efficiently as we could? and if not, why not? and how could we do better? Are we producing the "right" things? What are the "right" things? Who ought to decide this, and why? Is specialization always a "good" method of production? and in what sense "good"? Might we become too dependent on foreign supplies and does this matter? Is it better to buy goods produced in your own country? "Better" in what sense? Does it make one richer? or safer? or what? Is monopoly better than competition? always? sometimes? in what circumstances? Why does a factory worker usually earn less than a doctor? and what would happen if you insisted that they should get the same amount? Why does the Government settle some prices and not others? and who settles the price if the Government doesn't?

These are the sort of questions that a study of economics helps us to answer. They are also the kind of questions which underlie the issues on which the ordinary citizen votes at elections, but most people are likely to pay more careful attention to a TV "Do It Yourself" programme showing you how to make a garden path or mend a leaky tap than to one which attempts a serious analysis of economic problems. If a car breaks down nobody but a fool expects to be able to repair it without some elementary understanding of the mechanism, and the economic system is a good deal more dangerous to tinker with than a car. Unfortunately it is also much more difficult to understand. (p. 12)

Different economic introductory books have adopted very different approaches to explaining economics to the layman. Thus, Harrod (1983) has divided his book into three sections — depending on who makes economic decisions: *Personal* decisions about saving and spending; *Corporate* decisions by public and private organisations and *Government* decisions on such things as taxation and public spending. Others, like Brown (1970) have attempted to set economics in its historical and academic context. He has also attempted to spell out the axioms of human behaviour upon which the discipline is based:

(*a*) In normal circumstances we strive to keep ourselves and our families alive by taking action to avoid starvation, exposure or destruction by natural forces, wild animals and human enemies.

(*b*) We seek more satisfaction rather than less; such satisfaction may not necessarily be physical, and sometimes they may be bad for us; the economist tends to exclude as being too difficult to quantify such psychological satisfactions as a sense of security, self-respect, exercise of power, etc.

(c) Other things being equal, we prefer more remuneration to less, whatever form this takes as *wages, salaries, profits*, etc.

(d) Most of us prefer leisure to work, easy work to hard work, inactivity to activity, at least beyond a certain level of work.

(e) We prefer the cheaper to the more expensive among similar goods or services and also among goods or services that are a close *substitute* for each other, e.g. fish and meat, wool and nylon.

(f) As our income and purchasing power increase we prefer variety, and so, as each urgent *want* is satisfied, we move on to satisfying less urgent wants.

(g) Most of us do not want money for its own sake, to *hoard* like misers, but for what it will buy in goods and services (or perhaps in power over others).

(h) As our income rises we are more able and more prepared to use money to make more money, to *save* for the future in illness or retirement. (Brown, 1970, p. 18).

These simple facts of human behaviour, as Brown calls them, are assumed to be true of all peoples in all cultures. Psychologists as well as lay people might be very surprised to see the axiomatic truths spelt out like this, not to mention anthropologists, who have special interests in economic exchange differences in different cultures. Brown (1970) seems to be on safer grounds when he tries to define economic concepts: e.g. utility — the capacity of goods and services to satisfy wants.

Although economists appear to hold views about how individuals and more particularly groups of individuals behave in the economic world, they appear to have little interest in lay people's views of the economic world. Psychologists have been more interested in lay people's economic beliefs and behaviours (Furnham and Lewis, 1986). These methods have been employed to investigate lay "theories" in economics. The first is to look at statistics on buying, saving, consumption, etc., and to attempt to infer belief patterns or attitudes from them. The second is to investigate, through large scale surveys, attitudes and expectations and to attempt to assess consumer sentiment. The third method is, through smaller scale studies, to look at the structure and determinants of lay people's beliefs or theories about the economy.

6.2 Developmental Studies

One way of attempting to understand lay people's understanding of economics is to look at how these develop. There is, by now, a fairly extensive — if diffuse — literature on children's understanding of the economic world (Furnham, 1986d). Studies have looked at such things as the acquisition of specific economic concepts, like money (Sutton, 1962), exchange (Furth, 1980; Jahoda, 1979) and distribution (Berti *et al.*, 1982; Siegal, 1981). The literature seems to suggest that children go through various developmental stages in the development of economic ideas, but it is not until early to mid adolescence that they begin fully to comprehend, simple, but important, economic principles — such as profit or ownership. For instance, Jahoda (1981) studied Scottish children's conceptions of *banking* — a complex and often remote economic concept for children to grasp. Eleven-, 13- and 15-year-old children first role-played a shop transaction episode, where children playing shopkeepers bought products from retailers and sold them to customers, in order to ascertain whether they inderstood the notion of profit. They were then asked a number of questions about the functions of a bank such as "Supposing I put £100 into a bank, and after one year I take my money out again: would I get back more, less or the same?" and "Supposing I borrow £100 from a bank to pay back after one year. Would I have to pay back more or less or the same?" The response of the children fell into six different categories: no knowledge of interest (get back the same amount); interest on deposits only (get back more but pay the same); interest on both, but more on deposit; interest same on deposits and loans; interest higher on loans — not fully understood; interest higher on loans — fully understood. The developmental trends were striking and highly significant yet only a quarter of the 14-year-olds fully understood the function of the bank, a number which showed no increase for the 16-year olds. Thus it is quite possible that the majority of British school-leavers do not understand the concept of banking.

This study was, in fact, replicated by Jahoda and Woerdenbagch (1982) in Holland. They found that while primary pupils in both countries overwhelmingly saw the bank as simply a place that keeps money, compared with the older Scottish subjects, twice as many of the older Dutch subjects realised that one borrowed money from a bank. The authors concluded that the socio-cognitive pattern of development for economic ideas is much the same for all modern industrial societies. Ng (1983) replicated and extended Jahoda's (1981) study with 96, 6-13-year-old children from Hong Kong. Although he found much the same developmental trend, a full understanding of the bank emerged at 10 while the ideas of profit emerged at 6 years old. Thus, for both concepts, the Chinese children were more precocious than the Scottish and Dutch samples. Ng (1983) concludes:

> the exceptional maturity of the Hong Kong children probably reflected their high level of economic socialisation and consumer activity, and the business ethos of the society at large. Socially, life would be difficult for them if they did not grasp socio-economic concepts at an early age. Their maturity represents, in short, a case of socio-economic reality shaping (partly at least) socio-economic understanding" (pp. 220–221).

It may not, therefore, be valid to assume similar developmental trends across all societies. What is more important is the extent to, and volition with which, children participate in economic activity (by choice or necessity). Thus, poor children from a rural bartering society and rich children from an urban money orientated society may both acquire some economic concepts before children (in any society) who are sheltered from any form of economic activity. What is important to know is how the exposure to *which* economic *activities* (buying, selling, work), at *what age* relates to *which aspect* of economic understanding. Of course, it is possible that the causality between economic activity and understanding is bi-directional, such that a grasp of a concept gives the child the confidence to partake in the activity. Social class, exposure to the economic world, parental practices and formal teaching seem the most important determinants of children's economic knowledge and use of money, though there may well be other important determinants, such as their schooling experiences, the amount and type of economic activity in the town or country that they live in, etc. The importance of this area cannot be underestimated, as it seems possible that habits of using money (spending, saving, gambling, etc.) are established in childhood or at least early adolescence. Studies on children's pocket money for instance suggest that class attitudes towards money are established even before adolescence.

Developmental studies, then, have not proved very successful at pinpointing the major determinants of all economic beliefs. Because economic beliefs are to some extent determined by the economy itself they change as a function of national group, class structure and economic conditions. However, the *structure* of these beliefs, their *function*, and their *determinants* may be more resilient to changes in the economy.

6.3 Studies on adult economic beliefs

Research on lay people's economic beliefs has relied heavily on attribution theory. Hence, the research has been concerned with such issues as the *structure* of lay beliefs (are there dimensions or typologies which certain people characteristically follow?); the *functions* of these beliefs (do economic beliefs have defensive, aggrandising functions based on one's personal success or failure?); and the *determinants* of the beliefs (does education, age, sex and/or class in any sense determine these economic beliefs?).

The sort of economic issues that studies have covered are the largest macro-economic issues of concern to and understood by lay people. Four such areas will be reviewed: unemployment, poverty, wealth and inflation.

(1) Explaining the Causes of Unemployment

One reason why there has been an interest in lay explanations for unemployment is the suggestion by a number of writers that people out of work for long periods of time tend first to offer *societal* (external) attributions for their own (and others) unemployment, but that these explanations then tend to become *fatalistic*, and finally *individualistic*, with the unemployed blaming themselves for their plight (Hayes and Nutman, 1981; Furnham and Lewis, 1986). This pattern may prove, ultimately, very destructive, as attributions for unemployment may well effect the job search process. This may mean that a vicious circle develops, such that individualistic explanations for personal unemployment tend to lower self-esteem and expectations (Furnham, 1985c; Feather, 1982). However, expectations and confidence no doubt effect the job search strategy, which in turn lowers the probability of getting a job, so confirming the expectations. Hence, one may find examples of self-fulfilling prophesies (or reciprocal determinism) which may occur about the poor mental and physical health of the unemployed (Furnham and Lewis, 1986).

In one of the first studies done in this area, Furnham (1982bc) examined differences in the rated importance of explanations for unemployment in Britain as a function of whether people were employed or unemployed, as well as their age, sex, education and voting pattern. It was hypothesised that more unemployed people would find societal (external social, economic and political factors) and fatalistic (luck, chance, fate) explanations more important than employed people, who should find individualistic explanations (internal dispositional and personality factors) more important. It was also hypothesised that Conservative (right-wing) voters would find individualistic explanations for unemployment more important than employed Labour voters, who would find societal factors more important. The results showed a more-or-less predictable pattern of differences between the employed and unemployed, the former believing more in individualistic explanations and less in societal explanations than the latter (see Table 6.1).

However, whereas there were few sex and age differences, education and vote pattern revealed numerous differences in explanations for unemployment. Conservatives (capitalist) found individualistic explanations for unemployment more important than Labour (socialist) voters who in turn found societal explanations more important than Conservative voters. It was suggested that the results confirm the theses of a number of writers in the field (Tiffany *et al.*, 1970), that unemployed people will be more external in their attributions for the causes of unemployment than employed people, though this is only a matter of degree. Furthermore, according to Hayes and Nutman (1981), this pattern should increase the longer a person remains out of work. Also, the overall national unemployment figures probably affect this relationship (Furnham and Hesketh, 1988). As unemployment grows, even employed people tend to offer societal and fatalistic (external) explanations for unemployment, partly as a defence about becoming unemployed themselves.

Others have come up with rather different attributions. Feather and Davenport (1981) factor analysed reasons rated by unemployed Australian youths for their joblessness and found *two* major factors, called external difficulty (blaming government, industry, the unions) and competence deficiency (blaming own lack of education and experience). They found, as predicted, that more-depressed subjects were *less* likely to blame themselves for their unemployment, and *more* likely to blame external difficulties, such as the prevailing economic situation. Another study (Feather, 1983) grouped 19 explanations into three factors similar to Furnham (1982c) namely, individualistic, societal and fatalistic, though when factor analysed they

TABLE 6.1. *Means and F Levels for the Explanations for Unemployment Offered by Employed and Unemployed Subjects*†

Explanations	Employed	Unemployed	F level
A. Individualistic			
Unemployed people can earn more money on social security	5.21	5.31	0.17
Lack of effort and laziness among unemployed people	5.13	4.81	1.72
Unemployed people don't try hard enough to get jobs	3.15	4.21	13.22*
Unemployed people are too fussy and proud to accept some jobs	4.89	4.57	1.67
Poor education and qualifications among unemployed people	4.40	3.55	12.94*
Unwillingness of unemployed to move to places of work	4.32	5.51	10.60*
Inability of unemployed people to adapt to new conditions	4.77	4.38	3.44***
Lack of intelligence or ability among the unemployed	5.46	4.76	9.70**
B. Societal			
The policies and strategies of the present government	2.05	2.33	1.48
The policies and strategies of previous British governments	2.82	2.85	0.06
Inefficient and less competitive industries that go bankrupt	3.38	3.45	0.10
An influx of immigrants have taken up all available jobs	5.32	3.92	29.09*
Trade unions have priced their members out of a job	4.37	3.85	4.83***
Overmanning in industry which has occurred for too long	3.53	3.93	2.93
Incompetent industrial management with poor planning	2.94	3.46	5.98***
Weak trade unions that do not fight to keep jobs	4.80	3.58	26.05*
C. Fantastic			
Sickness and physical handicap among unemployed people	5.14	3.74	29.32*
Just bad luck	5.73	5.27	4.63***
World-wide recession and inflation	2.19	2.57	3.69***
The introduction of widespread automation	3.70	3.09	6.14***

† These numbers represent the mean on the following scale: Important 1 2 3 4 5 6 7 Unimportant.
*$p < 0.001$.
**$p < 0.01$.
***$p < 0.05$.
Reproduced with permission from Furnham, A. (1982c). Explanations for unemployment in Britain. *European Journal of Social Psychology, 12,* 335–352. Copyright (1982). Reprinted by permission of John Wiley & Sons, Ltd.

yielded *five* interpretable factors: lack of skill, lack of education, and interview/appearance inadequacy. A later study by Feather (1985) found *six* factors in an analysis of 265 university students' explanation for unemployment: lack of motivation, recession and social change, competence deficiency, defective job creation, personal handicap and specific discrimination. These factors were correlated with a number of terminal and instrumental values which supported Feather's point that lay economic explanations are not simply the products of neutral information processing, but are linked to their cognitive–affective system.

Other Australian studies have attempted to classify these lay explanations in terms of academic attribution theories (Gurney, 1981; Doring 1984). Similarly Hesketh (1984), in New Zealand, has classified possible explanations into effort, luck, ability and task difficulty.

Thus, although different studies have empirically derived rather different factors, it seems quite possible to categorise these into one or other theoretical framework: i.e. individualistic (internal, voluntary, effort, ability), societal (external, structural, task difficulty) and fatalistic (cyclical, luck, chance, uncontrollable). There is some evidence to suggest that these explanations or attributions for unemployment vary across national groups as a function of the prevailing economic conditions. Furnham and Hesketh (1988) tested the idea that as unemployment rises and becomes more commonplace in society, people will find it more acceptable and hence less blameworthy. They found, as predicted, the British tended to rate societal explanations as more important and individualistic explanations as less important in their country, with a 12% unemployment rate, than New Zealanders whose rate of unemployment was only 4%.

Furnham (1982b) also looked specifically at the relationship between Protestant work ethic beliefs and explanations for unemployment. As predicted, subjects who strongly endorsed the work ethic endorsed individualistic explanations for unemployment and were, by-and-large, more against welfare payments than subjects who did not strongly endorse these beliefs. This confirms MacDonald's (1971) finding that Protestant work ethic believers were proponents of the ethics of social responsibility which tend to blame people rather than "the system" for the source of their difficulty. It also confirms other findings which suggest that these beliefs — as measured by any of the Protestant work ethic scales — are part of a general conservative attitude pattern. Thus a high Protestant work ethic scorer is likely to explain poverty in terms of idleness and poor money management; wealth in terms of hard work honesty and saving; unemployment in terms of laziness and lack of effort; and he/she is likely to be against both taxation and social security (Furnham, 1982b, p. 283). This suggests that there may be coherent belief systems that discriminate between individuals and which in turn, relate to lay explanations for unemployment and other economic behaviour.

La France and Cicchetti (1979) were concerned with social class and employment status determinants of the perceived responsibility and blame for economic success and failure. Four groups of subjects (middle-class employed; middle-class unemployed; working-class employed; working-class unemployed) were asked a series of questions about a person that they had read about. They found that all the subjects were more concerned with praising the successful job seeker than with blaming the unsuccessful. The middle-class subjects distinguished significantly more between success and failure than working-class subjects, assigning more responsibility to the former and less to the latter. The middle-class also believed personality to be more influential than the working-class. Overall, employed subjects assigned more responsibility to the stimulus person and saw luck as being less influential in the successful outcome than did the unemployed.

Nearly all of the studies in this section on explanations for unemployment have used a limited and unrepresentative sample and a structured questionnaire. However, more recent studies have considered a free-response interview format with large, representative samples. In a free-response study Lewis and Furnham (1986) reported on 450 people's answers to the question about how they believed unemployment could be reduced. Most people gave answers which implied a stimulation of the economy, a number for the redistribution of jobs yet about 15% could provide no answer at all. When given six actual statements to rate, it was found that over 90% of the sample believed that the level of unemployment in Britain was unacceptably high while 66% argued that the Government should spend more money in order to reduce unemployment. There were some interesting and predictable sex, age and employment history differences: e.g. women were against sacrificing their jobs if their husbands were unemployed but did favour job sharing and reducing working hours; similarly younger people seemed more liberal than older people in that they did not believe in curbing immigration or women giving up jobs.

Using a large and representative sample, Lewis *et al.* (1987) asked 900 British people to explain the causes of unemployment. Content analysis using 13 economic codes revealed that 28% of the explanations concerned falling demand for goods; 23% the rate of inflation; 18% Government policy; 17% high wage demands. Curiously, there were very few demographic differences, though many were investigated (sex, class, age, housing, trade union membership). These explanations (many of which defied coding) were reclassified into the three categories used by Furnham (1982b) — 78% of the explanations were societal, 24% fatalistic and only 7% individualistic. What was particularly striking about the explanations offered for unemployment was the fact that so few were purely economic — that is, lay explanations for economic phenomena are often normative, moralistic, sociopolitical as well as economic. Furthermore, while some ideological differences arise, what differences there are in economic explanations from people of different age/ class/voting groups, may be explained primarily in terms of self-interest.

Furnham (1984c) has argued that a potentially important factor in helping to explain an unemployed person's response to unemployment may be how that person, or a significant other person, views the causes of not working. Two competing, but related, theoretical models have been proposed to explain relationships between causal attributions and reactions to stressful events. The theory of learned helplessness has shown how attributional/ explanational patterns affect levels of depression and other responses to uncontrollable negative events. For instance, internal (self-blame) attributions tend to lower self-esteem whereas external (societal attributions do not. Furthermore, stable (unchanging) attributions lower expectations of future success and increase the chronicity of helplessness in relation to a particular situation whereas unstable (changing) attributions do not. Considerable clinical evidence attests to the fact that there is a strong relationship between internal, stable and global attributions, and negative outcomes and depression — that is, people are likely to become particularly depressed if they believe themselves to be the cause of their plight, and that these causes are internal to them, stable over time and global across various issues.

The most severe, enduring, and generalised forms of depression and concomitant mental illnesses develop when aversive stimuli (in this case, unemployment) persist despite the person's best efforts to avert them (constantly seeks appropriate employment) and when the person feels hopeless and helpless to change the situation. Thus, one would predict a positive relationship between depressive effect and internal attributions (i.e. a person's holding himself or herself responsible) concerning the causes of unemployment. External attributions may also lead to depression but are more likely to lead to anger against the system.

A second, related model is based on expectancy-valence theory, which relates an action (behaviour or cognition) to the perceived attractiveness or aversiveness of expected outcomes. The theory predicts that frustration in the desire to find work is associated with negative affects such as depression and sadness, but that these effects will be most intense among people who perceive work as attractive, have high expectations of getting a job, and are very strongly motivated to find work.

Both models predict a relationship between depressive and other symptoms of mental illness (e.g. anxiety states) and causal attributions, but the direction of the causality is not clear. Hence, it may be that particular attributions follow or co-occur with depression rather than cause it. Moreover, expectancy-valence theory suggests that the relationship is mediated by other factors such as the person's desire for work. Finally, whereas learned-helplessness theory would suggest that internal attributions are associated with depression (low self-esteem), expectancy-valence theory does the opposite, associating external attributions with depression (nothing can be done).

Although most of the research on explanations for unemployment has been stimulated by other work within an attribution theory context, other conceptual frameworks have been put forward. Moscovici (1981) has argued that social representations (set of consensually held beliefs originating in daily life in the course of inter-individual communication) in fact determine people's attribution about such things as unemployment benefits. Whereas attribution theory is concerned with the way individuals attribute causes to events, the theory of social representations concerns how groups or individuals create a stable world in which diverse, unfamiliar or unpredictable behaviours are given meaning and become familiar and predictable. He maintains that people gather information, classify it into certain categories *and then* attempt to explain it. He believes that attributions follow from social representation and not the reverse. He, in fact, illustrates his point by reference to unemployment:

> Some think of the unemployed person as lazy, unlucky or as incompetent in looking for work; others consider him to be the victim of economic downturn, of social injustice and the contradictions of the capitalist regime. The former attribute the cause of unemployment to the individual, to his way of facing the world, and the latter to the general situation, to the individual's class affiliation and to the way in which the world treats him. Obviously this divergence is due altogether to their respective social representations. One representation gives precedence, under all circumstances, to personal responsibility, individual effort, and individual solutions to the problems of society; the other leads to a sharp awareness of social injustice and social responsibility, contemplating collective solutions to individual problems. (pp. 107–108)

(2) Explanations for Poverty

There is a fairly considerable literature on lay or everyday explanations for poverty. Some are simple national opinion surveys, where people are asked to attribute poverty either to internal (individualistic) or to external (societal) causes. For instance, a 1945 Opinion Research Survey in America asked a representative sampling "Why are some of the people always poor?" Relatively few people mentioned economic, political or structural factors, such as employment conditions, or educational differences; most spoke of lack of effort and initiative, money mismanagement, weak character or related causes. That is, they blame the victims of poverty for their own plight. Other studies have been more restricted in their scope, sample and methodology but have showed similar results, namely a preference for psychological rather than sociological or economic explanations.

In a influential study, Feagin (1975) asked over 1000 Americans to rate the importance of 11 reasons why some people were poor in America (see Table 6.2).

Feagin categorised these explanations into three groups:

1. *Individualistic*: which places responsibility for poverty on the behaviour of poor people.

TABLE 6.2

Reasons for poverty selected by Americans in national survey	Very Important %	Somewhat Important %	Not Important %
1. Lack of thrift and proper money management by poor people	58	30	11
2. Lack of effort by the poor themselves	55	33	9
3. Lack of ability and talent among poor people	52	33	12
4. Loose morals and drunkenness	48	31	17
5. Sickness and physical handicaps	46	39	14
6. Low wages in some businesses and industries	42	35	20
7. Failure of society to provide good schools for many Americans	36	25	34
8. Prejudice and discrimination against Negroes	33	37	26
9. Failure of private industry to provide enough jobs	27	36	31
10. Being taken advantage of by rich people	18	30	45
11. Just bad luck	8	27	60

Americans' explanations of poverty

Importance	Individualistic %	Structural %	Fatalistic %
Low	7	18	11
Medium	40	60	71
High	53	22	18

Adapted from Feagin (1975).

2. *Structural*: which places responsibility on extreme societal and economic forces.
3. *Fatalistic*: which places responsibility on luck and fate.

Furthermore, the results showed various socioreligious, racial, regional, age, income and educational differences. Individualistic explanations were favoured by white Protestants and Catholics, residents of the south and north-central regions, the over-50 age group, the middle-income group and groups with middle levels of education.

In contrast, black Protestants and Jews, the under-30 age group, the low-income group and the less well-educated tended to favour societal or structural explanations. Feagin (1975) argued that if people tend to indi-vidualise economic and social problems such as poverty, all attempts at redistributive reform will be impossible. He argues that individualistic views reflect "false consciousness and mesh well with establishment attempts to maintain the status quo, whereas structural interpretations lend themselves to attempts at counter-ideologies and at structural reforms in this society" (p. 126). Although he implicitly rejects psychological and individualistic expla-nations for wealth he does not put forward any arguments for how these explanations originate, save perhaps through simple self-interest.

Feagin's work is important for a number of reasons. First, his *a priori* classification of explanations into three factors has received fairly considerable backing from factor analytic studies (Feather, 1974; Furnham, 1982d; Singh and Vasudeva, 1977; Payne and Furnham, 1985). Secondly, his study has been replicated in a range of countries: India (Singh and Vasudeva, 1977), Israel (Rim, 1984), Britain (Furnham, 1982a), Australia (Feather, 1974), the West Indies (Payne and Furnham, 1985) and New Zealand (Stacey and Singer, 1986). Thirdly, the demographic variables of groups that discriminated between explanations for poverty (e.g. religion, age, education) have been replicated across many studies. Those variables which have shown most discriminatory power with regard to beliefs about poverty have been income and social class, age, rural–urban background, education, ideological beliefs, religion and, to a less extent, sex. Fourthly, he found that explanations for poverty are systematically linked to attitudes to welfare, so suggesting that people hold coherent theories about both the causes of, and cures for, poverty. That is, a person's world views about such things as justice and control determine the sort of explanations they give for poverty, as well as many other issues.

Feather (1974), who replicated this experiment in Adelaide, Australia, was interested in both a cross-cultural comparison and generational differences between parents and their children. He found that Australians were generally less likely than Americans to blame poverty on individualistic reasons, though the pattern of explanations was fairly similar. There were some significant differences in the 11 explanations for poverty offered by the subjects, who were differentiated according to religion, sex, occupation, education and income, though the major differences were between the two age groups (over 75% of the explanations). Younger subjects were less likely to blame poverty on individualistic factors. However, Feather suggests that values and beliefs, as well as macro-economic factors, should be considered in attempting to predict people's explanations of the causes of behaviour:

> In affluent societies, however, members may believe that there is plenty to go around and that, even though the poor have brought misfortune upon themselves, they should have some part of the plentiful resources that are available. One's reactions to inequalities would therefore depend upon the sometimes harsh economic and social realities of how much is available and whether it can be increased, as well as upon the dominant values, attitudes and modes of causal attribution that have emerged as complex products of one's socialisation. (p. 215)

The idea that socialisation is important in explanations of poverty was demonstrated by Furnham (1982d), who found that English public-school boys (traditionally from richer, middle-class homes) found individualistic explanations for poverty more important than comprehensive-school boys (from poorer, working-class homes), who in turn found societal explanations more important. This is consistent with other studies looking at the effects of schooling on values. In a similar study done on New Zealand adolescents,

Stacey and Singer (1986) emphasised the significance of the family, and downplayed luck and chance when explaining poverty (and wealth). Also, they tended to rate psychological consequences of poverty as being far *less* important than economic consequences.

A study by Singh and Vasudeva (1977) in India and a very extensive EEC study on the "Perception of poverty in Europe" (Commission of the European Communities Report, 1977) have examined demographic factors associated with explanations of poverty. The Indian study considered similar age, education and income related differences but few religious differences. The European study considered how people in the EEC saw and explained poverty. Overall the most common causes of poverty were believed to be — in rank order — poor luck, laziness and lack of willpower, injustice in society. However, as Table 6.3 shows there were considerable differences — the Italians and French tended to blame societal factors, the British and Irish the poor themselves and the Danes fate. Overall, the better-educated, and the better-off most often blamed social injustice, while the less well-educated and non-leaders tended to blame the poor.

More recently Payne and Furnham (1985) compared the explanations that adolescents gave for poverty in two West Indian islands — the relatively wealthy island of Barbados and the relatively poor island of Dominica. They predicted that poorer Dominican subjects would rate societal explanations as more important, and that, overall, societal explanations would be rated as more important than individualistic explanations for poverty. Whereas the second hypothesis was confirmed, the first was not, indeed the opposite was true. The authors believe that the unexpected result may be due to the fact that the richer Barbadians were exposed to inequalities in wealth. They were, however, concerned that explanations for the cause and persistence of poverty are moulded and sustained by economic conditions prevailing in each country.

A variable which has logically received attention is the relationship between political beliefs and poverty explanation. Many have suggested that left-wing people (and post-materialists) are more inclined to explain poverty in terms of social causes, while right-wing people are more likely to blame the victims. As predicted, Furnham (1982a) found Conservative (right-wing) voters found individualistic explanations for poverty more important than Labour (left-wing) voters, who found societal explanations more important than Conservatives, though fatalistic explanations showed no difference between the groups and were not rated as important in explaining poverty. Using a simpler questionnaire concerning the attribution of poverty but a more elaborate measure of political beliefs, Panday *et al.* (1982) found, as predicted, that politically neutral people and right-wingers attributed poverty more to individual habits and ability as well as fate, than the left-wing activists, who attributed poverty in India more to governmental policies and the economic dominance of the few in society. Williamson (1974) has

TABLE 6.3. Percentage of People Rating Explanations for Poverty in their Country

Italy (59%)*

1.	Deprived childhood	63%
2.	Lack of education	47%
3.	Too many children	36%
4.	Ill health	31%
5.	Laziness	29%
6.	Old age and loneliness	28%
7.	Lack of foresight	19%
8.	Drink	15%
9.	Chronic unemployment	9%

Luxembourg (50%)

1.	Drink	55%
2.	Laziness	39%
3.	Deprived childhood	30%
4.	Lack of education	29%
5.	Ill health	27%
6.	Old age and loneliness	23%
7.	Too many children	19%
8.	Chronic unemployment	13%
9.	Lack of foresight	10%

France (40%)

1.	Old age and loneliness	50%
2.	Deprived childhood	44%
3.	Ill health	38%
4.	Lack of education	37%
5.	Chronic unemployment	36%
6.	Drink	31%
7.	Too many children	26%
8.	Laziness	15%
9.	Lack of foresight	15%

Germany (39%)

1.	Deprived childhood	47%
2.	Ill health	42%
3.	Lack of education	41%
4.	Chronic unemployment	38%
5.	Old age and loneliness	32%
6.	Drink	31%
7.	Laziness	30%
8.	Lack of foresight	18%
9.	Too many children	17%

Ireland (36%)

1.	Drink	65%
2.	Chronic unemployment	56%
3.	Ill health	42%
4.	Lack of education	32%
5.	Old age and loneliness	31%
6.	Laziness	25%
7.	Too many children	23%
8.	Deprived childhood	16%
9.	Lack of foresight	8%

Belgium (31%)

1.	Old age and loneliness	46%
2.	Ill health	43%
3.	Deprived childhood	39%
4.	Drink	29%
5.	Laziness	28%
6.	Chronic unemployment	26%
7.	Lack of education	24%
8.	lack of foresight	20%
9.	Too many children	13%

United Kingdom (27%)

1.	Laziness	45%
2.	Chronic unemployment	42%
3.	Drink	40%
4.	Ill health	36%
5.	Too many children	31%
6.	Old age and loneliness	30%
7.	Lack of education	29%
8.	Lack of foresight	21%
9.	Deprived childhood	16%

Netherlands (18%)

1.	Deprived childhood	43%
2.	Lack of education	33%
3.	Chronic unemployment	33%
4.	Ill health	32%
5.	Drink	29%
6.	Old age and loneliness	24%
7.	Lack of foresight	22%
8.	Too many children	16%
9.	Laziness	11%

Denmark (14%)

1.	Drink	49%
2.	Ill health	46%
3.	Lack of education	44%
4.	Chronic unemployment	42%
5.	Deprived childhood	42%
6.	Old age and loneliness	14%
7.	Laziness	14%
8.	Too many children	10%
9.	Lack of foresight	7%

The % brackets after the country's name refers to the percentage of people in the respective countries who maintain that they have seen people in poverty.

proposed an ideological self-interest theory which predicts a negative correlation between socio-economic status and the perceived motivation of, and support for, aid for the poor.

Most, but not all, of the studies in this area have considered the causes of poverty among unspecified groups. Furnham (1982a) has argued that as different groups in a society are differentially likely to experience poverty, various explanations become salient in explaining these differences. This is also true of different historic periods. Thus, Huber and Form (1973) asked a sample of Americans why they thought people went on to social security during the Great Depression. Only 4% cited individualistic explanations, yet when asked why people had taken social security during the previous six years, 54% cited individualistic reasons. Similarly, Furnham (1982a) asked his subjects to imagine a poor person from one of four groups: black, white, middle-class and working-class and then explain why they were poor. It was established that explanations that may seem salient for one target group are not necessarily so for another. Although there was considerable agreement on the causes of poverty among those groups most susceptible to it, people began to differ radically in the causes of poverty ascribed to groups not usually thought of as poor.

Although it is not always easy to do so, some attempts have been made to verify public beliefs as to the causes of poverty. Feagin (1975) pointed out that figures available indicated that the public were wrong — or at least vastly overestimating the amount of people lying about having illegitimate children to increase their social security payments. Similarly, Goodwin (1973) found that the middle-class tended to underestimate the work values (ethic) and life aspirations held by the poor. Indeed, a considerable amount of psychological (Allen, 1970) and sociological (Davidson and Gaitz, 1974) research has demonstrated few differences in attitudes, beliefs and values between the poor and those not so badly off. Goodwin (1973) did a path analysis on the relationship between education, age, the work ethic and the perceived motivation of, and support for aid to, the poor. Naturally, those who believed in the work ethic believed the poor to be badly motivated and did not want to support them. They conclude that the work ethic is a fundamental element in popular ideology and that its change could lead to numerous important results.

Lay explanations for the causes, consequences and cure of poverty, then, tend to be psychological rather then economic but are shaped by both psychological *and* economic factors. Although people appear to differ in the extent to which they blame the victims of poverty for their plight, most people believe structural economic forces have an important influence.

(3) Explanations for Wealth

Probably because wealth is not considered to be a social problem it has attracted comparatively little research. Yet, quite naturally, the question of how one becomes rich is constantly discussed and is the topic of numerous popularist books (so much so that it seems writing those sort of books is the answer).

Yet there are a few studies of how lay people explain the causes of wealth. For instance Younger *et al.* (1977) asked a group of Canadian under-graduates to account for how a certain person "got to be who and what he is". In the financially successful condition he was described as earning $100,000 per annum; in the average condition he was described as earning $12,000 per annum; while in the failure condition he was described as unemployed. The students viewed the financially *successful* person as *least* responsible, and the *failed* person as *most* responsible for their condition. The successful person was seen as luckier than either the average or failure person but not more hardworking than the average person. The subjects did, however, believe that if the "target" person were asked to account for his/her own success or failure the successful would attribute their achievement to personal and/or situational factors while failures would attribute their circumstances pri-marily to situational factors. The authors point out that their explanations may serve a self-protective function:

> If one assumes that a high level of observed success functions as a threat to the subject's self-concept or self-esteem, then a conceivable strategy would be to attribute the perfor-mance to extra-personal causes. Such a defensive posture would no doubt serve to minimise feelings of one's own inadequacy or that of one's family. (p. 513).

In an American study of over a thousand male workers, Vecchio (1981) found that people who expressed external locus of control beliefs were themselves less wealthy, less well educated, less satisfied with their job and more likely to be black than workers who expressed internal locus of control beliefs. However, a study such as this could not determine whether locus of control beliefs were the cause or consequence of wealth and poverty. There is enough evidence to suggest that external control beliefs lead to low expec-tations of (occupational) success, which are subsequently confirmed beha-viourally. Thus, we may expect poor people to offer societal structure or fatalistic explanations for wealth and rich people to offer individualistic explanations.

In a large British study Lewis (1981) looked at the relationship between political beliefs (voting patterns) and attributions for wealth. Overall, the respondents felt that the wealthy have been luckier than others (54% agreement), received more help from others (60% agreement) rather than having worked harder (26% agreement), although they generally made more skilful use of their opportunities (52% agreement). However, as predicted, more right-wing voters (Conservatives) as opposed to left-wing voters (Labour Party Supporters) believed that wealthy people make more skilful use of their opportunities or generally work harder.

TABLE 6.4. *Means of the Three Voting Groups for the General Expectations for Wealth in Britain**

Explanations	Conservative	Labour	Liberal/other
Individualistic			
1. Careful money management throughout life	2.62	3.59	3.20
2. Hard work and great effort among the rich	1.89	2.78	1.76
3. Being very intelligent	3.78	4.35	4.58
4. The rich are ruthless and determined	4.41	3.17	4.44
Societal			
1. Very high wages in some businesses and trades	2.34	2.25	2.58
2. Being sent to certain schools and universities	3.91	3.60	3.61
3. Better opportunities for people from certain families	3.49	2.57	3.15
4. The taxation system favours the rich	5.25	3.34	4.69
5. Strong trade unions that get higher wages	4.61	4.78	4.37
6. The economic system automatically creates inequality	4.28	2.85	2.62
7. Society rewards those who work hard and take risks	3.19	4.54	3.84
Fatalistic			
1. Inheriting wealth from parents or relatives	1.44	1.09	1.22
2. Good luck in winning money at gambling	5.43	5.21	5.84
3. Having a lucky break	2.88	3.10	3.28
4. Being born with good business sense	2.50	2.95	2.78

*Low scores indicate high importance, i.e. the 7-point scale was *Important* 1 2 3 4 5 6 7 *Unimportant*.
Reproduced with permission from Furnham, A. (1983a). Attributions for Affluence. *Personality are Individual Differences*, 4, 31–40. Copyright (1983) Pergamon Journals Ltd.

In a similar study on a group of British subjects, Furnham (1983a) offered 15 explanations for wealth to subjects who were requested to rate them on a seven-point scale (important–unimportant) (see Table 6.4).

The results support the hypothesis that Conservative (right-wing) voters would find positive individualistic explanations for wealth, more important then Labour (left-wing) voters, who in turn find societal factors that maximise inequality more important than Conservatives. Thus, Conservatives believe that rich people are more hard working and thrifty (put more effort and have more ability) than do Labour Party supporters, who believe the rich to be significantly more ruthless and determined than do Conservative voters. That is, Conservatives support individualistic explanations when they portray the wealthy in a positive light, whereas Labour Party supporters support individualistic explanations for wealth when they portray the rich in a negative light. Similarly Labour voters believe that the rich had had better opportunities, and are more favourably treated by the tax and economic system, than Conservatives, who believe more than Labour voters that society rewards those who work hard and take risks.

These explanations differed for different groups, however. Thus, it (1981) studied Scottish children's conceptions of *banking* — a complex and wealth among blacks, while there was a considerable difference in explaining wealth among the whites. There were only three significant differences (one sex, and two education effects) in explaining wealth among working-class blacks, and no significant interactions. All the subjects believed that luck, business sense and intelligence were the most important factors to account for wealth among working-class blacks. Yet there were a number of differences between the subjects in their explanations for wealth among the middle-class whites, arguably the group most likely to achieve wealth. Apart from one significant sex and two education main effects, there were seven significant vote effects. They paralleled almost exactly the pattern of significant differences found in the explanations for general wealth — namely, Conservatives found positive individualistic explanations more important than Labour voters, who in turn, found societal explanations more important than Conservative voters.

Forgas *et al.* (1982) did a similar study in Sydney, Australia, though with a larger sample and somewhat different analysis. The first part of this study was based on a content analysis of the answers to the free-response question "Indicate the six most important reasons, in order of importance, why do you think some people are better off financially than others". They found that by far the most important explanatory categories used by subjects were family background variables (inheritance, good schooling), social factors (strong taxation), individual effort (hard work, savings) and luck (gambling).

Subjects made a total of five sets of attribution judgements for wealth, with the target being (1) a person in general, (2) a native-born working-class person, (3) a native-born middle-class person, (4) a migrant middle-class person and (5) a migrant working-class person.

Attributions to external/social causes such as taxation and the economic system were not affected by the target's class and ethnicity. These explanations applied uniformly to all target characters. It is interesting that attributions to internal/individual causes, such as thrift, hard work and business sense, were significantly more likely to be made when the target was a migrant, rather than a native-born Australian. This tends to confirm the common Australian stereotype of migrants as being particularly hardworking and motivated, in contrast with the easygoing, *laissez faire* attitude of native-born Australians. The third attributional category, family advantages (inheritance, good education, etc.), was significantly more likely to be used as an explanation of wealth in native-born rather than migrant, and middle-class rather than working-class, targets. The interaction of class and ethnicity on this variable indicates that family background was mainly seen as an important cause of wealth in native-born middle-class targets. Finally, the fourth attributional category, luck/risk taking, was significantly more likely to be seen as a cause of wealth in working-class rather than middle-class targets, irrespective of ethnicity.

Certain individual differences in attributions for wealth were also found.

The most powerful determinants were voting preferences, nationality and education. Finally Forgas *et al.* (1982) found that Australians estimated the necessary income for a "wealthy" person to be considerably higher than the British estimates of Furnham (1983). British subjects believed that considerably less income was sufficient for decent living than did Australians, while about twice as much income is necessary to be considered wealthy in Britain than in Australia.

What is particularly surprising is the significant and consistent differences between migrant and native-born subjects found here. Migrants to countries like Australia come from a variety of backgrounds, yet they appear to be unified in their belief that individual effort is a significant source of wealth. Migrants are also more likely to be seen by others as having acquired wealth through individual effort, and they have more limited estimates for income levels necessary to be "wealthy". The ideology of individual achievement is, of course, a well-known component of the migrant experience. It is still interesting to note that the Protestant work ethic finds its most devout followers not amongst the predominantly Anglo-Saxon native population, but within the heterogeneous migrant community.

Studies on lay explanations for the causes of wealth, though less in number than those concerned with poverty, have yielded similar results in terms of structure and determinants. This is perhaps to be expected, in that numerous researchers have argued that lay explanations for economic phenomena form a coherent system (Furnham and Lewis, 1986).

(4) Explanations for Inflation

Katona (1975) is one of the few economic psychologists to consider the psychology, as opposed to the economics, of inflation. He suggests that lack of confidence in money may occur *before* an increase in the circulation of money and restriction in the price of goods as a sort of anticipation of crisis (e.g. before a way). Thus, consumer sentiment itself may be a part *cause* of inflation. Also, whereas the psychological reactions to runaway hyperinflation are well documented much less is known about the more common phenomenon of creeping inflation. In fact, according to Katona, whereas the demand theory of inflation predicts that in inflationary periods consumers substitute goods for money by spending more and saving less, studies of consumer behaviour show the opposite. These studies showed that inflation was viewed in a negative light and that higher prices led people to believe that it was a bad time to buy. With a rise in prices people believe that more of their money has to go for necessities and less is available for discretionary items so that rising prices led to uncertainty which in turn induced people to try harder to save and accumulate reserve funds.

Katona's studies showed that at least 80% of people complained about being hurt by inflation, the poor more than the rich, which they believed should not and need not happen. Asked to attribute blame they felt the misdeeds of Government, business, consumers and trade unions to be the major causes of inflation. Respondents believed that the Government and consumers should spend less in an attempt to reduce inflation, but did not want to see taxes or interest rates raised. They quite categorically disagreed with the suggestion that one should create unemployment to slow down inflation, while also not wanting to make personal sacrifices, have wage controls or limit income gains.

Many current studies confirm Katona's findings (Williams and Defris, 1981). Others have become more interested in the effect of inflation on personal satisfaction. For instance, in an experimental study Levin *et al.* (1981) showed that factors such as a salary raise and inflation combine in a non-additive fashion to influence ratings of financial well-being and personal satisfaction. The respondents tended to compare a salary raise and inflation in determining their level of personal satisfaction, with the direction of change having a different effect from the magnitude of change. A small change in either could, therefore, produce a relatively large change in personal satisfaction. In a similar experimental study, MacFadyen *et al.* (1984) found that individuals do not react to combinations of inflation and a salary raise as a simple difference model might suggest. That is, the psychological research shows that there is no consistent relationship between a salary raise and inflation as these appear to operate under discontinuous processes.

Epstein and Babad (1982) looked at inflation as an economic threat by questioning 1512 alumni of Rutgers University and 500 alumni of Hebrew University at a time when the US inflation rate was 16% and the Israeli rate 150%. They were asked to provide basic demographic and economic information (including salary), subjective appraisals of inflation (comparative standard of living, concern about the future) and reported changes in economic behaviour (measures concerning consuming, spending, lifestyle and recreational activities). The results provided strong evidence that reported changes in economic behaviour is a function of the subjective *psychological* appraisal of aversiveness of inflation. "The observed pattern of findings was extremely similar in two societies strikingly different in important aspects of their economies" (p. 98). Perceived threat predicted self-reported changes in buying practices and leisure activities better than actual income. Interestingly, threat and income did not interact in predicting economic behaviour and none of the (over 10) demographic or economic variables differentiated between the Israelis or Americans who felt more, rather than less, threatened.

More recently Furnham (1988b) considered British respondents' explanations for inflation at a time of decreasing inflation but increasing unemployment. Respondents were asked, amongst other things, whether inflation has altered their way of life, how much their expenditure has changed on a number of items and to whom they attributed high inflation.

Some of these results for the seven explanations for unemployment can be

TABLE 6.5. *Percentage Responses to the Questions in the Three Sections*

A. Percentage of respondents who responded to the question "Has inflation substantially altered your way of life in the past couple of years?"
YES = 21%; NO = 79%

B. Percentage of respondents who reported having reduced, unchanged or increased expenditure during the past 2–3 years on seven factors

		Reduced	Unchanged	Increased
1.	Clothing	30.6	45.9	23.4
2.	Entertainment	36.5	36.5	27.1
3.	Holidays	38.0	37.3	24.7
4.	Eating Out	41.2	32.2	26.7
5.	Food	16.1	53.3	30.6
6.	Car Expenses	18.4	59.8	31.8
7.	Saving	36.5	42.8	20.8

C. Percentage of respondents who *agreed* (strongly, moderately or slightly), *were not sure*, or who *disagreed* (strongly, moderately or slightly) that the following factors were important in being responsible for inflation*

		Agree	Unsure	Disagree	Mean	SD
1.	Trade unions	63.5	13.3	23.1	4.79	1.97
2.	Previous Government	58.4	18.8	22.8	4.68	1.87
3.	Present Government	43.9	15.7	40.4	4.10	2.12
4.	Arab oil producing countries	74.1	14.9	10.9	5.33	1.61
5.	Big multi-national companies	48.6	27.8	23.6	4.57	1.74
6.	Joining the EEC	62.3	16.9	20.8	4.87	1.76
7.	Poor industrial management	67.4	20.4	12.1	5.14	1.56

*They were all rated on a 7-point agree – disagree scale For the purpose of this table 7, 6, 5 were collapsed into an agree score, 4 = unsure, and 3, 2 and 1 were collapsed into disagree. The mean and SD show more accurately the distribution of scores.
Reproduced with permission from Furnham, A. (1988b). Coping with inflation. *Applied Psychology*. London: Sage.

Some of these results for the seven explanations for unemployment can be seen in Table 6.5. The respondents believed Arab-Oil producing countries were the most important cause, and present British (Conservative) Government policies the least. A factor analysis of these seven items yielded three interpretable factors. *Socialism* (items 1 and 2 referring to Socialist Government policies); *external* (items 3, 4 and 5 referring to external and internal forces) and *Conservative* (items 6 and 7 referring to Conservative Government policies). Younger people who were Socialist–Liberal rather than Conservative tended to blame Socialist explanations, while older, better-educated subjects tended to blame external factors, but not Conservative policies. Furnham (1987) argues that these explanations are clearly self-serving with better-off, more Conservative people blaming Socialist ideologies for inflation, while less well-off, radical people blame the policies of the right-wing.

Unlike poverty, wealth or unemployment the explanation for inflation does not fit nicely into any established structure (e.g. individualistic, societal or fatalistic). This is no doubt because it is almost impossible to conceive of this macro-economic phenomenon in individualistic terms. This may well be true of various other macro-economic phenomena.

6.4 Conclusion

It is not always easy to disentangle lay economic and political theories as they are frequently related. Studies on lay theories and understandings of economics have shown that lay people are not particularly well informed though they tend to debate economic issues fairly frequently. Indeed, it is precisely because economic conditions have such an immediate and noticeable impact on ordinary people's lives that they are so frequently debated. Thus, in times of high unemployment, high inflation or boom people may be exposed to popular and professional economic debate which they may assimilate (or distort) into their private model or theory about how the economy works. Although there are introductory "teach yourself" guides for lay people on economics, it is probable that most people acquire their economic knowledge through direct experience or through media presentations and advertisements.

The economic model of behaviour is better at predicting behavioural outcomes in some areas of economics (such as consumer behaviour) than others (such as voting). Where the economic model has failed, various people have attempted to "enrich" it with various psychological ideas. One such attempt is the introduction of ideas from attribution theory, which is concerned with how people attribute the causes of phenomena. In this chapter lay theories or attributions for poverty, wealth, unemployment and inflation were covered.

Despite the fact that researchers from different countries, working with different methodologies and from different disciplines have investigated lay attributions for these economic phenomena, a consistent pattern of results seems to be emerging. First these attributions seem to have a clear *structure* — economic circumstances are attributed either to the effort, ability or behaviour of single individuals, or to controllable actions of large bodied and organisations like governments, trade unions, or big business, or economic conditions are seen as uncontrollable consequences of cycles, macro-economic trade forces, over which individuals or countries have no control. Second, economic beliefs seem to be *determined* by a number of specific factors like education, age, wealth, etc. Third, economic theories no doubt serve important psychological *functions* for the individuals that hold them. If for instance, one believes that the poor, the unemployed and the sick are personally responsible for their misfortune it is much easier to ignore their plight.

Lay economic theories seem very closely bound up with other lay beliefs, particularly political and moral beliefs. The central question of interest for sociologists and economists does not concern the structure, determinants and functions of these attributions, beliefs or theories so much as whether lay theories determine economic behaviour (such as saving, gambling, investing on the stock market) or the other way around. In other words, the issue of the direction of causality is most important because if lay theories were seen as epiphenomenal consequences of economic behaviour they would not warrant much research. If, on the other hand, it can be shown that lay theories actually predict or determine major aspects of economic behaviour, then, from an economic point of view at least, they are particularly interesting, in that they may be changed to change economic behaviour. As ever there appears to be evidence of bi-directional causality which is, nevertheless, an important admission because it suggests that lay attributions and theories cannot be ignored in an attempt to predict individual, or group economic behaviour.

7

Lay Theories in Statistics

7.1 Introduction

Perhaps it is because so many people have problems with basic numeracy that they hold such strong views about statistics (defined as the science of collecting, classifying and using numerical facts). Predictably, some appear to be in awe of statistics — indeed Florence Nightingale was attributed with remarking, "To understand God's thoughts we must study statistics, for these are the measure of his purpose". At the other end of the scale are those who distrust statistical inference or argument by statistical facts. They are fond of the quote from Benjamin Disraeli who noted sarcastically, "There are three kinds of lies: lies, damned lies and statistics". For some the statistics themselves invest a quality of meaning to data and are practically infallible, while for others they can be used to prove anything and, therefore, can prove nothing.

Reichman (1964) has likened statistics to a language, for a number of reasons. First, merely because people misuse grammar does not mean that grammar is itself bad, so the misuse of statistics does not condemn statistics as a whole. Second, being able to speak the language means that one cannot be fooled or misunderstood, so being familiar with statistics means being literate. Third, statistics has rules, symbols and concepts which are systematised into a dynamic grammar.

The use of the language analogy is a good one, as the use of statistics involves the learning of various meaningful symbols and letters (mostly Greek) and of some specific technical concepts (e.g. regression to the mean) as well as some general principles. Others, like Moore (1980), prefer to conceive of statistics as a form of logic, built on simple logical principles, applied to a wide range of problems.

It is probably true to say that people do not have lay theories of statistics or numbers. It is quite possible that people may be either statistophiles or statistophobes, in that they have an abiding love or loathing of statistics, but they are unlikely to have special "theories" about how statistics work. They may, however, be superstitious concerning certain numbers, like 3, 7, 9 or 13. Psychoanalysts, including Jung and Freud, documented many examples of patients being highly superstitious about numbers. Yet people do appear to have theories about such things as distribution, probability, etc.

Many studies have looked at people as intuitive statisticians attempting to make sensible inferences about the uncertain social environment. Peterson and Beach (1967), in their review, actually set out their paper as one might do in an introductory statistics book: they considered first intuitive descriptive statistics, such as the ability to judge proportions, means and variances, which people are moderately good at. People seem very conservative in their inferences about proportions and correlations and are only partially sensitive to all the relevant variables. Lay people's assumptions, it seems, are different from those of statisticians. For Kruglanski *et al.* (1984), however, this concept of the intuitive statistician has too strong a naturist ring. They believe, and suggest, that recent evidence supports their case that "far from being uniform, people's statistical intuitions may vary widely as a consequence of past learning and experience . . . and . . . as a function of the specific conditions determining the degree to which statistical notions are perceived as situationally applicable" (p. 516).

A great deal of the work on lay theories of statistics has concentrated on the fallible judgements of lay people when using statistical information and inference (Schweder, 1980). The catalogue of errors and biases, set out in the next section is long. Curiously, a lot of this research has also shown that educated and trained people (even scientists) are also prone to making many of these errors.

Using and manipulating statistical evidence is clearly important in any scientific enterprise. If people cannot interpret, or make correct predictions from, statistical evidence, however simply presented, it is highly unlikely that the theories they derive are correctly empirically based. The existence of consistent biases may be a crucial reason why people are overconfident in their judgements, persevere in their beliefs despite damning evidence and systematically distort evidence that they receive.

7.2 The Failure of Intuition

Psychologists have appeared to rejoice in revealing the mistakes of intuitive judgement or the inaccuracies in lay theories. There is a long list of errors, fallacies and biases of lay people. These include being insufficiently sensitive or mindful of *sample size* in interpreting statistics or generalisation; the *reliability* of information used to support or refute an argument; the *accuracy* of information retrieved from *memory* with all its attendant biases and failures; the relevance of paying attention to *base-rate* frequencies; the necessity of testing *disconfirming information*, etc.

In each case psychologists have demonstrated that lay people make erroneous assumptions or incorrect calculations in dealing with statistical manipulations. Although people probably do not have statistical theories, they do appear to have ideas about order, randomness, etc., which dictate their statistical behaviour. For instance, many lay people feel threatened by randomness and lack of control and, hence, operate as if the former did not occur and they, therefore, were able to experience some kind of control over events.

Without doubt the authors who have contributed most to the understanding of lay statistical inferences are Kahneman and Tversky with their work in the 1970s. In looking at people's probabilistic predictions they specified various heuristic rules (three in particular) that people use, as well as systematic biases associated with them.

(1) Representativeness

In judging whether people are representative of a class or group people often ignore several factors which should influence their probability judgements (e.g. if we know someone is shy, withdrawn and unhelpful; neat and tidy with a need for order and structure, how ideally is this person suited to being a librarian?) These include:

(a) *Prior probabilities*: base-rate frequencies of the absolute number of people in any category must be taken into account, before judging their representativeness of that group or category. (i.e. how many librarians have the characteristics of our applicant?)

(b) *Sample size:* results drawn from small samples are seen to be equally, and sometimes even more, accurate than results drawn from larger samples, which is incorrect. (i.e. The larger the sample the more accurate the probabilities.)

(c) *Misconceptions of chance*: people have a belief in the appropriate law of small numbers in that they inappropriately expect that a sequence of events generated by a random process represent the essential characteristics of that process even when the sequence is short. (Therefore people overestimate the replicability of findings based on small populations.)

(d) *Insensitivity to predictability*: people appear to be insensitive to the reliability of the evidence upon which they make their predictions and do not know the rule that the higher the predictability the wider the range of predictable values. (That is, if the evidence is unreliable, all outcomes are equally possible.)

(e) *Illusion of validity*: the more supposedly representative a sample or item is, the more confidence people have in the validity of their judgement, even when they are aware of the many factors that limit accuracy. (For example people still conduct interviews despite repeated demonstrations of their weaknesses.)

(f) *Misconceptions of regression*: people do not develop correct intuitions about this phenomenon when it is bound to occur or they invent a spurious causal explanation for it. Essentially, the phenomenon is incompatible with the belief that the predicted outcome should be maximally representative of the input, and, hence, that the value of the outcome variable should be as extreme as the value of the input variable.

(2) Availability

This refers to the fact that when people judge the frequency or probability of an event they bring to mind available instances or occurrences of that event which they have themselves experienced. Availability problems lead to predictable biases:

(a) *Retrievability (Recall) of instances*: where instances are easily retrieved from memory, they appear more numerous than those events, of equal frequency, whose instances are less retrievable. Similarly, more recent or more salient events' frequencies are overestimated compared with less recent and less salient occurrences. (i.e. the more easily something is remembered, for whatever reason, the more validity it acquires.)

(b) *Effectiveness of search set*: the ease of search for information, based on a set of strategies leads to errors in judgement because items more easily retrieved are thought of as more frequent.

(c) *Imaginability*: the extent to which the problem can be imagined influences judgements — the more easy salient issues can be imagined, the more their effects will be overemphasised and vice versa. Thus, the more abstract and/ or unimaginable a phenomenon, the less weight given to it in various judgements.

(d) *Illusory correlation*: this judgement of how frequently two events co-occur is often based on the strength of the associated bond between them — when this is strong, people conclude that the events have been paired even though they have not. Thus people might overestimate the association between physical features (e.g. flapping ears) and delinquency despite the fact that there is *no* evidence of this association.

(3) Adjustment and Anchoring

A mistake in the initial value or starting point frequently leads to computational errors. Three particular problems frequently occur:

(a) *Insufficient adjustment*: this occurs when calculations are based on initial figures which anchor the answers and are never sufficiently adjusted thereafter, even when the first "guess" was badly wrong.

(b) *Biases in evaluation of conjunctive and disjunctive events*: frequently people tend to overestimate the probability of conjunctive events (e.g. drawing a red marble, with replacement, seven times in succession from a bag containing 90% red marbles) and underestimate the probability of disjunctive events (e.g. drawing a red marble once in seven times from a bag containing 10% red marbles). This is because the overall probability of conjunctive events is lower than the probability of each elementary single event, whereas the overall probability of a disjunctive event is higher than the probability of each elementary event.

(c) *The assessment of subjective probability distributions*: subjects tend to state overly narrow confidence intervals which reflect more certainty than is justified by their knowledge about the assessed qualities.

Tversky and Kahneman (1974) argue that these cognitive biases resulting from the reliance on heuristics is found among lay people *and* experts. What they do find surprisingly is not that people use these heuristics but rather that they fail to learn rules like "regressions to the mean" even when they (both experts *and* lay people) have been exposed to this phenomenon so often. Their work has attracted considerable research, mainly confirmatory.

Kahneman and Tversky (1982) have argued that there are numerous good reasons for the study of errors in statistical reasoning: they expose our intellectual limitations; they reveal the psychological processes which govern judgement and inference; they map which principles are intuitive or counter-intuitive. For them, intuitive judgements are those reached by an informal or unstructured mode of thinking; those that are compatible with our lay view of the world; and those that we apply in the procedure of our normal conduct. They argue that one should distinguish between errors of comprehension and errors of application because although people may understand a particular statistical law they may not recognise when it should be applied.

Table 7.1 shows a list of some sources of error and bias commonly found among lay people, specifically those relating to the acquisition, output and feedback of information on judgements.

7.3 Lay Psychometrics

With the belief that people can reason statistically accurately about familiar kinds of events that they encounter on a daily basis, so long as they are also able to code them clearly, Kunda and Nisbet (1985) set out to investigate lay psychometric knowledge. They point out that inferring the probability that one will enjoy a film given that a close friend likes it involves the processing of different statistical information (base rate of generally liking films; degree of co-variation; aggregation principle).

There is, however, considerable evidence supporting the hypothesis that people make consistent errors about such things as the consistency of the behaviour of others. Also, not understanding the aggregation principle properly, lay people do not realise that predictability of social behaviour on single occasions (items, situations) is frequently very low. In a series of seven studies Kunda and Nisbet (1985) set out to demonstrate their point. For instance, they demonstrated:

(a) People do not appreciate the aggregation principle (the rule that the

TABLE 1.

	Bias/source of Bias	Description	Example
1.	Acquisition of information		
	Availability	Ease with which specific instances can be recalled from memory affects judgement of frequency	Frequency of well-publicised events are over-estimated (e.g. deaths due to homicide, cancer); frequency of less well-publicised events are under-estimated (e.g. deaths due to asthma and diabetes)
		Chance "availability" of particular "cues" in the immediate environment affects judgement	Problem solving can be hindered/facilitated by cues perceived by chance in a particular setting (hints set up cognitive "direction")
	Selective perception	People structure problems on the basis of their own experience	The same problem can be seen by a marketing manager as a marketing problem, a financial problem by a finance manager, etc.
		Anticipations of what one expects to see bias what one does see.	Identification of incongruent objects — e.g. playing cards with red spade — are either inaccurately reported or cause discomfort
		People seek information consistent with their own views/hypotheses	Interviewers seek information about candidates consistent with first impressions rather than information that could refute those impressions
		People downplay disregard conflicting evidence	In forming impressions, people will underweight information that does not yield to a consistent profile
	Frequency	Cue used to judge strength of predictive relationships is observed frequency rather than observed relative frequency. Information on "non-occurrences" of an event is unavailable and ignored	When considering relative performance (of, say, two persons), the absolute number of successes is given greater weight than the relative number of successes to successes and failures (i.e. the denominator is ignored). Note, the number of failures is frequently unavailable
	Concrete information (ignoring base rate, or prior information)	Concrete information (i.e. vivid, or based on experience/incidents) dominates abstract information (e.g. summaries, statistical base rates, etc.)	When purchasing a car, the positive or negative experience of a single person you know is liable to weigh more heavily in judgement than available and more valid information e.g. in consumer reports

Bias/source of Bias	Description	Example
Illusory correlation	Belief that two variables co-vary when in fact they do not. (Possibly related to "Frequency" above)	Selection of an inappropriate variable to make a prediction
Data interpretation	Order effects (primary/recency)	Sometimes the first items in a sequential presentation assume undue importance (primacy), sometimes the last items (recency)
	Mode of presentation	Sequential vs intact data displays can affect what people are able to access. Contrast, for example, complete listed unit-price shopping vs own sequential information search
Data presentation	Mixture of types of information e.g. qualitative and quantitative	Concentration on quantitative data, exclusion of qualitative good, or vice-versa
	Logical data displays	Apparently complete "logical" data displays can blind people to critical omissions
	Context effects on perceived variability	Assessments of variability, of say, a series of numbers, is affected by the absolute size (e.g. mean level) of the numbers
2. Output		
Question format	The way a person is required or chooses to make a judgement can affect the outcome	Preferences for risky prospects have been found to be inconsistent with the prices for which people are willing to pay
Scale effects	The scale on which responses are recorded can affect responses	Estimate of probabilities can vary when estimated directly on a scale from zero to one, or when "odds" or even "long-odds" are used
Wishful thinking	People's preferences for outcomes of events affect their assessment of the events	People sometimes assess the probability of outcomes they desire higher than their state of knowledge justifies
Illusion of control	Activity concerning an uncertain outcome can by itself induce in a person feelings of control over the uncertain event	Activities such as planning, or even the making of forecasts, can induce feelings of control over the uncertain future

	Bias/source of Bias	Description	Example
3.	Feedback		
	Outcome irrelevant learning structures	Outcomes observed yield inaccurate or incomplete information concerning predictive relationships. This can lead, *inter alia*, to unrealistic confidence in one's own judgement	In personnel selection you can learn how good your judgement is concerning candidates selected, but you usually have no information concerning subsequent performance of rejected candidates
	Misperceptions of chance fluctuations (e.g. gambler's fallacy)	Observation of an unexpected number of similar chance outcomes leads to the expectation that the probability of the appearance of an event not recently seen increases	So-called "gambler's fallacy" — after observing say, 9 successive Reds in roulette, people tend to believe that Black is more likely on the next throw.
	Success/failure attributions	Tendency to attribute success to one's skill, and failure to chance. (This is also related to the "Illusion of Control" — see above.)	Successes in one's job, e.g. making a difficult sale, are attributed to one's skill; failures to "bad luck"
	Logical fallacies in recall	Inability to recall details of an event leads to "logical" reconstruction which can be inaccurate	Eyewitness testimony
	Hindsight bias	In retrospect, people are not "surprised" about what has happened in the past. They can easily find plausible explanations	The "Monday morning quarterback" phenomenon

magnitude of a correlation increases with the number of units of evidence on which it is based) in that they think total to total correlations no greater than item to item correlations. Thus two groups of people are more likely to agree than two individuals, because observations at the group level are more stable than at the individual level that is reflect the true score and less error.

(b) People tend to overestimate the agreement between any two individuals, but underestimate the agreement between any two groups of individuals.

(c) Even if experts do understand the aggregation principle in the abstract, they are unable to apply it to important real world evaluations.

(d) Both lay and expert subjects were more accurate about correlations that obtain for abilities than those that obtain for traits.

From the experimental evidence the authors conclude:

> Recognition of the aggregation principle seems to be well developed only in domains where people are able to detect covariations at more than one level. The recognition of the role of chance in producing events and the realisation that the covariations at one level of aggregation are far from perfect do not suffice to prompt recognition of the aggregation principle. Even when subjects accurately perceive item to item correlations to be very low they do not use the aggregation principle to extrapolate to total correlations unless they have also had the opportunity to perceive that the total to total correlations are high. Accurate covariation detection in a given domain, at more than one level of aggregation, may be required if the rule is to be induced in that domain.
>
> Thus, ironically, people are probably able to apply the aggregation principle best for domains for which they already have had substantial opportunity to observe covariation. They are unable to benefit from its use in domains where it would be most beneficial - domains where they are familiar with covariation at only one level of aggregation, or at no level. As a consequence, people make very serious errors when assessing covariation in such domains. When they are familiar only with covariation at the item to item level, as in several of the domains we examined, they tend to grossly *underestimate* covariation at the total to total level. It seems likely that when they are familiar only with covariation at the total to total level they would tend to grossly *overestimate* covariation at the item to item level. And when they have no familiarity with a domain, they seem sure to make at least one of these errors. (p. 41)

Thus, for people to be good psychometricians they need to be familiar with the data they are using to be able to code it; and to know whether the data that they are correlating is drawn from distributions of the same kinds of events. But they need also to understand such crucial factors as probability, as well as the difference between cause and correlation.

Lay people are also notoriously inaccurate at making probabilistic judgements despite often being very confident in them, even in the face of contrary evidence (Kahneman and Tversky, 1973; Einhorn and Hogarth, 1978). Experiments using all sorts of material have come up with very much the same answers. For instance, Blackmore and Troscianko (1985) looked at lay people's beliefs in the paranormal and they divided them into sheep (believers) and goats (non-believers). Using a variety of tasks including coin-tossing they found, as predicted, that goats were better than sheep at tasks involving judgements about probabilities. Also sheep had the illusion of control because they did not understand the random nature of the task and thought they could exercise some control over the outcome. This study seems to suggest that people's beliefs in paranormal phenomena are intricately linked to this (mis)understanding of simple statistical rules.

At the heart of much scientific and lay thinking is the notion of cause, which is not the same as correlation. A correlation between A and B may exist because A causes B; B causes A; A and B show reciprocal causative effects; A and B are both caused by C. Many lay people infer cause from correlation and it is often difficult for scientists themselves not to fall into this trap.

The concept of correlation can be traced back almost exactly 100 years to Galton, who noted that two things co-relate when the variation for the one is accompanied on the average by more or less variation of the other, and in the same direction. In an intriguing study Valsiner (1985) found only 13 out of 95 subjects demonstrated an adequate understanding of the correlational co-efficient and that some individuals shift their interpretation from the population level analysis, where they belong, to the individual level. Valsiner argued that lay people tend to operate at first in terms of quantitatively heterogeneous classes where a correlational co-efficient is calculated, but then switch their thinking to the qualitatively homogeneous view as they interpret it. In other words correlational data based on inter-individual variability of specimens within a class gets translated into knowledge that is believed to be applicable to individual cases.

Given the above findings there appears little doubt about the fact that the layman is not potentially a very competent psychometrician. But it is quite possible to educate people about statistics. Fong *et al.* (1986) demonstrated that people reason statistically by using (often incorrect) abstract rules but that by directly manipulating these rules (through education) their reasoning about a wide variety of content domains can be affected. They note:

> It seems to us that courses in statistics and probability theory concentrate almost entirely on calculus while often ignoring its common-sense roots . . . If introductory statistics courses were to incorporate examples of how statistical principles such as the law of large numbers can be applied to judgements in everyday life, we have no doubt that such courses would have a more far-reaching effect on the extent to which people think statistically about the world. (pp. 281–282)

A good deal of work has gone into the law of large and small numbers, which basically, states that larger samples are more representative of the population from which they are drawn than smaller samples.

7.4 Gambling

Apart from the day to day arithmetic and probabilistic calculations that people have to do, largely concerned with their own finances, there are one or two other areas where they are required to make numerous probabilistic decisions. One such area is gambling, on which there has been a good deal of psychological research. Studies in this area throw light on lay statistical knowledge and practices.

Furnham and Lewis (1986) have noted that most research has been concerned with compulsive gamblers. Compulsive gambling (which is defined as a chronic and progressive preoccupation with gambling and urge to gamble, and gambling behaviour that compromises, disrupts or damages personal, family and/or vocational pursuits) has received a great deal of interest. Descriptions of chronic gamblers are remarkably similar to those of alcoholics. Extensive biographical, social and psychological data have been gathered on a very limited number of individuals (Lesieur, 1977). All studies show a prevalence of male over female compulsive gamblers (Custer, 1976). There are no reliable data to show how social class, occupational or religious differences affect the evidence of compulsive gamblers, but the literature suggests that the compulsive gambling system affects all types of people (Greenberg, 1980).

Furnham and Lewis (1986) have suggested that there are essentially five main types of psychological theories. Psychoanalytic theories tend to stress that the compulsive gambler is driven by overwhelming desire to lose and savour victimhood and injustice and, hence, revel in remorse and self-pity. Personality theories tend to suggest that the compulsive gambler gambles because he or she is psychophysically predisposed to high arousal levels. Some have suggested that gambling is in fact a surrogate for the risk-taking which has been removed from everyday life. It has also been suggested that choice of occupation is related to gambling: both those with very high- and very low-risk jobs would indulge in high-risk gambling, while those in middle-risk jobs would take part in low-risk gambling. Thirdly, there are a number of sociological theories. Devereux (1968) developed a structural-functionalist theory which saw gambling as the perfect scapegoat for the contradictions of capitalism. Capitalism seeks to encourage economic self-interest of a "rational" kind; competition with a visible correlation between effort and reward; institutional mechanisms of banking and credit which service both producers and consumers, and the Protestant work ethic which stressed rationality and avoidance of reliance on risk and luck. Gambling survives and flourishes because it meets personal and social needs frustrated in capitalist societies, or acts as a protest against budgetary constraints, rationality and ethics, while providing thrills, aggression behind a playful façade, and artificial and short-time problem-solving issues differentiated from real life. More importantly, gambling is counter-religious because it stresses ultimate ignorance and helplessness over luck, which has to be constantly tested. This, according to sociologists, accounts for the many contradictory and ambivalent attitudes to gambling in the West where it is tolerated in practice and yet often illegal in principle. This ambivalence is strongest in the middle-class, where the Protestant work ethic values are at their strongest.

Fourthly, there are social psychological theories which stress, amongst other things, the determinants of attitudes to gambling and the relationship between attitudes to, and habits of, gambling.

Furnham (1985d) has argued that the types of, motivation for, satisfaction derived from, attitudes to and habits of gambling are interrelated and multidimensional. In most Western countries gambling takes many forms, some of which are favoured by some members of society more than others and which are considered more or less acceptable by them. The motivation for gambling — ranging from social contact through psychophysical arousal, to the desire to lose and punish oneself too — are as varied as the satisfactions derived from gambling. Hence, attitudes to gambling are manifold: some concern the psychopathology of this possibly irrational activity; others the moral and legal aspects of gambling; while others concern the financial possibilities. Any attempt to measure gambling beliefs and attitudes needs to take this complexity into consideration. Furthermore, as one might expect, gambling attitudes are not independent of gambling habits. Those who gamble frequently and in a variety of ways find the activity harmless and exciting and resist legal or financial restraints, whereas the opposite is true of those who rarely, if ever, gamble.

Fifthly, some researchers have attempted to describe and identify key environmental features which stimulate, maintain or suppress the incidence of gambling. Factors which have been considered include:

1. The frequency of opportunities to gamble, such as the regularity of lotteries, the number of betting shops, fruit machines, etc., and the number of horse/dog race meetings.
2. The pay-out interval, which refers both to how long people have to wait before they know of the result of the bet and how long they have to wait for their winnings.
3. The range of odds and stakes available, which may be quite variable.
4. The degree of personal participation and the exercise of skill, as gamblers feel more active when present at the gambling event, and when they are able to select the odds of the bet.
5. Probability of winning an individual bet and pay-out ratio.

Another approach is based on classic learning theory and the principles of operant conditioning, which stress schedules of reinforcement. Gambling usually provides intermittent schedules of reinforcement (variable ratio, variable magnitude reinforcement schedules) which, though not the best schedule for establishing a particular response pattern, is probably the most addictive — that is, maintaining the response pattern over long periods of time. Experimental studies have looked at resistance to extinction as a function of the duration of previous reinforcement with mixed results. But there are very wide differences in behavioural terms between different forms of gambling, such as event frequency, expected values, etc. Thus, it may be that the reinforcers differ from person to person, and from one type of game to another. Precisely what is reinforcing (feedback, exercise of skill, excitement, etc.) is extremely important.

Is it true that people who properly understand the odds at most gambling games do not play? So why are there professional gamblers? Do statistical experts fare any better at card games? Wagenaar and Keren (1985) tested professional blackjack dealers, statistical experts and lay people concerning the probabilities of card combinations in the game of blackjack. Contrary to some predictions, the results showed that experience and statistical expertise do not make people better in this task.

Yet there is a considerable literature on gamblers' erroneous evaluation of probabilities and payoffs, such as the well-known "gamblers' fallacy" which is a negative recency effect which erroneously claims that the chances of winning are increased by betting against a long run of one colour or number. These fallacies relate primarily to the judgemental heuristics covered in Section 7.2. Another area of research in this field refers to the illusion of control. Gilovich and Douglas (1986) demonstrated that people generally attach more diagnostic significance to successful, rather than unsuccessful, outcomes, even though both are randomly determined. It is this bias in evaluating success vs failure that increases resistance to extinction that is produced by intermittent reinforcement. The major effect of this bias is to produce the impression that one's previous performance is in fact better than the objective records show.

Cornich (1978) has argued:

> It is clear that incorrect or inappropriate beliefs about probability theory, the role of skill in determining outcomes, and about the means by which natural events can be influenced may distort perception of the probabilities of winning or losing a gamble, and hence — by extension — the attractiveness of gambling at all. The belief that the occurrence of winning sequences in games of chance can be predicted and controlled by use of appropriate theories, skills and ritualistic practices may also have arisen as a consequence of these games' original purposes. . . . Games of chance seem to have emerged from the divinatory aspects of religious ceremonies within primitive animistic cultures, their purposes in such circumstances being those of "quizzing the supernatural". Preparation for divination requires elaborate rituals, incantations and propitiatory ceremonies to ensure the best conditions for a favourable outcome. It may be that behaviours such as talking to the dice and other superstitious practices in modern games of chance still fulfill for some players the functions of trying to secure the benevolence of fate, and that the feelings of luckiness — or reduction of anxiety — induced by these rituals may distort players' perception of probabilities. (pp. 101–102).

7.5 Limitations and Artefacts of the Current Research

Most, but far from all, of the studies on lay statistical inferences have involved giving people certain amounts of statistical evidence, and then requiring them to guess, infer or calculate some other statistical feature. As has been shown lay people make characteristic errors. However, it should be pointed out that this particular methodology may lead to possible artefacts.

(1) Information Presentation vs Search

In many studies of lay statistical inference subjects are "presented" with all the information that they need, and frequently ignore much of it (Evans and Bradshaw, 1986). In everyday life people have to seek out this information. It may be that how they seek this information, in which order and how much trust they put in it, best summarises lay theories of statistical inference. A number of studies — some concerned with statistical and some with causal inference — have supported this point. For instance, Lalljee *et al.* (1984) argued and demonstrated that people have specific hypotheses about causality and seek information which will disambiguate or confirm their hypotheses, rather than engaging in a general inductive process. They argue:

> The importance attached to obtaining the correct explanation, time constraints and the costs of obtaining more information are obvious candidates for exploration in a context where sequential information search is investigated. Further, individual differences in information search strategy as a function of depression or locus of control may also be fruitfully explored. (p. 21).

Consider, for instance, the task of predicting an exam candidate's mark in one subject such as theology, where he or she is writing at least three exams (theology, philosophy and psychology). What information would one want: the candidate's previous marks in theology (consistency), other classmates' marks in theology (consensus), the candidate's marks from other subjects (distinctiveness). People might require other information as well (e.g. the sex of the lecturer, the time of the exam). Further, they are bound to weight this information differently. But if they are active agents in the pursuit of information, rather than passive recipients of all the salient information (as judged by the experimenter), a very different set of cognitive processes may occur (they may, for instance, bias, or systematically "forget" certain information). As people have most frequently to seek out the information that they use for their judgements, rather than get it presented to them, it seems important to look as much at statistical information search strategies.

(2) The Context of Calculation

Various studies have demonstrated that people who have never been formally educated tend to solve mathematical problems rather differently from people who have been to school. Carraher *et al.* (1985) actually hypothesised that the same differences between informal and school-based routines exist within people, such that the same person could solve problems at one time or place in a formal, and at other times and in other places, in an informal way. In a study on adolescents in rural Brazil, they found subjects using computational strategies different from those taught in schools. They found that performance on arithmetic and statistical tasks was better when set in a real-life market place context than when it was more abstract or context-free.

In other words, the context in which one is tested usually implies the abstractness of the statistical problem to be solved. Experimenters nearly always require people to make abstract inferences or de-contextualised calculations. If people find these more difficult, or actually use cognitive strategies different from more common day-to-day statistical problems, of equivalent complexity that they can and do solve, the results obtained may be unrepresentative of lay people's ability and ungeneralisable to a wide variety of situations.

(3) The Role of Experience

By and large, the role of individual differences has not been stressed when considering lay statistical inference. Of course, one would predict that age, education and socioeconomic status might each affect ability. But added to this is the role of experience. Wason and Shapiro (1971) showed that certain types of experience in a reasoning problem can help, and others hinder, problem solving — thematic experience is more helpful than abstract experience. Thus, both the type and salience of experience of statistical problem solving may affect a person's ability to get the correct answer. Unless these possibly confounding variables are taken into account, results may not be representative of lay people's general statistical ability. Thus, experimental artefacts may have important consequences for experimental findings. There is considerable evidence to suggest that the external validity of decision-making research that relies on laboratory simulations of real-world decision problems is low. Seemingly insignificant features of the decision task and measures cause people to alter their decision strategies. The context in which the decision problem is presented, the salience of alternatives, the number of cues, the concreteness of the information, the order of presentation, the similarity of cue to alternative, the nature of the decomposition, the form of the measures, and so on, seem to affect the decisions that subjects make.

Similarly, Kunda and Nisbett (1985) have argued that many lay people fail to apply, in simple laboratory tasks, statistical principles that they can apply to everyday life problems with content that is familiar and with elements that are codeable.

The existence of these limitations and artefacts has been recognised by many (but not all) researchers in this field. Certainly, studies that do not take the above into consideration may have poor ecological validity and, hence, poor generalisability.

7.6 Conclusion

Research in this area has concentrated on the shortcomings of the layman's ability to reason statistically, particularly with reference to such things as cause (Einhorn and Hogarth, 1986) and probability (Teigen, 1983; Cohen,

1982). Most studies have pointed out how poor lay people are at a range of tasks, but there have been exceptions. For instance, Nisbett and Kunda (1985) found that lay people were good at estimating social distributions while Ceci and Liker (1986) demonstrated that horse racing enthusiasts could use mental models containing multiple interactions and non-linearity to predict racing handicaps!

Less attention has been paid to how people acquire statistical information. Harding *et al.* (1982) demonstrated that the mode of presenting statistical information (proportion, percentage, pre-chart bar chart) affected people's reactions to it. For instance, they found that when relatively small probabilities were concerned, pictorial presentation of risks lead to a decrease in perceived importance of that information, which did not occur if the risk was described in absolute terms without reference to the base rate. Certainly, the way in which people present statistical information through which they aim to persuade us (politicians, advertisers, health educators) can have a powerful effect on the comprehension of that information. Similarly, Sherman *et al.* (1983) found that statistical judgements are based either on facts available in memory at the time of judgement or on the basis of previous summary impressions.

Nisbett *et al.* (1983) attempted to answer interesting questions concerning the use of statistical heuristics: "What factors encourage statistical reasoning and what factors discourage it? For what kinds of events and for what kinds of problems is statistical reasoning most likely to be used? Does purely formal training modify the untutored heuristics of everyday inductive reasoning?" (p. 340). They argue that three factors are likely to increase the use of statistical heuristics: where the clarity of the sample space and process are clear (the conceptualisation of what one has to predict is clear); the recognition of the operation of chance factors is possible; cultural prescriptions that encourage a particular type of reasoning. Hence, they could make predictions such as people who are knowledgeable about events of a given kind should be more inclined than less knowledgeable people to apply statistical reasoning, because both the distributions of the events and the chance factors influencing the events should be clearer to such people.

In the same paper, Nisbett *et al.* (1983) consider the results of training in statistical reasoning. They suggest that training is apt to facilitate three phenomena: the recognition of event distributions and their statistical parameters; the recognition of the role of chance in producing events; the ability to improve the clarity, accessibility and repertoire of statistical rules. They also find that people are becoming more and more statistically sophisticated, no doubt because of the education they receive and the sort of information they are regularly exposed to.

8

Lay Theories in Law

8.1 Introduction

Legal concepts such as justice, rules and retribution are well understood and used by lay people. Children are very concerned with fairness and appropriate rules or laws by which groups, communities and societies live. Adults in most countries are assailed by legal and related issues: much television concerns law infringements and detection; in some countries lay people sit on juries and judge the behaviour of apprehended suspects; and in their capacity as parent or leader many adults have to enforce various rules and laws in just ways.

Various lay questions concerning the origins of crime are frequently debated. These include: how might crime be related to personality; might genetic factors play any part in crime or criminality; which environmental factors encourage crime, etc. Similarly, not only people in the legal profession but other social scientists have interests in legal issues. For instance, Lloyd-Bostock (1984) has suggested that psychology and law have certain issues in common, such as *mens rea*, the nature of probability and the issue of responsibility as well as jury decisions and eyewitness testimony. Similarly, lawyers frequently appeal to common sense. As Loyd-Bostock (1981) notes, lawyers use the term common sense in many different ways, many of which are highly vague and value laden. However, she argues that when either lawyers or psychologists investigate lay people's legal attributions they should realise that these are observable, rule governed, social acts that take place in a particular context with its particular constraints and may in fact be negotiated (Lloyd-Bostock, 1983). Lawyers and psychologists have been primarily interested in such things as the *process* by which the ordinary man or woman perceives causality and makes judgements of responsibility. Depending on the particular interests of the researcher, various different factors have been put forward to account for how judgements of cause and legal responsibility are arrived at by an active constructive process full of error and bias. These include the structure of natural language; the motives, values, experiences, etc. of the judge; the specific context of the attributions; and the anticipated consequences of the attributions.

Others have been more interested in the *contents* of people's knowledge.

For instance, in a chapter entitled "Crime and Punishment" Nicholson and Lucas (1984) devised a quiz, no doubt to surprise readers. There were ten questions and readers were required to stipulate true or false. Many subjects got the answers wrong, in many cases over 50%.

1. The elderly run the greatest risk of being attacked. (False: old people are the least frequent victims of violence — the most frequent are young men.)
2. Psychopaths are typically withdrawn and controlled. (False: psychopaths are usually outgoing, impulsive and uncontrolled.)
3. Most victims of rape know their assailants. (True.)
4. Your chances of being robbed are lower than your chances of being admitted to hospital as a mental patient. (True.)
5. Most rapists are armed (False: about 30% are armed.)
6. The typical householder must expect to be burgled every couple of years. (False: houses are burgled less often than they catch fire.)
7. Young offenders under seventeen in Britain are responsible for less than 20% of all crime. (False: the true figure is 36%.)
8. Most crimes are not reported. (True.)
9. Anti-shoplifting signs increase shoplifting. (True.)
10. Once he's married, a man is likely to turn his back on crime. (True and false. Getting married reduces criminality among men in their twenties, but those men who do continue their criminal activities after marrying actually commit more crimes than before.)

8.2 Attribution Theory

Attribution theories have naturally been interested in public views of crime causation and prevention (Kidder and Cohn, 1979). Experimental studies of the causal roles of offenders and deviants have shown up some very interesting results. Studies varying the details of the offender and victim, such as their attractiveness and previous record, have found that lay people, policemen and parole officers usually regard offenders of all sorts as responsible for their actions, hence they expect them to repeat the offence.

In an extensive study of personal theories about the causes of crime Kidder and Cohn (1979) found that people speak primarily about the *victim's* or the *offender's* role in bringing about crime. A second dimension concerns distal and proximal factors that lead someone to become either a victim or an offender. *Distal* factors, such as time, physical distance or a presumed chain of social conditions, are those that are further removed from the crime in several ways, while *proximal* causes are close to the event both in time and space. Distal causes are not necessarily less powerful than proximal causes, and people may have the idea of a causal chain. The authors thus attempted to taxonomise lay beliefs about the causes of crime in the 2 x 2 matrix shown in Table 8.1.

TABLE 8.1. *Examples of Proximal and Distal Causes of Crime for Victims and Offenders*

	Victims	Offenders
Proximal causes	"You come in dressed up and looking affluent, and you become a target." "It's an unfortunate fact of life that senior citizens are an easy target." "I think they [victims] are careless as a rule. They leave their lights on. They don't lock the doors."	[Why do kids snatch purses?] "To buy their booze and drugs. . . . Actually, I think the booze is more than drugs . . ." [One cause of crime is that] "the judge lets 'em off too easy." "The problem was not that the community wasn't organised against crime but that the court system put convicted criminals back on the street.
Distal causes	"This area breeds crime. And it's very hard to organise, because the population is so transient." "As soon as I'm able, I want to live in the country . . . This isn't the kind of place now that I'd like to raise a family." "The most important facet of crime prevention is neighbourhood awareness. Unfortunately, people don't want to get involved if a crime happens . . ."	"young adults . . . bumming around because they don't have jobs." [One cause of crime is that] "parents don't care enough. . . ." [The structure of society causes crime] "It should go more socialistic." "I'd say the main reasons for our problems are (1) the projects . . . (2) the lack of employment and (3) welfare." "Sociologists say that's the root of crime anyway . . . deteriorated housing and lack of jobs."

Reproduced with permission from Kidder, L., and Cohn, E. (1979). Public views of crime and crime protection. In: I. Frieze, D. Baral and J. Carroll (Eds.). *New approaches to social problems*. San Francisco: Jossey-Bass.

TABLE 8.2. *The Most Frequently Mentioned Causes of Crime in Field Work Interviews and Two Sample Surveys*

	Michigan survey	Oregon survey	Field work interviews
First mention	Drugs/dope	Poverty	Economic situation; poverty, unemployment
Second mention	Kids; lack of activities and parental guidance	Environment	Drinking/drugs
Third mention	Unemployment; poverty	Alcohol	Kids; lack of activities, parental neglect
Fourth mention	Insufficient law enforcement; need for stricter laws	Insufficient law and order	Insufficient law enforcement

Reproduced with permission from Kidder, L., and Cohn, E. (1979). Public views of crime and crime prevention. In: I. Frieze, D. Baral and J. Carroll. (Eds.), *New approaches to social problems*. San Francisco: Jossey-Bass.

Other studies using different samples have shown different causes. Erskine (1974) noted that national surveys seem to show *six* major perceived causes of crime: unrest, polarisation, student protest, moral decay, drugs and youth problems, while Hindelang (1974) cites *four* major causes: lenient laws or gentle penalties, drugs or drug addiction, lack of parental supervision and poverty or unemployment. There have been other small- and large-scale surveys and Kidder and Cohn (1979) have attempted to classify these (see Table 8.2):

Interestingly, they found that certain explanations offered to the survey population were rarely endorsed as being a major cause of crime. These included: laziness, lack of religion, mental disorder, kicks, lack of moral standards and attitude towards the Government. The above results are, however, interesting for two reasons: the first is that people tend to mention external, environmental causes first rather than internal or personality dispositions. Secondly, although there are clear differences in the rank order of the results in the different surveys there is a fair degree of agreement between them. However, what these and other surveys do not tell us is which characteristics (psychographic or demographic) determine which causes a person will offer or endorse. Nor does it tell us the person's perceived relationship between causes. For instance, do people believe that poverty has an effect on drinking or drug taking and vice versa. But, as Furnham and Henderson (1983) point out, theories about the causes of crime, or more specifically delinquency, do not necessarily follow the same structure as lay theories about how to prevent crime.

In an attempt to codify crime prevention strategies within their 2 x 2 (Victim/Offender; Proximal/Distal) framework Kidder and Cohn (1979) note a paradox: When people *talk* about the *causes* of crime they stress social conditions and distal causes but when they decide to *act* they engage in victimisation protection. This may be because as individuals, people feel they cannot cure social injustice but they can personally prevent crime happening to them.

In other words, although crime is seen as a social problem caused by unemployment, poverty, drug addiction, etc., people attempt not crime-prevention but victimisation protection. People appear to operate with two disparate sets of theories — those about the causes of crime and those about the prevention of victimisation.

8.3 Lay Theories of Delinquency and Deviance

Probably because it frequently affects them personally, lay people often advance explanations, based on theories, of the causes of delinquency and deviance. In many ways lay people have as many, and as complex, theories as criminologists, which can be variously classified into *strain* theories (delinquency is the result of socially induced tension), *labelling* or control theories (certain people and acts are processed as deviant by agencies of social control) and *drift* theories (people drift into delinquency by the suspension of ordinarily accepted moral and legal obligations). Others have grouped or classified academic theories of crime and delinquency rather differently. For instance, Sullivan *et al.* (1985) have mentioned three quite different perspectives: *Functionalist* — crime and delinquency result from structural flaws in society not individual problems but because people are not fully integrated into the society; *Conflict* — delinquency is a social problem only when it threatens the values and interests of some group with the power to make its consensus felt; *Interactionist* — delinquency is a social problem to the extent that influential groups define it as such (i.e. there is consensus).

However one categorises academic theories, it is probably true to say that all explicit academic criminological theories of delinquency tend to the view that delinquency has a multiplicity of causes and is a complex phenomenon. Lay theories too reflect the complexity of the phenomenon. Yet, occasionally, the methodology employed in eliciting explanations or theories tends to imply they are, in fact, more simple than they really are. For instance, a number of polls have been carried out concerning beliefs about crime and delinquency. In the 1960s an American Gallup Poll asked "Which in your opinion is more to blame for crime and lawlessness in this country — the individual or society?" Nearly 60% felt that society was to blame compared with 35% who blamed the individual. In the 1970s the first two Gallup Polls found 60% of people interviewed favoured "clearing up social conditions as a promising method of crime reduction", while just under 40% chose improving conditions for rehabilitation in jails. A later poll, however, found that support for "law and order" techniques of crime control increased while belief that problems can be solved through social reform or treatment had declined. More recently a CBS/*New York Times* poll in 1977 (Jensen, 1981) found two-thirds of respondents felt that "a lot of the blame" for crime and delinquency could be attributed to "conditions of poverty and unemployment" and the "leniency of the law" while about 60% felt a lot of blame could be placed on "the way judges apply the law" or "the breakdown of religion and morality in families".

Erskine (1974) reviewed the findings of eight American polls from 1936 to 1973. She summarised her review of the polls thus:

> Six out of ten Americans blame society and its pressures for its own crime rate. Only a third would hold the individual wholly responsible for his unlawful acts. People excuse the individuals by laying the burden on the atmosphere of permissiveness that pervades today's society as a whole, the home and the criminal justice system alike. Though the public thus seems to take a sophisticated view of the individual's helplessness in his environment, they nevertheless sound authoritarian in their analyses of the crime problem. The trend, indeed, is for Americans to take an increasingly hard line in favour of severity in handling lawbreakers. (p. 288)

However interesting the results of these opinion polls might be they do not attempt any more than a very superficial analysis of the data. Furthermore, Jensen (1981) has noted " opinions about the causes of crime in the United States vary among people with different social backgrounds . . . there is evidence of variation by occupation, age, education, political party and region as well" (p. 8).

Simply asking binary questions, or getting people to endorse three or four statements about deviance in no way does sufficient justice to the complexity of their ideas.

Other studies have, however, attempted a more systematic investigation of people's ideas of the causes of deviance. In Britain, Banks *et al.* (1975) carried out a large survey on public attitudes to various aspects of crime and the penal system. Informants were presented with ten statements offering explanations for crime and were asked to choose those they thought most important. They concluded: "The main thing that seems to stand out from all these surveys is the general agreement about the causes of crime. A majority of people everywhere think that crime can be attributed to lack of parental discipline, although this feeling tends to be stronger in America than in Britain" (p. 240).

However, as Reuterman (1978) found in a study specifically focused on lay explanations of delinquency, while there are systematic variations among various segments of the public regarding views of causation, the general public seems to regard delinquency as resulting from different, possibly interrelated, causes. Although he found some demographic differences — notably that women blame home and family circumstances more than men — there was no systematic variation in the general (American) public along the dimensions of age, sex or socioeconomic status. These results should meet with virtually equal amounts of support or lack of support from various segments of the general public, "The public generally seems to regard delinquency as resulting from a multiplicity of causes" (p. 41).

There exist both sociological and psychological studies of specific groups' explanations or attributions for deviant behaviour. For instance, Hardiker and Webb (1979) examined the explanations of probation officers and found that they varied more than they originally anticipated, encompassing both determinist and voluntarist accounts. However, they did establish that the more serious the offender's criminal history or personal problems the more likely it was that the probation officer thought in determinist terms.

A few studies have attempted to look systematically at lay explanations of delinquency, by examining both the different dimensions (or theories) underlying lay explanations, as well as individual differences in the extent to which lay people rated the explanations as important. Furnham and Henderson (1983b) offered over 300 people, 30 explanations for delinquency in Britain which they were required to rate on a seven-point importance scale. Factor analysis yielded six clear factors. The first factor, which accounted for just under a fifth of the variance, contained items concerning a delinquent's *defective or inappropriate socialisation*. All of these items were rated as fairly important. The second factor, which accounted for nearly a tenth of the variance, contained items which tended to explain delinquency in terms of the young person's *mental instability or genetic deficit*. Overall, the subjects tended to find these explanations less important than those mentioned above. The third factor contained items which tended to reflect the belief that delinquents are *tempted by easy opportunities* to break the law or achieve easy money. The fourth factor contained items referring to the *excitement* that young people experience when performing delinquent acts. The fifth factor contained items which appeared to be related to anomie or the *alienation* theory of delinquency. The final factor contained explanations which refer almost exclusively to the *parents* of the delinquent being for some reason the cause of the delinquency.

Furnham and Henderson (1983b) also looked at various demographic differences, specifically sex, age and political beliefs. They found that females preferred explanations which referred to the delinquent's socialisation in the home and the school, while males placed more importance on explanations involving education and the inability to resist temptation. However, voting pattern showed the most difference (over 40%). The three which revealed greatest differences between the voting groups all referred to education/socialisation: "They have never been given strong parental guidance", "They have not had enough discipline at school", and "There has been a neglect in religious and moral education". On each factor right-wing voters thought the explanation more important. On the other hand, left-wing voters thought four explanations significantly more important in describing the causes of delinquency: "The existence of police prejudice and unfairness", "They see the obvious unequal distribution of wealth and income", "There exist no job opportunities and high unemployment", and "They have had an irrelevant education which has failed them". Two of these four loaded on factor 5 (alienation) which showed significant differences. Hence, whereas right-wing Conservatives see delinquency as a failure of socialisation, left-wing Labour voters see it as a consequence of an unjust society.

Whilst age and sex are the most commonly researched respondent variables, other variables have been shown to be of importance: these include socioeconomic status (Lentz, 1966; Reuterman, 1978), personality (Gudjonsson, 1984) and having an occupation involved with offenders (Hardiker and Webb, 1979; Reuterman and Cartwright, 1976).

However, not only do different groups of people have different theories for delinquency, but they vary according to the perception of the *offender*, and also the type of offence (Silverman *et al.*, 1984; French and Waites, 1982). In two studies Hollin and Howells (1987) set out to compare lay explanations for three types of crime — burglary, robbery and sexual assault. They found that whilst burglary and robbery were most likely to be explained by failing in education and parenting, sexual assault was most strongly explained in terms of mental instability. There were also various sex and age effects which, by and large replicated previous results. A second study replicated the first but did not find evidence of differences in explanation as a function of the race of the offender.

Both Furnham and Henderson's (1983) and Hollin and Howells' (1987) studies found that lay people tend to stress socialisation — particularly education and parents — which appears to have been neglected or understressed by sociological thinkers and only occasionally mentioned by psychological researchers under the rubric of differential association theory. Researchers in this area have attempted to describe some of the implications of lay theories of human behaviour. Hollin and Howells (1987) argue that these lay beliefs are related to beliefs about types of social control, may affect jurors' decision-making and may be important in the selection and training of such groups as probation, police and prison officers. Furnham and Henderson (1983), on the other hand, believe that the type of explanation that one offers for delinquency implies the sort of remedy that is necessary to suppress or eradicate it. Thus, if one believes that the primary cause of delinquency is due to poor education (neglect of moral education, no discipline in the schools) it is logical to attempt to change educational practices so as not to encourage delinquency (introduce religious and/or moral education, encourage greater discipline in schools). On the other hand, if one believes that delinquency is primarily due to social factors such as no job opportunities or inadequate leisure and recreational facilities, attempts to prevent delinquency would involve such things as Government expenditure on job creation schemes and/or more opportunities for recreation. If, however, one believed in personality/genetic explanations of delinquency it seems unclear as to which preventative measure is most appropriate, save the detection and incarceration of "delinquent-types".

8.4 Theories of Justice

Do people hold general theories or beliefs that enable them to apply general moral principles to specific events and to assess whether their own or others, behaviour is, in fact, just? Psychologists from various traditions — some interested in developmental, others in organisational and still others in social psychology, have suggested that people adhere to various "theories" which they apply to circumstances to evaluate justice.

(1) Equity Theory

It was Aristotle who distinguished between equality (where rewards are divided equally among individuals) and equity (where rewards are distributed according to merit). Equity theory — which is to be found in various forms in a number of social science disciplines like anthropology, economics and psychology — has a number of simple axioms: that people try to maximise their outcomes (outcome equals rewards minus costs); that groups can maximise their collective outcomes by developing fair systems of rewards and costs; and that the experience of inequity is unpleasant and that people will try to restore equity if it does not apply. The theory provides a scheme, or system, by which relationships are enacted according to rules about what is fair or just. The dominant principle is the ratio between inputs (investments) and outcomes. An easy, somewhat disputed, formula is as follows:

$$\frac{O_A}{I_A} = \frac{O_B}{I_B}$$

Where O is output, I is input and A and B are people. Thus a relationship is equitable where each participant's proportionate share of outcomes equals his/her proportionate share of inputs. In inequitable situations people may make adjustments to attempt to create equity by: altering one's own inputs or outputs; adjusting the other's outcomes or inputs and/or subjectively distorting the outcomes or inputs of either party.

Thus, equity theory may be applied to legal settings where one has to determine the equity between harm doers and victims, such as how much the harm doer should suffer or how much punishment should be prescribed. This may be demonstrated empirically in laboratory based studies. Thus, Austin *et al.* (1976) asked student subjects to determine the sentence of somebody who, in the getaway from a purse snatching, caused wounds (either moderate or severe) to the victim. As predicted, the less the victim was seen to suffer, the more lenient was the punishment assigned.

Thus, one may attempt to assess the extent to which people believe in equity theory and apply its principle to problems requiring decisions about justice. But the issue of *equity* or how much is contributed to an outcome is only one principle that one may apply. Another viewpoint is that of *equality*, namely that everybody should be equally rewarded independent of any level of input. A third principle is that of *need* where a calculation of input or output is not seen to be relevant — rather it is the extent to which people are in need.

There may, therefore, be different principles that individuals may apply to decisions involving justice. It is quite possible that with problems in a specific domain equity principles are applied, while with a different set of problems equality or need principles apply. Furthermore, if a person applies equity principles to a particular problem it is not certain which of a number of equity-restoration principles are applied.

(2) Justice Motives

There is a substantial literature on the just world hypothesis (Lerner, 1980; Rubin and Peplau, 1975) which may be stated thus: "Individuals have a need to believe that they live in a world where people generally get what they deserve. The belief that the world is just enables the individual to confront his physical and social environment as though they were stable and orderly" (Lerner and Miller, 1978, p. 1030). That is, there is an appropriate fit between what people do and what happens to them. Studies on the determinants of just world beliefs have shown that believers in a just world tend to be more authoritarian, religious, have internal locus of control beliefs, believe in the Protestant work ethic and are more likely to admire political leaders/social institutions, and to have negative attitudes towards the underprivileged (Rubin and Peplau, 1973). A number of American studies have shown that believers in a just world tend to be hostile and unsympathetic towards victims of social injustice, especially in cases where their suffering cannot be easily alleviated — hence people's desire to live in a just world leads not to justice but justification (Rubin and Peplau, 1975).

Most of the empirical work has concerned how, when and under what circumstances, people blame or derogate victims. It has been argued that an individual's major concern is his/her own deservingness of rewards and punishments. Concern with justice towards oneself often means that people ignore evidence of injustice, yet, not being personally threatened, they may actually offer help. However, when people's own state of deservingness is threatened they tend to blame victims and see them as direct causes of their own fate.

Thus, the extent to which one believes that there is a just world may substantially affect one's perception of what constitutes justice. However, as Furnham (1985e) pointed out, the just world concept in fact relates to two basic concepts, in that it is quite different believing that the world is *not* just (or *ajust*) as opposed to it being *unjust*. In the former case rewards and

TABLE 8.3. *Taxonomy of Ethical Ideologies*

Idealism	Relativism	
	High	Low
High	Situationists	Absolutists
	Rejects moral rules; advocates individualistic analysis of each act in each situation; relativistic	Assumes that the best possible outcome can always be achieved by following universal moral rules
Low	Subjectivists	Exceptionists
	Appraisals based on personal values and perspective rather than universal moral principles; relativistic	Moral absolutes guide judgments but pragmatically open to exceptions to these standards; utilitarian

Reproduced with permission from Forsyth, D. (1980). A taxonomy of ethical ideologies, *Journal of Personality and Social Psychology*, *39*, 175–184. Copyright (1980) by American Psychological Association. Reprinted by permission of author.

punishments are random, as there is no necessary or causal relationship between actions and their rewards. However, if the world is an unjust place the just and the good are punished, or at very least remain unrewarded. People may believe that the world is just, unjust or not just and these beliefs may in turn play a large part in their understanding of law, justice, punishment, etc.

(3) Ethical Ideologies

Based on the work of Sharp (1898) on individual moral judgements Forsyth (1980) has suggested that moral judgements may be parsimoniously described in terms of two factors: relativism and idealism. In the case of the former, some people reject universal moral rules in favour of relativism, while others believe in, and make use of, moral absolutes when making judgements. In the case of the second dimension, some individuals assume desirable consequences can be obtained if the right action is taken while others admit that often undesirable consequences mix with desirable ones. Hence, according to Forsyth (1980), there are essentially four basic ethic ideologies (see Table 8.3).

As Forsyth (1980) has noted, the situationist ideology is found in the works of Fletcher and the absolutist ideology in the works of Kant. He demonstrated that a person's ethical position predicted well their attitudes to contemporary moral issues, such as test-tube babies, mercy killing, marijuana use, homosexuality and abortion. Thus absolutists, more than all others, felt that test-tube creation was immoral; mercy killing should not be tolerated; marijuana use, homosexuality and abortion were wrong. On the other hand the situationists were the most liberal, particularly in regard to euthanasia. Later Forsyth (1981) in a study concerned with the attribution of responsibility found, as predicted, that absolutists judged a hypothetical actor more harshly than exceptionists, but only when the described actor had foreseen or intended to produce a highly negative consequence.

> Absolutists relative to others, attribute extra responsibility to those who produce negative outcomes, judge these outcomes less favourably and attribute less morality to those who are to blame. Exceptionists, on the other hand, tend to be more favourable, due to their willingness to overlook negative consequences and situationists are less likely to allow for justifying factors when extremely negative consequences are involved. (p. 223)

More recently, Forsyth and Berger (1982) found that although variations in ethical ideology may predict individual differences in moral judgement they do not predict differences in moral behaviour. However, they did find that self-devaluation was most pronounced among absolutists; exceptionists reported increased happiness the more they cheated, situationists' self-ratings were not clearly related to the morality of their actions, and subjectivists showed signs of fear of detection. Once again, then, the particular ideology that a person holds may affect his or her legal judgements.

Of course, these three concepts — equity theory, just world beliefs and ethical ideologies — may overlap and it may be possible to determine a person's position on all three if one knows their position on the one. Many interesting questions remain, however: What is the aetiology of these beliefs? How and when do they change? Are they situation specific or general? Nevertheless, they remain interesting and potentially useful cognitive individual variables that may be used to predict lay legal behaviour.

8.5 Attitudes to Punishment

The role of punishment in learning or controlling behaviour has been of interest not only to psychologists and sociologists but also to philosophers and ethicists. Of course, lay people have also debated the efficacy and morality of punishment and proverbs reflect this. Thus we have "spare the rod and spoil the child" and "an eye for an eye, a tooth for a tooth". For many years arguments have been put forward as to the efficacy of punishment. Consider the conclusions of Walters *et al.* (1972):

> The evidence suggests that moderately intense consistently administered punishment can be effective in suppressing undesired behaviour and that . . . side effects of punishment may even be facilitating via increments in attention to elements of the task at hand. Moreoover, the absence of punishment is frequently taken as tacit approval of behaviour. Thus in attempting to use non reward to eliminate undesired behaviour the agent may be inadvertently strengthening these behaviours. Furthermore, the use of indirect methods such as withdrawal of attention or redirection of attention may not provide as clearly the important information upon which to base subsequent choices. Thus direct punishment may have the advantage of promoting the child's ability to make a conscious choice relative to indirect techniques of discipline. (p. 383)

The arguments in favour of punishment as an effective way of shaping behaviour are essentially threefold. First, punishment is an effective way of eliminating undesirable behaviour if (and only if) alternative behavioural responses are available and rewarded. Second, because avoiding a threatened punishment can be rewarding, in that it is a reduction of anxiety, a symbol of actual threatened punishment such as a policeman can be very effective. Third, punishment can be informative, in that it can provide useful feedback on behaviour.

On the other hand, some have argued that punishment is not only morally wrong but an ineffective way of controlling behaviour. Often punishment does not prescribe an alternative behaviour; it simply tries to suppress an existing one. Thus, it is feasible that an even more undesirable behaviour may be substituted for the punished one. Secondly, it has been established that punishment can "fix" or encourage a behaviour (such as bed wetting) rather than punish it. This may be due to the fear or anxiety induced by the punishment or fear of punishment. Thirdly, certain by-products of punishment such as the hatred of the inflictor or a phobia about the place of punishment may result which are, in themselves, highly undesirable. Furthermore, various psychological studies seem to indicate that, frequently, punishment temporarily suppresses behaviours, it does not weaken them, and that as soon as the punishment ceases the behaviour returns.

Hogarth (1971) has suggested that there are essentially three punishment philosophies (or sentence strategies) widespread among lay people, philosophers and lawyers though this a rather old-fashioned trichotomy. These are:

1. *Punishment* (retribution): The attempt to impose a just punishment on the offender, in the sense of being in proportion to the severity of the crime and his culpability, whether or not such a penalty is likely to prevent further crime in him or others. 2. *Reformation* (rehabilitation): The attempt to change the offender through treatment or corrective measures, so that when given the chance he will refrain from committing crime. 3. *General deterrence* (deterrence): The attempt to impose a penalty on the offender before the court sufficiently severe that potential offenders among the general public will refrain from committing further crime through fear of punishment. (p. 70)

In a study using measures of this system McFather (1978) found: "Deterrence sentences were the most severe for all crimes, whereas the rehabilitation sentences were the least severe for serious crimes only. Surprisingly, the rehabilitation group subjects consistently blamed the victim of the crime more than did the other groups" (p 41).

As well as general beliefs about the efficacy and morality of punishment there have been various surveys of public attitudes to specific crime and punishment. In a study of over 3000 members of the British public, Hough and Mayhew (1985) found that recommended punishments varied as a function of the crime, but also found a fair degree of congruence between the courts and the public in terms of imprisonment. Consider the example set out in Table 8.4.

Although prison is a popular form of punishment, this was not true for all

TABLE 8.4. *Sentences for 25-year-old Offenders: Preferences of the Respondents compared with Court Practice for Selected Offences*

	Robbery (%)	Burglary (%)	Shop-lifting (%)	Car theft (%)	Drugs (%)
Respondents' preferences (offender aged 25 with previous convictions)					
Prison	85	62	12	23	15
Discharge/caution	1	1	16	10	23
Community service	5	10	18	17	7
Other disposal	10	27	54	50	55
Total	100	100	100	100	100
Court practice for offenders aged 25 (including first offenders)					
Prison	92	61	10	31	11
Discharge/caution	1	2	11	6	11
Community service	1	8	5	11	2
Other disposal	6	29	74	52	76
Total	100	100	100	100	100

Reproduced with permission from Hough, M., and Mayhew, P. (1985). *Taking Account of Crime*. London: HMSO.

crimes. This is all the more true because of overcrowding and violence in prisons. Hough and Mayhew (1985) found that:

in response to questions about ways of reducing the prison population:
* 86% of respondents said that it was a good idea to "make some non-violent offenders do community service instead of going to prison";
* 82% favoured "making some non-violent offenders pay compensation to their victims instead of going to prison";
* 69% favoured "giving shorter sentences to people guilty of non-violent crimes";
* 67% favoured "fining people guilty of non-violent crimes instead of sending them to prison";
* 58% favoured weekend imprisonment;
* 51% favoured extending the parole system; and
* 40% thought that it was a good idea to release prisoners on remission after serving half their sentence, rather than the present two-thirds." (p. 45–46)

Various attempts have been made to assess people's general attitudes towards punishment or punitiveness (Viney *et al.* 1982).

A number of attempts have been made to examine specific psychological belief systems and attitudes to punishment. For instance, Viney *et al.* (1982) believed general beliefs about free will vs determinism would predict attitudes to punishment. Specifically they hypothesised that libertarians (those that believe in free will) would consistently recommend more punitive measures for behavioural deviations than determinists. They found the precise opposite, however, and believed this may be due to the burdensome moral responsibility which punishment represents to those who believe in free will and hence demand it is administered with scrupulous attention to fairness and justice. However, they concluded that "there is no empirical basis for believing that libertarians are categorically more punitive than determinists; the opposite is also true'' (pp. 945–946).

Similarly, Ryckman *et al.* (1986) did not find that high, as opposed to low, authoritarians endorsed the use of harsher strategies for all crimes. High authoritarians were more likely to endorse harsher strategies (specific and general deterrence), but only when judging harsher crimes like murder, rape and manslaughter — not for lesser crimes such as burglary and robbery.

It seems, then, that lay people's beliefs about the efficacy and desirability of punishment are multidimensional. Nevertheless, there appears to be a general dimension of pro- vs anti-punishment. It seems intuitively reasonable that conservative beliefs are associated with punishment and retribution and liberal beliefs with education, though, as the literature has shown, this intuition may be too simple.

8.6 Legal Reasoning

A training in law provides, no doubt, many skills. It is important to know the law but also to present one's case persuasively. Although lay people may not actually know much law, except those with which they frequently come into contact, they may nevertheless be able to reason and argue legal points.

The following problems have been set to test the legal thinking of lay people. The vignettes offer the possibility of a variety of arguments:

> Below you will find two sets of rules, one relating to Murder, one relating to Negligence. You will also find various sets of facts, which give rise to the question of whether a murder is committed, or whether a person is negligent. On the basis of the rules provided in this paper, you will be expected to indicate your conclusion in relation to one or more of these set of facts, giving reasons wherever necessary. In some cases, you may consider that the full and strict application of the rules leads to a result which is unfair or unreasonable: in such cases, you are asked to formulate in your own mind the text of a further rule designed to mitigate the harsh or unreasonable effects of the rules already given.
> (A) *Murder*
> > Rules: 1. If someone deliberately kills another person, then that is murder;
> > 2. If someone causes serious injury to another, who subsequently dies of those injuries, then that is murder.
> Consider the following situation:
> * Peter stabs John, a Jehovah's Witness. Because of his faith John refuses the blood transfusion that he knows will save his life. He dies. Murder/Not Murder?
> * Michael fires a high velocity hunting rifle at Tony. His shot misses, and hits Barbara, who dies. Murder/Not Murder?

* Dennis and Tom are bank robbers. As they speed away in their getaway car, public spirited Louis backs his car into their path. They swerve, hit a lamp post, and both are killed Murder/Not Murder?
* Margaret puts a drawing pin on Arthur's seat. Arthur, a haemophiliac, bleeds to death. Murder/Not Murder?

(B) *Negligence*

Rule: A person is liable in negligence if his careless act causes foreseeable loss or damage to another person.

Consider the following situations:

* John has his leg broken by Peter's careless driving. With his leg in plaster he has great difficulty on stairs. He falls, and fractures his skull, for which he sues Peter.
* Dave falls from the deck of Larry's yacht after tripping on carelessly arranged ropes. Alexis dives into the icy water to save Dave, but drowns. Larry himself dives in and rescues Dave. Alexis' next of kin wish to sue (a) Larry and (b) Dave.

The number and type of arguments that people put forward in favour of a particular case allow one to ascertain the sort of legal reasoning processes that people go through. Clearly some lay people are more able, confident and persuasive than others. Precisely which factors determine this ability are unclear, though no doubt education and intelligence are important factors.

8.7 Fear of Crime

Fear of crime refers to a person's fear or anxiety about becoming a victim of crime, especially that of burglary, mugging and rape. Fear of crime is not the same as assessment of risk (Garofalo and Lamb, 1982), as someone may believe their chances of being a victim are high but remain relatively unworried (perhaps fatalistically) while another person may know that the actual chances are remote yet be highly anxious. This fear of crime or anxiety about victimisation is determined not only by the perceived likelihood of falling victim, but also by expected consequences and, therefore, people have different reactions to similar incidents.

Various people have attempted to categorise the variables that may determine fear of crime. Yin (1980) has suggested these factors, "fearful individual" (demographic characteristics, residential locale); social determinants (previous victimisation, social support systems, etc.) and psychological determinants (perceived probability about being victimised). Another way of characterising salient variables according to Kennedy and Silverman (1985) are demographic (age, sex, income), environmental (household, neighbourhood), behavioural (socialisation patterns) and social psychological (satisfaction with police protection).

Various large- and small-scale studies have been conducted in Britain and America to assess people's fear of crime. For instance, in a large-scale nationwide study done in Great Britain, Hough and Mayhew (1985) looked at such things as the extent and pattern of fear; how fear relates to risk and affects its behaviour, perceptions of risks, etc. They summarised their findings thus:

  * Women, the elderly and those in inner cities registered most anxiety about walking alone in their neighbourhood after dark. Fear of falling victim to robbery or "mugging" plays a large part here, though more diffuse and unfocused anxieties appear to be implicated too.

  * Asked how worried they were about different crimes, women expressed most fear of rape. Four out of ten women under 30 said they were "very worried". Aside from the alarming nature of the offence, exaggerated estimates of its likelihood may underpin some of this worry.

  * Burglary causes widespread anxiety, in particular among women. The degree of worry in different areas tracks actual burglary risks, suggesting that most people have some grasp of the *relative* likelihood of break-ins. On the poorest council estates, where risks were highest — 19 attempted and actual break-ins per 100 homes in 1983 — four out of ten residents said they were "very worried" about burglary.

  * Even so, people in all areas tended to exaggerate the risks of burglary. Over half of respondents saw it as the most common crime in their area. Overestimation of actual risks is highest in areas where burglary is relatively infrequent, and those who overestimate most express most anxiety.

  * Worry about becoming the victim of "mugging" is as widespread among women as worry about burglary, though relative to other age-groups neither elderly men nor women appeared disproportionately worried. Again, people overestimated the risks of mugging: nearly one in six people thought they were very or fairly likely to be a victim in the next year.

  * Fear of crime restricts people's behaviour. Half the women in the sample, for instance, said they avoided going out unaccompanied after dark; in high-crime areas one person in 25 said they *never* went out after dark wholly or in part because of fear of crime. The figure for the elderly in these localities was 18%.

  * Across the country as a whole, crime and vandalism are outranked as the worst problems of local areas by other social and environmental factors. However, crime and vandalism takes the lead in multiracial areas and in the poorest council estates. Crime levels and fear of crime were also highest in these areas. (p. 41)

There have also been many fear of crime studies in North America. Many studies have attempted to identify the most salient predictors of fear of crime among certain sub-groups. For instance, Kennedy and Silverman (1985) found the most significant factors associated with fear of crime among the elderly was sex, social isolation, type of housing, length of residence and area of the city. Further, social interaction with neighbours and friends reduced fear of crime among the elderly. Many factors have been suggested such as loneliness, but in many studies sex appears to be the most powerful determinant with females being more afraid than males (Silverman and Kennedy, 1985). Studies on television viewing and fear and mistrust are relevant to fear of crime. Studies done in the 1970s in America tended to show that heavy television viewing was associated with greater fear of being victims of crime and violence, greater mistrust of authority and less hope for the future (Gerbner and Gross, 1976). For instance, when asked "During any given week, what are your chances of being involved in some kind of violence?" Americans said one in ten, while police records indicated less than one in a hundred, yet at the time of analysing over 64% of fictional characters became involved in some form of violence. Similarly, when asked "What percent of all crimes are violent crimes like murder, rape, robbery and aggravated assault?" respondents said 25%, while official statistics suggested 10%, yet 77% of fictional crime was of this sort.

Gerbner *et al.* (1977) write:

> Violence plays a key role in television's portrayal of the social order. It is the simplest and cheapest dramatic means to demonstrate who wins in the game of life and the rules by which the game is played. It tells us who are the aggressors and who are the victims. It demonstrates who has the power and who must acquiese to that power. . . . In the portrayal of violence there is a relationship between the roles of the violent and the victim. Both roles are there to be learned by the viewers. In generating among the many a fear of the power of the few, television violence may achieve its greatest effect. (p. 180)

However, attempts to replicate this finding in other countries have not succeeded (Wober, 1978). This could be due to actual national differences, various methodological problems or the more plausible fact that real levels of violence in different localities jointly determine views of the reality of social threat *and* the amount of viewing done if people watch TV, so escaping what they perceive to be a frightening world.

Studies done in other countries such as Australia, Holland and Sweden have provided equivocal findings. A major problem in this area, however, is that all the studies are correlational, hence it is difficult to infer direction or causality, or the possibility of other mediating variables. Much of this work is based on the cultivation theory, which has a number of assumptions. Firstly, television viewers see fictional programmes depicting people and events considerably different from those in the real world. Secondly, a "reality shift" occurs such that viewers are influenced in their view of the real world by the content of what they see on television, and this is more true of heavy viewers. Thirdly, the imagery on television not only affects viewers' beliefs about the real world, but also produces feelings to correspond with those beliefs. Value systems may change and with them related behaviour such as calls for stricter law enforcement, more police, harsher treatment of criminals, etc.

More recently, Gunter and Wakshlag (1986) showed that television viewing patterns were relatively weak and inconsistent indicators of judgements about crime once six other more important factors were taken into account. These were the perceived likelihood of victimisation for others and self; fear of victimisation for self; demographic characteristics of respondents; their direct experience with crime; but most of all their confidence in personal ability to defend themselves against an unarmed attacker. However, heavier viewing of soap operas and crime drama was associated with various beliefs such as the greater perceived likelihood of personal victimisation in one's own neighbourhood. Heavier television viewing in total was related to greater fear of victimisation in many areas, while heavier viewing of action adventure programmes was associated with greater concern for personal safety close to home. The authors concluded from their research:

> There was once again (with one exception) little evidence of any relationship between likelihood perceptions concerning involvement in crime or fear of self victimisation and viewing specifically of content-relevant (i.e. crime-drama) television programming. With respect to fear of crime, viewing of particular categories of programmes seemed to be less relevant than simply how much television is consumed overall. This may indicate that if television is the causal agent, it really does not matter which programmes individuals watch. Rather, it is general levels of exposure that are most significant. Alternatively, it could be that television is the affected agent, with viewing levels being influenced among other things by the fearfulness of individuals. Those who have greatest anxieties about possible dangers to self in the social environment may be driven to spend more time indoors watching the box. Probably nearest to the truth though may be a notion of circulinity in the relationship. Greater fear of potential danger in the social environment may encourage people to stay indoors, where they watch more television, and are exposed to programmes which tell them things which in turn reinforce their anxieties. (p. 19)

8.8 Is There a Criminal Type?

Lay people, as well as early writers, have suggested that criminals are characterised by particular personality profiles or physical appearances. This is a popular approach, though it remains uncertain as to which individual differences lead to crime or how, indeed, this occurs.

However, it should be pointed out that some lay people prefer sociological or psychoanalytic explanations for crime. Sociological explanations link crime with poverty, inequalities in wealth, capitalism, etc. People who prefer psychoanalytic-type explanations stress the importance of unconscious thought processes and infantile experiences on adult behaviour. But the majority of lay theories are psychological, in the sense that they believe certain traits or individual differences are the major causes of crime.

Although there are a few theories relating antisocial behaviour and individual differences, the most celebrated and empirically tested theory is that of Eysenck (1964). The theory, which is derived from both psychobiology and learning theory, suggests that criminals and delinquents tend to score more highly than non-delinquents on measures of extroversion, neuroticism and psychoticism. It is supposed that extroverts are less socialised than introverts due to poor conditionability and, hence, are more prone to antisocial behaviour. In other words, they do not learn right and wrong as quickly and effectively. Furthermore, neurotics with habitual antisocial responses will tend to repeat antisocial acts more than non-neurotics since anxiety is said to act as a drive which multiplies with habit. Finally, tough-minded people who are less likely to feel empathy, guilt or sensitivity for the feelings of others are more likely to engage in antisocial acts than those who are not as tough-minded.

Although the studies on known groups of criminals and delinquents are equivocal, studies of self-reported delinquency and antisocial behaviour among "normal" populations have tended to confirm Eysenck's (1964) hypothesis. It is, however, quite possible that the theory applies more to normal non-delinquent populations than to delinquent populations. Early studies did not find much confirming evidence for this theory. Little (1963) found that a large group of borstal inmates did not differ significantly from the norms of a normal non-delinquent sample and that inmates who were released from the institution relatively quickly did not differ in their personality scores from those discharged later from the institution. Similarly, Hoghughi and Forrest (1970) found persistent young offenders not to be significantly more extroverted but introverted, so casting doubt on Eysenck's theory.

Studies on non-delinquent populations provided more support for the theory. Allsop and Feldman (1976) found a positive significant relationship between extroversion and tough-mindedness on both self-reported and teacher-assessed measures of "bad" behaviour. Similarly, Shapland et al. (1975) found extroversion (but not neuroticism) scores significantly related to a self-report measure of delinquency, particularly among girls. More recently, Rushton and Chrisjohn (1981) found clear support for a relationship between high delinquency scores and high scores on both extraversion and psychoticism, but not neuroticism. Similarly, Putnins (1982) found that the tough-mindedness, but not the extraversion or neuroticism, scale discriminated between groups differing in offender status (in his case male non-delinquent high school vs delinquent boys aged 15–18). The discrepancy and lack of consistency in the findings of extraversion, neuroticism and tough-mindedness scorers with studies of offenders casts doubts on the status of the theory.

However, some of the above experiments have looked at antisocial and amoral rather than illegal and immoral behaviour (Allsop and Feldman, 1976), while others have used comparatively small samples (Shapland et al. 1975) and some have ignored sex differences (Rushton and Chrisjohn, 1981).

Finally, none of the researchers have suggested why neuroticism has not been shown to be linked to delinquency as Eysenck (1964) predicted.

Yet there remains considerable evidence for Eysenck's theory (Furnham, 1984). But this is not only personality or individual difference theory. Social skills theorists have argued that criminals and delinquents are socially inadequate and not able to communicate effectively with others. It has been suggested that some people commit antisocial acts and behave maladaptively because they lack the requisite social skills to do otherwise or have no legally acceptable ways of achieving their desired goals. Numerous studies to test this hypothesis have been done on young prisoners (Fawcett *et al.*, 1979), arsonists (Rice and Chapman, 1979) and sex offenders (Able *et al.*, 1976).

However, some studies have looked specifically at juvenile delinquents. Rotenberg (1974) compared delinquents and non-delinquents on a cognitive role-taking (guessing game) and an affective role-taking task. Whilst the two groups showed a similar level of ability in predicting another's mental state (cognitive role-taking skills), the delinquents scored significantly lower on the disposition to decrease another's suffering (affective role-taking skills). Similarly, Freedman *et al.* (1979) found that delinquent males' verbal responses to a series of problem situations were rated as less competent than those of a non-delinquent control group matched for age, intelligence and social background. The delinquents used a more limited range of response alternatives in solving interpersonal problems and tended more to verbal and physical aggression. More recently, Spence (1981) compared 18 male delinquent offenders with a group of non-delinquent controls matched for age, academic performance and social background on a short standardised interview. In this careful behavioural study Spence found the delinquent group less socially skilled than the non-delinquent group. Furnham (1984d), however, found no evidence that there was an association between social skills and self-reported delinquency.

The evidence, therefore, for both academic schools of thought about crime and individual differences is equivocal. This, however, does not prevent lay people believing that there are criminal types. As can be seen from the introduction to this chapter, as well as the section on lay attributions for delinquency, people do have fairly complicated theories, most of which do imply some sort of criminal type.

8.9 The Police the Public and Crime

One of the more practical aspects of lay theories of crime concerns lay people's attitudes to crime detection and prevention, and more specifically, the role of the police.

More work appears to have been done on the police themselves than on attitudes to the police. For instance, Burbeck and Furnham (1985) reviewed a large number of studies concerned specifically with individual differences between the police and other groups. Studies have looked at general values, conservatism and authoritarianism, as well as personality and intelligence. They have, by and large, failed to describe the "typical police personality" or shown policemen and women to be very significantly different from non-police people. More importantly, where differences exist it is unclear if these are due to predispositional or socialisation factors. In other words, is it that people with particular personalities and beliefs (e.g. high in authoritarianism) join the police force (the predispositional model) or that the experience of being in the police force shapes and changes one's values, beliefs and cognition (the socialisation model).

However, the public's beliefs about, and attitude towards, the police probably shows most clearly people's lay theories as to the role, function, efficacy, etc., of the police. Although some studies have concentrated on very specific features, such as attitudes to policewomen (Koenig and Juni, 1981), there have been some general studies on lay people's beliefs about, and attitudes towards, the police. For instance, Belson (1975) reported on a fairly large study of the attitudes, beliefs and behaviours of adults in London, in relation to the Metropolitan Police force. Some 1200 adults, 503 young people and 1000 police officers were sampled in the study, which considered everything from the social philosophy of the police and their views about the characteristics of the public to the public's knowledge about the duties of policemen and of policing arrangements.

These studies on lay theories of policing are interesting but limited. Firstly, they are restricted in time and context, in that these attitudes may be fairly volatile and liable to change as a consequence of personal experience (be it positive or negative, or widely reported events). Furthermore, they are, no doubt, context specific, in that people from different sub-groups (e.g. natives vs migrants); in different parts of a country (e.g. urban vs rural); and from different countries (e.g. democratic vs non-democratic) have quite different attitudes and beliefs. Secondly, as has been consistently demonstrated, attitudes are not necessarily predictive of actions and thus could not be used as a substitute for behavioural information.

Nevertheless, attitudes to the police — their behaviour, function and efficacy — are bound up in lay people's attitudes to beliefs about, and theories of, the law, legal practice and justice.

8.10 Conclusion

Although some research has been concerned with lay people's knowledge of the law, crime statistics, etc., the most interesting work in this field stems from an attribution theory viewpoint. Most studies have been concerned with taxonomising lay explanations for the causes of crime; lay beliefs about most effective crime prevention methods and lay theories of delinquency and deviance.

Once again, it seems that lay theories to a large extent mirror academic theories. Hence, lay people may offer economic, psychological or sociological theories for the origin of delinquency, though they, like criminologists and other experts, do appear to believe that crime arises through a multiplicity of causes. Similarly, certain demographic and psychological features of people appear to be systematically related to the explanation or theory they tend to support. Perhaps the two most interesting suggestions to emerge from this research which suggests that lay explanations are crime-specific and thus general theories or explanations do not apply equally to all crimes and delinquent acts. The second suggestion, for it is no more than that, is that people appear to be more certain about punishment than cause and thus may infer the latter from the former, rather than the other way around.

The chapter also reviewed a number of belief systems concerning justice. These are widely held beliefs or hypotheses about the world that lead people to think and act in characteristic ways. They are, in a sense, "personality" variables and have been treated as such in the literature. They may, for instance, predict a lay person's attitudes to the efficacy of, and necessity for, punishment, a topic that has been much debated by social scientists and lay people alike.

A topic that has received comparatively little attention is the extent to which lay people can, and do, reason and argue as lawyers. That is, are the logical principles of argument from legal definitions and crime facts found among lay people as well as trained barristers and attorneys? Interesting though this topic is it appears to have received very little attention.

The sort of topic that has interested psychologists is whether there is a criminal type — whether some individuals, due to their personal history or unique personality are more predisposed to criminal acts than others. The evidence is equivocal, though there is sufficient evidence that certain personality features are associated with apprehended acts of crime and delinquency to suggest that there is indeed some merit in the suggestion.

Finally, some literature on attitudes to the police was reviewed. Far fewer studies have been concerned with attitudes to judges, juries, probation officers and other bodies and officials concerned with the administration of law and justice. Though these studies may be restricted in both time and space they do give an insight into lay theories of legal justice and practice.

9

Lay Theories in Education

9.1 Introduction

Lay theories, as well as explicit formal theories, of education usually cover a wide range of issues. Frequently they concern not only *what* should/or should not be taught to *whom*, and *when*, but more importantly *how* this should be done. Furthermore because education is supposed to develop certain qualities (knowledge, understanding, compassion, etc.) it becomes an issues of debate which qualities need to be encouraged and which not. It is precisely because lay theories in education cover such wide issues that professional and lay people become so passionate about educational issues.

It is customary for philosophers of education to make conceptual distinctions between education, schooling, instruction and pedagogy. Richmond (1975) notes that education is to schooling as theory is to practice: schooling is what we get, education is what we are supposed to receive. Schooling provides instruction, custodial care, socialisation and classification. Thus schooling is necessarily formal and deliberate, but education can be both informal and non-deliberate. Education is what one makes of schooling and is perfectly possible in the absence of schooling.

Although the term education is more widely used, most lay, but not academic theories are about schooling. A good deal of the philosophy and sociology of education involves an explication of different theories of *both* education *and* schooling. Some have debated the very nature of that theory (Hirst, 1960), others the virtue of theory building, possession and use (Richmond, 1968). Some theoretical approaches are concerned with the *aims* of education, others with the *content*, and still others with the *method*, though more sophisticated and integrated theories are naturally concerned with all three (Hirst and Peters, 1975).

For Carr (1986) current academic theorising adopts one of four approaches: *Common sense* — here principles are not derived from theory but the obverse, in that they are generalisations acquired through observation and analysis (recovery and articulation) of practice and tested pragmatically in practical situations; *Applied science* — questions about means (of teaching) but not ends (because they involve value judgements) can be treated empirically in line with approach of any applied science; *Practical* — this is an

TABLE 9.1. *Examine your Perspective on Education. Circle the Number that Describes your own Commitment to Basic Aims of Education in Society*

Individual	1	2	3	4	5	6	7	Society
Child-centred	1	2	3	4	5	6	7	Subject-centered
Guidance	1	2	3	4	5	6	7	Instruction
Discussion	1	2	3	4	5	6	7	Lecture
Pupil planning	1	2	3	4	5	6	7	Teacher planning
Intrinsic motivation	1	2	3	4	5	6	7	Extrinsic motivation
Insight learning	1	2	3	4	5	6	7	Drill and practice
Growth	1	2	3	4	5	6	7	Achievement
First-hand experience	1	2	3	4	5	6	7	Vicarious experience
Freedom	1	2	3	4	5	6	7	Dominance
Democratic	1	2	3	4	5	6	7	Authoritarian
Subjective world	1	2	3	4	5	6	7	Objective world
Spontaneity	1	2	3	4	5	6	7	Conformity

anti-empirical process, case-study or naturalistic approach which aims to reveal the tacit and previously unacknowledged assumptions inherent in education; *Critical* — this approach seeks to explain how objective factors constrain teachers' perceptions and beliefs and distorts knowledge and hence hopes to promote self-knowledge. In other words, these four approaches represent theories of theory *and* practice in that they are concerned with recovering the logic of educational practice implicit in the conceptive structures of educational theorising.

But more than a concern with the relationship between educational theory and practice are basic debates about the aims of education in society as a whole. There is a whole range of issues which divide lay people.

To some extent it may be suggested that the above list falls nicely into two sides — the more one endorses values on the left the more liberal or modern one is in one's aims, while the more one tends to the aims in the right-hand column the less liberal but more old fashioned one is in one's views. That, however, would be too simple, as one could easily demonstrate empirically. Nevertheless, the table provides a useful list of the major dimensions or arguments that underly lay beliefs about the aims of education.

Apart from the conceptual work which has gone into making various distinctions in this area, there have been a number of *public opinion surveys* in all countries which give some insight into people's lay theories of education. For instance, Madaus *et al.* (1979) tried to determine the opinions of the Irish public on educational goals. Whereas 72% find the amount of emphasis schools place on the teaching of traditional subjects "just right", 58% found the emphasis on religion "just right" and 25% "too little". While 70% felt "too little" emphasis was placed on preparing students for married life and 52% said "too little" emphasis was placed on helping children value music, art and literature. Again 53% found schools emphasise "too little" education for work and 44% said schools emphasise "too little" helping children achieve financial success. Overall, there were many more differences between urban and rural respondents, and the parent and non-parent groups which indicated that rural respondents who were themselves frequently less well educated were far less critical of the educational goals and achievements in their country.

Kelleghan *et al.* (1981) investigated a large adult Irish population's views on educational innovation. The majority saw a number of changes as beneficial: raising school age to 15 (93%); change in school management (76%); provision of sex education in schools (68%); having boys and girls in the same class (68%); comprehensive schools (65%) and the abolition of corporal punishment (58%). As part of the same study Fontes *et al.* (1983) looked at public opinion about examinations. Over two-thirds of the 1000 subject sample thought the public exam to be a fair assessment of what a child learned at school (69%) and that the skills measured by examinations do matter in later life (67%). The group believed that having the school-leaving certificate affected one's choice of further education (93%); the kind of job one gets (90%); one's promotional prospects (73%); and one's social status (61%) but not the amount of money one makes (52%).

There have also been large studies in America (Gallup 1983). The American public sees things such as lack of discipline, use of drugs, poor curriculum and standards, and lack of proper financial support as major problems confronting the schools as well as to a lesser extent, difficulty in getting good teachers, teachers' lack of interest, and parents' lack of interest. Lack of discipline was blamed on a number of different causes: lack of discipline in the home (72%); lack of respect for law and authority throughout society (54%); students who are constant troublemakers often cannot be removed from school (42%); some teachers are not properly trained to deal with discipline problems (42%). A majority of respondents believed elementary school children (61%) and high school students (65%) were not required to work hard enough. A majority (40%) were in favour of increasing the length of the school year. There seemed to be considerable agreement about the most useful subjects in school. In rank order they were: mathematics, English, history, science, business and foreign language. A majority also believed the following subjects should be taught in schools: drug abuse, alcohol abuse, driver education, computer training, parent training, dangers of nuclear waste, race relations and communism/socialism.

The 1983 Gallup study showed that respondents rank ordered the most desirable personal qualities in teachers thus: ability to communicate/understand/relate, patient, ability to discipline to high moral character, friendliness/sense of humour, dedication/enthusiasm, ability to motivate, intelligence and caring about students.

These surveys are interesting for a number of reasons. They give a snapshot of public opinion of a particular population at a particular time. Hence, comparisons can be made over time to determine the effect of educational changes. Surveys can also show which demographic variables (e.g. age or wealth) show major differences in opinions about education though they do not necessarily give any insight as to why these differences occur. Thirdly, the surveys can show the relationship between various aspects of lay opinions about education, i.e. perceptions of the most useful disciplines, the use of corporal punishment and the most desirable qualities in teachers. Though rarely done, this sort of analysis can reveal some structure to the underlying theories of education as a whole.

9.2 Common Sense

There is no shortage of books and papers in education which purport to discuss "common sense" or at least have the term in their title. Wilson (1979), for instance, has argued "that when things go badly wrong in education, the chief cause is not ignorance or lack of empirical research, or practical incompetence or shortage of resources, but the operation of some powerful (and often unconscious) fantasy that prevents us from approaching the subject seriously and from using our common sense" (p.3). Fantasies are thus contrasted with reasonably held ideas and beliefs though it is unclear how to distinguish the two.

Others appear to contrast common sense to academic writing. Thus Elvin (1977) notes:

> There is a considerable area where we should not be afraid to argue from general good sense, no doubt supplemented by such specialist reading as we can manage; and that in particular it is important for teachers and student teachers to bring their own good sense to bear even though the writings of specialist, philosopher sociologists and psychologists may seem frighteningly recondite. (p.73)

> What moral and analytical philosophers have written on these things is important but a great deal of what ought to be said can be said at the level of hard-thinking yet sensitive commonsense. (p.89)

Goodnow (1980) has described these common-sense notions of education and development as "everyday" theories and has argued that there are three central questions in this area: What is the content of these theories/models? What techniques can we use to discover them? What use can we make of them? She has argued that we can frequently discover these from looking at people's ratings of desirable outcomes of education — e.g. obedience, respectfulness, hard work. In other words, we can get at common-sense views of education by examining the desirable goals — the ends elucidates the means.

This chapter will be concerned with the common-sense theories of the groups concerned with education: teachers, pupils and parents. Part of the aim of this exercise will be to contrast these perspectives and hence see how common is common sense about education.

9.3 Divergent Perspectives

In her constructivist book on personality, Hampson (1982) has suggested that there are three quite distinct perspectives on personality — that of the personality theorist; that of the lay person concerned with others; and the self-perspective concerned with one's own personality. Because these three groups have different concerns and investigate/observe personality from different vantage points they have come up with different concepts and theories of personality.

The same is true in education where there are also three rather different perspectives. The first is that of *educators* — teachers, administrators, psychologists, planners and so forth, who have theories as to what, how and why education should proceed in the way in which it does. Secondly, there is the perspective of the *pupils* or students on the whole education process as well as particular aspects of it. Finally, there is the perspective of *parents* and relatives who are concerned that the education process is maximally beneficial for those they are personally responsible for, namely the education of their children.

However, it may be that the first group — educators — needs to be divided into further quite different groups. For instance educational psychologists and teachers — both educators — may have rather different perspectives on the same issue. For instance, consider the issues of punishment and streaming. Teachers and parents may be more closely aligned on the issue of punishment against psychologists and pupils. While on the issue of streaming, teachers and psychologists may share views anti-thetical to both parents and pupils who themselves would not agree.

Most empirical studies have compared and contrasted the views of two or more groups on specific issues. Hence O'Hagan and Swanson (1986) compared the views of teachers and educational psychologists about the latter's role and showed as predicted, numerous differences. For instance, 4.5% of the psychologists compared with 41% of the teachers agreed that it is not the psychologist's business to encourage parental involvement in schools. While *no* psychologists and 45% of teachers agreed that when there is conflict between school and parents, the psychologist's role is to support the school's position.

Similarly, an American study comparing perceptions of these two groups found significant disagreement in the areas of desired direct services to children, usefulness of consultation, severity of referred problems, usefulness and adequacy of communication, usefulness of information given to teachers, how informed both groups were about each other, and how helpful services provided by school psychologists were to teachers and children (Barton and Garbach 1985).

Another study looked at the adults' and children's beliefs about emotional reactions. Zelko *et al.* (1986) tested pre-school 3rd grade (9-year-old), 6th grade (12-year-old) children and adults asking them to predict reactions to eight different types of experiences. Adults and the older school-going children had identical perceptions but not with pre-schoolers, partly because of an absence of developmental considerations in their implicit theories of children's emotional responsiveness.

However, there have also been a number of studies which have attempted to examine divergent perspectives on education-specific issues. For instance, the BPS (1979) report on corporal punishment in schools looked at attitudes of parents, pupils, teachers, and other concerned bodies of which there were many. They summarised their otherwise long and complicated report thus: Corporal punishment is often preferred by children to alternative sanctions; but parents display a diversity of opinions about its use. Although a majority of British teachers appear to favour the phasing out of the use of corporal punishment, there is an active minority in positions of authority who hold retentionist views. Teachers' unions, institutions which train teachers, and nearly all professional organisations concerned with the welfare of children favour the abolition of the use of corporal punishment. However, the arguments for and against are manifold: the case *for* argues that corporal punishment is requested/supported by parents; the only effective sanction; without it the teachers are deprived of adequate support; it is effective in the context of positive and caring relationship; pupils prefer it; denial of the right to use it is the thin edge of the wedge of other rights; it is preferred by teachers to suspension or expulsion; and it is needed for persistent offenders and defiant or aggressive pupils. On the other hand, it is argued that it is ineffective if the teacher's feelings are of no importance to the pupil; it is illogical if violence is deplored; alternatives are available and should be used; its effectiveness is dubious; it is demeaning to the teacher using it; it causes resentment; teachers are often reluctant to use it; anywhere it is used *and* respect is retained, it is probably easily dispensed with.

The issue of punishment, which has been touched on in Chapter 8, is therefore multi-faceted. Few of the studies address the interesting question of why the majority of pupils but minority of teachers and parents favour corporal punishment.

Perhaps the most relevant studies on divergent perspectives in education are those concerned with ability and examination success and failure. There is some evidence to suggest that teachers prefer certain pupil thinking styles (convergent) more than others (divergent) but that this probably interacts with the personal style of teachers themselves (Biggs *et al.* 1972). But how do teachers, pupils and parents attribute academic success and failure? One approach has been to investigate how people process information. For instance, imagine one had to explain why a particular person failed an exam. One could examine class lists for consensus information on how others had done; report cards for consisting information for how the pupil did in the past; and find exam grades for distinctiveness information to see how the person did in other exams. Less work, in this attribution theory tradition, has gone into the information people seek than into the way in which they process the information that they have.

For instance Bar-Tal and Guttman (1981) hypothesised that teachers, pupils and parents would offer different explanations for pupil exam success and failure. They partially confirm two predictions: whereas teachers would tend to attribute their pupils' *success* mainly to their own teaching ability, pupils would tend to attribute it to their own abilities and parents to the children's ability and their own influence, while teachers would attribute failure mainly to characteristics of pupils, the pupils and their parents would attribute it to various reasons other than themselves. The result showed:

(a) Teachers tend to attribute pupils' success mainly to pupils diligence, effort, interest and their own teaching of explanations, and failure to lack of effort, difficulty of material and home conditions.
(b) Pupils attribute success to own efforts, teachers' explanations, personal diligence and ability, and failure to lack of parental help and difficulty of tests.
(c) Parents attribute success mainly to home conditions and teachers' explanations, and failure to home conditions, child's lack of interest and ability.

They point out in their study that the alternative explanations from the three groups may be the result of differences in their information-processing of the facts that they have *and/or* their motivational biases to protect their self-image.

In a large-scale study of educational objectives Raven (1977) looked at both teachers' and students' perceptions of the importance of educational objectives. Some of the more dramatic discrepancies in the two groups assessments are set out in Table 9.2.

The analysis of the data was neither sophisticated nor systematic and the author did not attempt to explore the factors which led to variance in pupil perceptions such as school type and social class.

Studies such as the above are extremely interesting but do not give sufficient insight as to *why* these differences occur. Presuming that the comparative methodology is satisfactory (that is, that there are matched equivalent populations; equivalence of meaning of the question) it becomes necessary to explore the causes of major divergences. Very little attempt has been made to explain the aetiology of beliefs in a single culture, let alone why they should be different among different culture groups.

TABLE 9.2.

(A) *Objectives which come near the top of the pupils' list of important objectives, but which were considerably lower down in the teachers' list*

Ensure that you leave school confident, willing and able to take the initiative in introducing changes (21st in teachers' list, 1st in boys' and girls' lists)

Make sure that you know how to apply the facts and techniques you have learned to new problems (16th in teachers' list, 5th in boys' and girls' lists)

Tell you about different sorts of jobs and careers so that you can decide what you want to do (14th in teachers' list, 6th in boys' list, 8th in girls' list)

Help you to understand the implications and responsibilities of marriage (29th in teachers' list, 9th in boys' list, and 10th in girls' list)

Ensure that you leave school intent on being master of your destiny (28th in teachers' list, 10th in boys' list, 17th in girls' list)

Help you to do as well as possible in external examinations (23rd in teachers' list, 3rd in boys' list, 13th in girls' list

Sex education in school (boys only) (35th in teachers' list, 16th in boys' list).

(B) *Objectives high in teachers' list but of relatively little importance to the pupils*

Encourage them to have a sense of duty toward the community (4th in teachers' list, 38th in boys' list, 37th in girls' list)

Help them to develop a considerate attitude toward other people (7th in teachers' list, 30th in boys' list, 16th in girls' list)

Ensure that all students can express themselves clearly in writing (9th in teachers' list, 30th in boys' list, 16th in girls' list)

Teach them about right and wrong (10th in teachers' list, 32nd in boys' list, 26th in girls' list)

(C) *Objectives at the bottom of the pupils' list but fairly high in teachers' list*

Ensure that you are aware of aspects of school subjects which you do not have to know for the examination (16th from bottom in teachers' list, 5th from bottom in boys' list, 7th from bottom in girls' list).

(D) *Objectives at the bottom of the teachers' list but considerably higher in the pupils' list*

Encourage them to have a good time (bottom in the teachers' list, 16th from bottom in boys' list, 10th from bottom in girls' list)

Introduce them to new subjects, e.g. philosophy, sociology, archaeology (3rd from bottom in teachers' list, 14th from bottom on boys' list, 18th from bottom in girls' list)

Provide the pupils with sex education in the school (5th from bottom in teachers' list, 35th from bottom in boys' list)

Teach them things that will be of direct use to them when they start work in their jobs or careers (10th from bottom in teachers' list, 33rd from bottom in boys' and girls' lists)

Reproduced with permission from Raven, J. (1977, p. 78) *Education, values and society.* London: H. K. Lewis.

9.4 Teacher Expectations: Fulfilling Prophesies and Confirming Theories

It has long been known that teachers' attitudes, perceptions and expectations are of paramount importance in determining children's academic advancement. This may occur in many ways: if a teacher regards a standard of work above the capabilities of a child he/she will probably not teach it, so limiting possible development; if a pupil is led to believe he/she is capable of little (or a lot) he/she will have low (high) expectations and poor (good) motivation and hence will under- (over-) achieve; teachers will confirm their hypotheses in their marking schemes.

Downey and Kelly (1980) have noted how teachers' written reports, whose threefold aims are to assess, diagnose and plan, are variably effective and do not lead to bias and self-fulfilling prophesies *only* if they are skilfully formulated. Precisely because of concerns with bias and distortions in teachers' judgements of children, written reports, which act as records, need to be made as accurate, unbiased and value-free as possible.

Without doubt, the most interesting and provocative research in this field is that of Rosenthal (1966) and Rosenthal and Jacobson (1968) who were concerned with self-fulfilling prophesies in the classroom — more specifically how teachers' perceptions and expectations were powerful, though unintended, determinants of pupils' intellectual competence. That is, children whose teachers expected them "to bloom" showed greater gains in tests and IQ measures, than those children whose teachers did not expect them to bloom.

Rosenthal and Jacobson's study has naturally not escaped criticism. The nature of the IQ tests, the test administration and statistical analysis have all been criticised. Yet the phenomenon has been replicated in a wide variety of settings with different groups of subjects including experimental studies (Skarzynska, 1975) and using slightly different methodologies. However, there are some caveats which should be noted: Cooper (1979) has noted that one should be able to identify expectation-effect-prone teachers whose behaviour serves to *sustain* pre-existing achievement variations among students. That is, expectations frequently maintain rather than change below (or above) average performance. More importantly, perhaps, it is *both* student and teacher expectancies that need to be taken into consideration (Zanna *et al.* 1975).

The crucial question remains *how* do communicated expectations influence student performance. Most frequently five factors (all necessary and none sufficient) have been specified:

1. *Climate or socioemotional atmosphere* — many more positive emotional verbal behaviours are displayed by teachers to students believed to be bright.
2. *Verbal inputs* — the quantity and quality of teacher attempts to explain or teach new or novel material is associated with their expectations.
3. *Verbal output* — teachers tend to pay closer attention to, give more clues to, and allow longer responses from those they believe to be bright.
4. *Frequency of interaction* — teachers initiate and engage in more interactions with high- than with low-expectation students.
5. *Feedback* — teachers tend to praise high-expectation students more, and proportionately more per correct response, while low-expectation students are criticised more, and proportionately more per incorrect response.

Thus, the argument goes, because of different treatment one finds different performance — students taught less difficult material with less enthusiasm and less novel instruction show poorer performance. Cooper (1979)

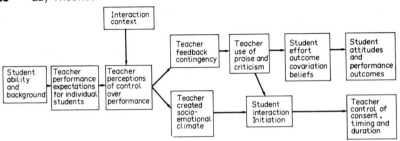

FIG. 9.1. A Model for Expectation Communication and Behaviour Influence. Reprinted with permission from Cooper, H. (1979) Pygmalion grows up. *Reviews of Educational Research*, *49*, 389–410. Copyright 1979. American Educational Research Association.

has attempted to explain these factors in a single model that suggests: teachers form differential expectations for student performances; expectations in conjunction with the interaction context influence teacher perception of control over student performance, that control perceptions influence teacher feedback information and the socio-emotional climate of the classroom; that feedback differences influence student beliefs concerning the importance of effort in producing personal outcomes; and that effort-outcome perceptions influence the quality of, and motivation behind student performance. This model is summarised diagramatically in Fig. 9.1.

But it is not only teacher expectation but their meta-perceptions that have attracted empirical work. Thus, Jackson (1968) was concerned with teachers' perceptions of pupil perceptions of their school. School pupils completed a 47-item questionnaire which was scored and categorised and teachers had to estimate within a narrow range-band the satisfaction or dissatisfaction of pupils. Teachers' predictions were classified as "hits" or "misses" and they were found to be able to predict student attitudes with greater-than-chance accuracy. But the teachers could identify "satisfied" students more accurately than "dissatisfied" students because the opinions of the former were somehow more visible. Also, teachers tended to overestimate the amount of satisfaction to be found among the students with high IQs and the amount of dissatisfaction among students with low IQs. In other words, teachers appear to hold to the belief, quite simply, that the pupil who succeeds at school thinks well of it despite the fact that consistently research has shown that students' liking for and satisfaction with school is negligibly correlated with their scores on achievement tests.

Similarly, a teacher's general belief system influences the classroom atmosphere created and the students' general behaviour. Harvey *et al.* (1968) confirmed previous findings which demonstrated that the abstractness vs concreteness of a teacher's belief system had powerful deterring effects on children's behaviours. Greater abstractness of the teacher was associated with greater student involvement, greater co-operation, more activity, less nurturance seeking, higher achievement, greater helpfulness and less concre-

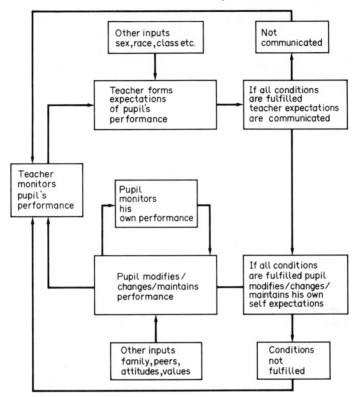

FIG. 9.2. The Role of Feedback and Pupil Self-expectancy.
Reprinted with permission from Blease, D. (1983) Educational Studies, Volume 9, p. 127, Carfax Publishing Company, Abingdon.

teness on the part of students. That is the concreteness–abstractness of teachers' belief systems affect their overt resourcefulness, dictatorialness and punitiveness in the classroom. Clearly, teachers' theories and thinking styles have substantial effects on school-pupils' education.

Other studies have suggested that the sex of the teacher and the sex of the pupil are both important factors in "objective" behavioral ratings. Levine (1977) found male pupils tended to be rated more poorly than female pupils, and male teachers tended to use more conservative ratings than female teachers.

This work has attracted a great deal of research. Many confirmations (Beez, 1972) have led researchers to conclude that one should be very careful as to what information a teacher should receive about a pupil, lest these facts lead to a behaviour pattern that is detrimental to the child.

What remains most in doubt about the self-fulfilling nature of teacher expectations is the mechanism whereby they occur. Blease (1983) has attempted to do precisely this in terms of various feedback mechanisms. This is set out in Fig. 9.2.

Clearly what is most interesting about the work is how lay theories (or expectations) lead to specific self-fulfilling behaviours. What the approach does not concern itself with is how these theories develop in the first place or, indeed, whether teachers adhere to different types of "educational" theories. Thus, if one would taxonomise teachers' lay theories into a relatively small number, one may begin to see how a theory leads to expectations, which in turn confirm the theory.

There is a vast literature on teachers' attitudes and perceptions to general educational theories (Todman and Farquharson 1983), particular branches of education like further-education (Young, 1980) or sixth-form (12th grade) education (Reid and Holly, 1974) or specific issues such as the relative effectiveness of reforms for motivating pupils and alleviating behaviour problems (Burns, 1977). Some studies attempted to look at the dimensions of teachers' beliefs, such as Wehling and Charters (1969) who found eight. However, as Breubeck (1971) has pointed out, these beliefs and theories change over time as a function of teaching experience and that it is possible to distinguish the theories, beliefs and behaviours of good vs poor teachers.

Rather than simply investigating teachers' attitudes to specific educational topics some researchers have attempted to investigate the structures of these attitudes and provide a crude taxonomy. Oliver (1953) attempted to ascertain if the implicit unformulated philosophies of practising teachers formed a similar taxonomy to these explicit systematic theories of educational philosophers. He found evidence for four philosophies based on two dimensions:

1. Authoritarian Idealism (Plato);
2. Liberal Idealism (Frobel);
3. Authoritarian Naturalism (Marx);
4. Liberal Naturalism (Rousseau).

Later work by Oliver and other researchers has suggested that teachers' philosophies can be more parsimoniously described in terms of Eysenck's (1947) two dimensions of social attitudes: radicalism–conservatism; tough–tender mindedness. Empirical support for this comes from a study by Wilson and Bill (1976), who found evidence for three orthogonal factors underlying teachers' beliefs about education: tender/tough mindedness, radical/conservative and naturalism/idealism. This may provide a useful beginning to a taxonomy in this area, which may well apply to other groups such as parents, pupils and educational administrators.

9.5 Parents' Beliefs

There have been a number of studies on parents' beliefs about child-rearing, parenting and education as well as studies on their knowledge of behavioural principles (McLoughlin, 1985). Some have been concerned mainly with pre-school children where, for instance, Lawton et al. (1984)

found that parents appeared to be more certain of their actual parenting and its relation to their children's social development followed by intellectual development, and least certain of its relation to their physical development. Others have been interested in how parental beliefs (particularly about sex-typing) influence the behaviour towards the child, and still others have been interested in attitudes to particular types of education (ILEA 1985).

"Naive" or lay theories of child development are, however, culture specific. Keller *et al.* (1984) found numerous differences between German and Costa Rican mothers' beliefs about child development and optimal parenting. For instance, German women expect infants to see, think, understand words and identify pictures of objects earlier than do Costa Ricans. This study suggests that parental ideas of development and education would be culture-specific, and also, possibly, class-specific.

There are a number of reasons why the study of parental beliefs has been considered important. Goodnow (1984) has argued that parents' beliefs illuminate effects of culture and class, but more importantly because parental beliefs relate to childrearing practices, which in turn have developmental outcomes in the child. A few general questions appear to have guided research on parents' beliefs about children:

(a) *What the beliefs are* — general belief systems about childhood and also specific predictions of particular abilities and developmental milestones.
(b) *The origin of the beliefs* — what experiences form, shape and modify these beliefs.
(c) *The relationship between beliefs and behaviour* — how, when and why parental beliefs influence childhood behaviours.
(d) *The effects on the child* — how parental beliefs relate to measures of development in the child.

There is also evidence for systematic bias between parents' and children's explanations. For instance, Compas *et al.* (1982) showed that when asked to explain behaviour, parents made more attributions than their children to the characteristics of the child, rather than the environmental factors. More interesting, however, was the finding that parents and children differed in their locus of attributions (to what they attributed the cause of behaviour) when interviewed individually, but that these differences were not present when families were interviewed with both parents and children present. This suggests attribution, attitudes, beliefs and theories are expressed and formulated quite differently, depending on the context.

Others have attempted to define how parents categorise and conceptualise their children's behaviour. Bacon and Ashmore (1985) found a number of evaluative and descriptive schemes that parents use to categorise their children's behaviour including hostile/aggressive - non-hostile/non-aggressive, normal--problem, typical-not typical, and shows-does not show sexual interest. However, they suggest that the most basic category is simply, behaviour I should do something about – behaviour I don't need to do anything about.

Of course, parental attitudes and beliefs are modified by their experiences of the child, especially if the children are not normal. For instance, Banner (1979) found that compared with mothers of normal or over-achieving 11-year-old children, mothers of under-achieving children tend to be more dominant, rigid, restrictive and protective. However, the crucial question remains as to whether these attitudes and behaviours were the cause or consequences of educational performance.

Less work has been done on the educational theories of people with and without children; before and after they have children; parents from different socio-economic groups. There is sufficient evidence from studies on social mobility, to suggest that parents' beliefs and resources are the major determinants of the educational outcomes of their children.

9.6 Pupils' Perceptions and Expectations

Of course, pupils at all levels have perceptions and expectations of certain aspects of schooling and the education system. Recently, Burdsal and Bardo (1986) factor analysed results from over 40,000 questionnaires concerned with students' perceptions of teacher effectiveness. Six factors emerged: attitudes towards students, work load, course value to students, course organisation and structure, grading quality and level of material. These divisions may well underlie most pupil and student attitudes, beliefs and expectations about education.

Nicholls *et al.* (1985) attempted to evaluate American high school students' theories of education and, more specifically, what the aims of education should be, their personal goals in school and their perceptions of the causes of success in school. For the authors, the logical consistency in these beliefs was an indicator of the existence of a theory. They found that the view that school should prepare pupils to be socially responsible and useful, to understand the world and be motivated to continue learning are all associated (consistent) are related to beliefs that academic success follows from interest, effort, attempts to understand and collaborative learning. Similarly, students who are induced to feel successful when they do well without effort, are more likely to believe that effort and interest are necessary for success as much as the ability to impress people and act if they like the teacher. The authors maintain that their research suggests evidence for educational ideologies and goals in adolescents, some of which were not in with explicit or official views. For instance, they found that the view that school should enable students to enhance their wealth and status were negatively correlated with commitment to learning and positively correlated with academic alienation.

Studies since the 1930s have been concerned with children's perception of teachers and have yielded fairly comparable results. For instance, Musgrove and Taylor (1969) found that where teachers placed great emphasis on the personal qualities of a good teacher, school children at various ages placed most emphasis on the teacher's teaching skills. The pupils seemed more interested in teaching skill than personal qualities, organising abilities or preferred methods of discipline. The authors concluded by speculating that there may be a curvilinear relationship between teachers' effectiveness and their friendliness to pupils, despite some theories which suggest that this relationship is linear.

O'Hagan and Edmunds (1982) examined pupils' attitudes to teacher strategies for controlling disruptive behaviour. They found predictably, that certain strategies were preferred. The results also indicated that initiatory aggressive strategies which were effective in controlling misbehaviour are in fact deleterious in their consequences. In a review of this topic McCann (1978) concluded thus:

> Most children, but particularly those at pre-adolescence see school discipline as an extension of parental discipline, and see teachers as needing to exercise much the same kind of control as their parents do. Most children would appear to accept punishment, even corporal punishment as a fact of life . . . Essentially then they do not view punishments as being "humiliating" or "degrading", but as fair or unfair, merited or unmerited. (p. 172)

Interestingly, sociological perspectives on pupils expectations and perceptions have been grouped into various approaches. Meighan (1981) has suggested three different approaches: structural functionalist, structural conflict or interactionist. Whereas the former do not see the relevance in consulting pupils for their views, the latter considers them most important. Although Meighan (1981) remains uncertain of the necessity or usefulness of considering pupils' views, he considered the relevant research and summarised the findings thus:

1. Primary school children tend to enjoy school, whereas secondary school children tend to be less happy with their school experiences.
2. Both "successful" and "unsuccessful" pupils in secondary schools record dissatisfaction. It is not just a reaction of the "failures".
3. The dissatisfaction appears to be marked, and not a minor feature. Only the minority of secondary schools appear to achieve even a pass mark in the eyes of the pupils.
4. The views of the pupils are not merely negative. They are sympathetic to the difficulties of teachers. They are able to offer a wide range of constructive, and mostly feasible, alternatives.
5. The perceptions of pupils show high degrees of reliability and validity.
6. The pupils' views about preferred teachers show a high degree of consensus, as do their views of "bad" teachers.
7. Pupils are able to recognise some aspects of the hidden curriculum and some of the labelling processes, and record their feelings of alienation that result.
8. A structural functional view tends to dominate educational thinking, so investigations of the pupils' views are often seen as radical even when they are not.
9. The pupils' layer of meaning is rarely known to teachers in any systematic way, so findings are often disturbing and represent "uncommon sense".
10. The pupils' preference for "nice strict" over "nasty strict" disappoints the beliefs of both transmission educationalists and radical educationalists.
11. The experience of schooling of girls may well differ from that of boys, therefore making generalisations about the pupils' view open to question. (p. 37)

TABLE 9.3. *Dimensional Characteristics of the Causal Attributions*

	Internal attributions Stable	Unstable
Controllable	Stable effort	Unstable effort
Uncontrollable	Ability	Mood

	External attributions Stable	Unstable
Controllable	Other's stable Effort	Other's unstable Effort
Uncontrollable	Task difficulty	Luck

9.7 Beliefs about the Causes of Success and Failure

One topic in educational psychology that has attracted a great deal of research concerns lay assumptions about the causal relationships that produce various effects observed in the school. A great deal of this research has been derived from Weiner's (1985) attribution-based model of achievement motivation which suggests three dimensions — locus of causality (internal vs external), stability (stable vs unstable) and controllability (controllable vs uncontrollable) — underlie all attributions for success and failure.

This "system" allows for eight types of attributions as shown in Table 9.3.

This system, or adaptations of it, has been used in nearly all studies in this area (Frieze and Snyder, 1980). Of course, there are many other explanations which can be offered but researchers have, by-and-large, had little difficulty in getting them into the framework (Little, 1985). Studies on pupils from various groups have shown that success is usually attributed to stable internal factors and failures to external, unstable causes. However, research projects have shown that this differs as a function of age (Little 1985); ability (Raviv *et al*. 1980); personality (Satterly and Hall, 1983); culture (Fry and Ghosh, 1980); sex (Callaghan and Manstead, 1983); perception of others' attribution (Karnlol, 1987) and socio-economic states (Bar-Tal *et al.* 1984; Butler, 1986).

It has been suggested that many of these attributions are functional rather than rational, in the sense that they function to protect and/or enhance self-esteem. In this sense these explanations can be seen in motivational, rather than information processing, terms. Thus, students would like to be perceived more as having ability than exerting effort to achieve academic success (Raviv *et al.* 1983). However, it has been demonstrated that teachers take effort into consideration in their marking when a student with low ability fails or when a student with high ability succeeds (Bar-Tal *et al.* 1981).

These schemes that ordinary people use to make sense of the ability-linked performances of themselves and others are usually attempts to infer trait or stable dimensions underlying performance. Darley and Goethals (1980) have considered various factors involved in the process, such as the difference between short- and long-term exercises; explaining single vs multiple performances; the difference between an "objective" vs "involved" observer. They provide a simple quasi-mathematical function which assesses performance in terms of ability, motivation, task difficulty and luck which, they argue, people use systematically to "discover" abilities, maintain and enhance their own self-esteem and the regard others have for them.

However, these causal attributions are not only interesting in terms of their structure and function but also because of their consequences. Attributions are closely linked to expectations which then affect performance (Vollmer, 1986).

9.8 Conclusion

Dann (1986) has argued that lay (or subjective) theories on education — whether held by teachers, parents, pupils or any other lay audience — have four axiomatic features:

1. They are relatively stable cognitive structures (or mental representations) which are, nonetheless, possibly changed through experience.
2. They are often implicit, yet parts of them may be accessible to the lay person's consciousness in certain circumstances.
3. They have a similar structure to scientific theories and a quasi-logical base.
4. They are one of the important factors determining behaviour.

His work and that of other colleagues in Germany, particularly on the perception of aggression, tends to support the above axioms, which are indeed some of the axioms of this book. Certainly, the fragmented but extensive research in this area leads one to believe that lay people have theories of education not unlike those of academic philosophers of education. Indeed, many educationalists strive after what they call common-sense perspectives.

Two important themes underlie the research reported in this chapter. The first is that lay theories of education tend to be rather different, depending on the interests of the party to which people belong. Thus, teachers, educational psychologists, pupils, administrators and parents may differ on specific or general aspects of educational aims and practice, depending on their perspective. Furthermore, these patterns of similarities and differences in beliefs are neither fixed nor identical for all issues.

More importantly, perhaps, than the similarity and differences in theories/ beliefs between different groups is the work on the consequences and functions of these beliefs. Research from an attributional and expectancy — value theoretical viewpoint has highlighted how theories may be self-fulfilling. Thus, the attribution patterns of pupils may serve to perpetuate excellence or failure, while the expectations of teachers may have a powerful and long-lasting effect on the success or failure of children.

10

Conclusion

10.1 Introduction

This book has been concerned with various aspects of lay theories — everyday, novice, implicit understandings of issues and problems in the social sciences. They have often been contrasted with "scientific" theories although there is considerable debate in the philosophy of science regarding their actual status (Chalmers, 1986). Indeed, within disciplines like psychology there are serious controversies and crises regarding the states of "scientific" theory (Westland, 1978).

Theoretical and empirical work from a large range of disciplines was examined. Some areas were omitted, such as lay beliefs about sex roles, lay political theories and lay beliefs about anthropological issues, though all of these were touched upon tangentially. Certainly, enough general issues were considered in order to derive some general points about the nature of lay theories. Hargreaves (1981) has posed a number of important and salient questions concerning lay theories, some of which have been attempted by researchers mentioned in this book. They include:

> If adults can display competencies in the use of complex common-sense models of action, how do children come to acquire these competencies? Common-sense models of action may or may not rest on a relatively unchanging and underlying model of "deep-structure"; but certainly some aspects of common-sense change from age to age . . . how are these changes in common-sense models to be explained and what are their consequences? . . . Are the common-sense models of action and explanations to be found in Western Europe and North America applicable in other cultures? The practical application of psychological theory and research often requires man to modify his common-sense model. How can this change be affected unless we fully understand the nature of the model to be displaced? (p. 223)

Many researchers, particularly psychologists, have been fascinated by the similarities and differences between lay common sense and scientific theories. Most investigations have shown, predictably, both similarities and differences, but perhaps more surprisingly, more similarities than differences. That is, according to many of the features of lay theories as outlined in Chapter 1, the theories of lay people and academic scientists are relatively similar. To some this will come as no surprise, perhaps least of all to academics and "scientists", while to others eager to preserve their image this may seem a disappointing admission, that their research only proves what we already know. This is not to suggest that there are no examples where there are counter-intuitive scientific theories as opposed to intuitive lay theories; that lay people fully understand the complexities and niceties of academic theories; or that lay people vs academics would derive the same conclusions or policy implications from the same or similar theories. However, it does appear that scientific, explicit theories are not as sophisticated and unambiguous as presupposed, nor are lay theories as muddled or fallacious.

Very few studies have considered through longitudinal or cross-sectional design the development of lay theories, how they change over time and what are the most powerful predictors of who holds which theory. Some factors like education, socio-economic status and other associated demographic and psychographic features appear to be strong determinants of what sort of theory people hold. However, these factors vary from one theoretical area to another. Furthermore, it is possible that there are numerous feedback loops such that a theory determines a behaviour which in turn determines a theory. Hence, it may be difficult to disentangle cause and consequence in lay theories of human behaviour.

Some work has been done on the relationship between lay beliefs within and between the same area. Hence, one may find dimensions like individualism–collectivism (psychology vs sociology) underpinning many theoretical positions. Certainly, the research on lay theories of economics and lay theories in the law appear to suggest stable underlying patterns, from which one may predict the relationship between lay beliefs on similar issues. These theories may be highly idiosyncratic (Swede and Tetlock, 1986) or shown by groups of individuals.

A theme running through much of this work is the issue of the function of lay beliefs. Many researchers have pointed out that people do not hold beliefs for simple rational, logical and dispassionate reasons. Theories nearly always serve a function, such as to bolster or maintain self-esteem, to ensure group solidarity, to provide a social or moral framework through which to comprehend new facts. Lay theories, then, appear to be much more psychological than logical in nature.

The functional nature of lay theories has implications for their stability, consistency and change. Presumably the more central and important the function that the theory serves, the less likely it is to change and the more stable it is over time. The issue of consistency of the theory is, however, more complex. There are different types of consistency — absolute, relative, coherence — which may work at different levels. A logical analysis of lay theories often reveals them to be fairly inconsistent in the sense that antonymous presuppositions are simultaneously held by people who may be unaware of, or simply not concerned by, contradiction. Indeed, this concern with internal consistency may be particular to Western cultures, which appear most obsessed with balance and dissonance, compared with non-Western cultures.

In that theories fulfil important psychological functions it is important to take these into account in the changing or manipulation of these beliefs. That is, a logical campaign may be less successful than an emotional campaign, as many health educators have discovered. Thus, if one can determine the psychological function that a theory fulfils and either change the need for that function (to bolster self-esteem) or replace the theory or behaviour by another that equally or more effectively changes the function, the original theory may be changed. The manipulation of lay theories and beliefs has, however, not been very extensively discussed in this book.

A great deal of the research has been concerned with the structure of lay beliefs. This has nearly always involved empirical attempts at taxonomisation. Presumably these attempts at discovering the underlying structure of lay beliefs fulfil two functions. First, they allow one to compare the structure (and hence relationship) between lay and scientific theories. Second, it is frequently argued that description and taxonomisation precedes explanation as we first need to know what people believe, how those beliefs are related and integrated into a theory and, finally, how that theory operates.

Perhaps the major interest in lay theories has been in the consequences of lay beliefs for the believer. The cognitive movement in psychology has placed great stress on the importance of cognitions determining all kinds of behaviour, from drug-taking to depression. It has been argued that lay theories or styles of thinking and attributing causes are major causal factors in determining behaviour. Hence the extensive interest in cognitive therapies aimed at changing specific cognitions thought to be maladaptive. Precisely what role cognitions or theories play is open to dispute, some arguing that they are epiphenomenal and others that they are primary. Nevertheless, this cognitive revolution has led to a considerable interest in the social and behavioural consequences of lay theories.

10.2 A Terminological Note

Throughout this book the terms model, theory, belief system, metaphor, attributional style, etc., have been used rather loosely and, frequently, interchangeably. What has determined the choice of one item over another has usually been which one was used most frequently within an area of research which may be dominated by a quite different tradition. Hence, the term attributional style is closely associated with psychological research, and folk metaphor with anthropology. Shoemaker (1984) has noted that the term theory means many things to many people but is essentially an attempt to make sense out of observations:

> To the lay person, a theory often suggests a wild speculation, or set of speculations, an unproved or perhaps false assumption, or even a fact concerning an event or a type of behaviour, based on little, if any, actual data. To some scientists, or philosophers of science, a theory consists of a set of descriptions or classification schemes concerning a particular

phenomena. To others, a theory is a systematic collection of concepts and statements purporting to explain events or behaviour. (p. 8)

Some researchers have suggested that it may be misleading to use one term rather than another. Objecting to the term lay theory in preference to lay beliefs, Fitzpatrick (1984) noted: "The term 'theory' implies a high degree of consistency, order, stability, and rationality, properties that may not be essential to lay concepts" (p. 17). One reason for this is that many of these beliefs are drawn from a variety of originally disparate, distinct sources and later integrated and reworked into a hybrid, often highly idiosyncratic theory.

Norman (1980), however, favours the term belief system because it merges cognitive and social science. Belief systems are interesting, he argues, not only for their contents of cultural knowledge but also because they influence memory, perception, problem solving, etc. Clearly, the term system implies the *integration* of a set of beliefs and attitudes rather than a single isolated group of beliefs.

Not only are there problems with academic distinctions but ordinary people use a wide variety of terms to describe phenomena. In a fascinating paper on metaphors, Lakoff and Johnson (1980) set out some of the metaphors people use to describe abstract concepts: ideas are people (cognitive psychology is still in its infancy); ideas are plants (she has a fertile imagination); ideas are products (he produces ideas at an astonishing rate); ideas are commodities (he won't buy that plan); ideas are resources (that idea will go a long way); ideas are money (he has a wealth of ideas); ideas are cutting instruments (she cut his argument with razor sharp wit); ideas are food (that's food for thought); and ideas are fashion (that idea is old hat). They note:

The way ordinary people deal implicitly with the limitations of any one metaphor is by having many metaphors for comprehending different aspects of the same concept. As we saw, people in our culture have many different metaphors for *IDEAS* and *MIND*, some of which are elaborate in one or another branch of Psychology and some of which are not. These clusters of metaphors serve the purpose of understanding better than any *single* metaphor could — even though they are partial and very often inconsistent with each other. Scientists, however, have tended to insist on complete and consistent theories. While consistency is generally desirable, there are times when it does not best serve the purpose of understanding. In particular, the insistence on maintaining a consistent extension of one metaphor may blind us to aspects of reality that are ignored or hidden by that metaphor. We would like to suggest that there are times when scientific understanding may best be served by permitting alternative metaphors even at the expense of completeness and consistency. If Cognitive Science is to be concerned with human understanding in its full richness and not merely with those phenomena that fit the *MIND IS A MACHINE* metaphor, then it may have to sacrifice metaphorical consistency in the service of fuller understanding. The moral: Cognitive Science needs to be aware of its metaphors, to be concerned with what they hide, and to be open to alternative metaphors — even if they are inconsistent with the current favourites. (p. 208)

Thus, just as the metaphors lay people use to describe phenomena give one an insight into their "theory" of that phenomena, so the term (theory, belief system, attributional style) social scientists use of lay people's ideas gives an insight into the former's "theory" of the latter's "theories"!

10.3 Common Sense

Textbooks in many of the social sciences continue to contrast science and common sense in a somewhat simplistic strawman way. Compare the way Kerlinger (1973) contrasts the two along five dimensions.

1. While the man in the street uses "theories" and concepts he ordinarily does so in a loose fashion . . . The scientist, on the other hand, systematically builds his theoretical structures, tests them for internal consistency, and subjects aspects of them to empirical test . . .
2. . . . the scientist systematically and empirically tests his theories and hypotheses. The man in the street tests his "hypotheses" too, but he tests them in what might be a selective fashion . . . The sophisticated social scientist knowing this "selection tendency" to be a common psychological phenomenon, carefully guards his research against his own preconceptions and predictions and against selective support of his hypotheses . . .
3. . . . the scientist tries systematically to rule out variables that are possible "causes" of the effects, he is studying other than the variables that he has hypothesised to the "causes". The layman seldom bothers to control his explanation of observed phenomena in a systematic manner . . .
4. . . . the scientist consciously and systematically pursues relations. The layman's preoccupation with relations is loose, unsystematic, uncontrolled. He often seizes, for example, on the fortuitous occurrence of two phenomena and immediately links them indissolubly as cause and effect . . .
5. The scientist, when attempting to explain the relations among observed phenomena, carefully rules out what have been called "metaphysical explanations" (p. 35).

Despite this vision of the heroic scientist vs the muddled layman Kerlinger (1973) attempts to dispel erroneous stereotypes of science! However, later his definition of scientific research was "systematic, controlled, empirical and critical investigation of hypothetical propositions about the presumed relations among natural phenomena" (p. 11). Not all psychologists are as dismissive of common sense in favour of disinterested empiricism (Hargreaves, 1981).

However, within the academic scientific community there is frequently antipathy to disciplines that investigate common sense, or by ignoring common sense rediscover it. Giddens (1987), who considered sociological research, argued that at the heart of objections to the discipline is the idea that sociologists state the obvious but with an air of discovery. Worse still, in that it offers explanations that do not ring true, sociology is doubly redundant because it not only tells us what we already know, but parades the familiar in a garb which conceals its proper nature.

Giddens attempts to rebut these arguments thus: first, that common knowledge (Britain is particularly strike prone; there has been a sharp rise in one-parent families) is frequently wrong and may lead to prejudice, intolerance and discrimination; second, correct knowledge may be the consequence of sociological research; third, that common knowledge about behaviour differs from one group/milieu to another; fourth, that people are normally able discursively to identify only a little of the complex conventional framework of their activities; fifth, that behaviour may have unintended as well as intended consequences and that ways of acting, thinking and feeling may exist outside the consciousness of individuals; sixth, that ordinary language is too ambiguous for dispassionate analytic scientific description.

A major problem in the social, as opposed to the natural, sciences is that the theories and concepts invented by social scientists circulate in and out of the social worlds they are coined to analyse. But while lay concepts obstinately intrude into the technical discourse of social science, the opposite is also true. Hence, the most interesting and innovative ideas in the social sciences risk becoming banal:

> the achievements of the social sciences tend to become submerged from view by their very success. On the other hand, exactly because of this we can in all seriousness make the claim that the social sciences have influenced "their" world — the universe of human social activity — much more strongly than the natural sciences have influenced "theirs". The social sciences have been reflexively involved in a most basic way with those transformations of modernity which give them their main subject-matter. (p. 21)

The topic of what is common sense, how it differs from scientific fact, who has it and who has not, remains at the heart of the research covered in this book (Furnham, 1988). With the rise of interest in constructivism and other socio-cognitive approaches to behaviour this trend is likely to continue.

10.4 Constructionism and Ethnomethodology

It should not be thought that all social scientists share views on scientific metatheory or methodology. Within psychology and sociology, for instance, there are quite distinct and theoretically opposed traditions. Many of these alternative approaches have a particular interest in lay theories (Douglas, 1974).

For instance, the social constructivist orientation is principally concerned with the processes by which people come to describe, explain or otherwise account for behaviour. Gergen (1986) has specified some of the major assumptions of this movement.

1. Knowledge of the world is *not* the product of induction, or of the building and testing of general hypotheses. It is argued that lay beliefs and theories are either highly circumscribed by culture, history or social context, or altogether non-existent.
2. The terms in which the world is understood are social artefacts, products of historically situated interchanges among people, lay theories are the result of an active, co-operative enterprise of persons in relationship.
3. The degree to which a given form of understanding prevails or is sustained

across time is not directly on the empirical validity of the perspective in question, but on the vicissitudes of social processes of communication and negotiation.

4. Forms of negotiated understanding are of critical significance in social life, as they are integrally connected with many other activities in which people engage. Hence, there is an extensive interest in the images and metaphors people use to describe human action.

This approach rejects positivism and empiricism with its emphasis on objective, individualistic, ahistorical knowledge. It argues that scientific theories are not the result of impersonal applications of rigorous, decontextualised methods but a social communicative construction between people. In other words, neither the layman nor the academic scientist is a true scientist in the Western empirical tradition as all theories are shaped by socio-historical and cultural forces and changed during the course of social interchange. The layman, no more or less than the scientist, socially constructs theories of the world. The constructivist tradition has recently informed studies of lay conceptions (Semin and Krahé, 1987).

Another more established anti-empirical tradition comes from sociology and it is known as ethnomethodology Garfinkel (1959), which is the study of everyday methods of practical reasoning used in the production and interpretation of social action. Central to this approach is the idea that social scientists have paid too little attention to the implications of their own membership of, and familiarity with, the subject matter of their inquiries. The focus of ethnomethodology is the study of folk methodology comprising a range of "seen but unnoticed" procedures or practices that make it possible to analyse, make sense of and produce recognisable social activities. According to ethnomethodologists many theoretical problems in the social sciences result from a longstanding eagerness of researchers to regard their own native competencies as a resource rather than as a topic for investigation itself. This approach involves a marked shift away from deterministic traditions which seek to construct formal *causal* theories of social behaviour. Ethnomethodologists are more interested in explaining *how*, rather than why, social conduct occurs.

There is then, and has been for a long time, a tradition that has never "compared and contrasted" lay vs scientific theories. Based on different suppositions these alternative approaches have always placed more stress on the importance of common-sense constructions and understandings of the world.

10.5 Current Research Concerns

A browse through a wide range of psychological journals — in applied, experimental, personality and social psychology — shows a surprisingly large number of papers concerned with lay theories. Various different terms exist for the lay perspective: implicit psychologists (Six and Krahé, 1984), every-day conceptions (Semin and Chassein, 1985), common-sense conceptions (Semin and Rosch, 1981), novices (Isaacs and Clark, 1987), intuitive perso-nologist (Lamiell *et al.*, 1983).

Some of these current concerns are not new, reflecting consistent interests in psychology while others are more recent. Some of the more current concerns are as follows:

(1) Everyday Knowledge of Particular Issues

One topic that has seen a revival of popular interest is that of intelligence. Forty years ago Flugel (1947) asked 300 lay people, including housewives, civil servants and factory workers, 16 questions about intelligence and found about 10 issues where there were major differences and only four where there was agreement. For instance, speaking of the layman the author notes: "He distinguishes less clearly between intelligence and achievement . . . He overrates the importance of knowledge in intelligence tests . . . He is inadequately informed concerning the relative constancy of the IQ" (p. 152).

Various opinion poll type studies have been done on intelligence in many different countries at specific points of time (Fontes *et al.*, 1983). More recently, studies have attempted to elucidate tacit (or rarely expressed or stated) knowledge from experts, novices and lay people (Wagner, 1987; Wagner and Sternberg, 1985).

Lay theories of personality, particularly dimensions such as introversion-extroversion continue to attract attention (Semin et al., 1981). Semin and Chassein (1985), for instance, have again demonstrated that hypothetico-deductive models of personality rely primarily on ordinary language descrip-tions of persons and, hence lay people do not differ from academic theorists to any significant degree. But not all studies have been concerned with the *content* of lay knowledge — some have looked at lay theories of process. For instance, Six and Krahé (1984) presented psychology undergraduates with the method section of 20 published papers, all concerned with the relationship between attitudes and behaviour. Despite the fact that most studies showed a modest, but positive and significant correlation betweeen attitudes and behaviour, most subjects were unable to predict the results. The authors note:

> The present results show the implicit psychologists' difficulties in estimating empirically determined attitude–behaviour consistencies. They are supportive of the claim of scientific psychology to be able to produce non-trivial results, suggesting that other people's reactions in situations where both attitudinal and behavioural variables are involved cannot be adequately accounted for by common-sense psychological knowledge. (p. 82)

(2) The Structure of Implicit Taxonomies

There remains an abiding interest in lay taxonomies of various processes. For instance, Russell and Steiger (1982) demonstrated a three-dimensional (pleasure–displeasure, arousal–sleepiness and dominance–submissiveness) structure to lay theories of emotions. Almost as soon as a new concept or research area has been established attempts are made to establish its underlying structures.

(3) Information Search and Lay-Hypothesis Testing

The issue of how people gather information to test hypotheses in theories remains an interesting empirical area of research. Skov and Sherman (1986) have found evidence for three different lay information-seeking strategies: evidence being sought to the extent that it is more likely under the hypothesis being tested than under the alternative. The tendency to ask questions that will have the effect of making the hypothesis under test appear to be true, a preference for evidence that is most differentially probable under the hypothesis than its alternative. In other words, strategies may be aimed at confirming hypotheses or diagnosing effects. To a large extent the way in which people seek out information to test hypotheses or theories establishes how different or similar they are to scientists.

(4) Self-Other Discrepancies

There remains an interest in the difference between lay theories of one's own behaviour and of others' behaviour. For instance, Turnbull (1981) considered the deterministic paradox concerning naive conceptions of free will which predicts that in judging past events people assume that their behaviour has been free, but that the behaviour of others, and surrounding events have been determined. Though this belief in control may be generally psychologically adaptive, the idea that one may have acted differently, and so avoided negative outcomes, may lead to the perception of personal blame. If the consequences of this action were in fact chance-determined, uncontrollable or beyond personal control, the reason (i.e. self-blame) may in fact be psychologically harmful.

Wilson *et al.*, (1982) was interested in the accuracy and use of shared theories and found, as other have, that it is unparsimonious to assume people are better able to predict their own versus others' behaviour because they had some sort of privileged information about their own thought processes or behaviour. They found that even when judging a response as important as their own mood subjects cling tenaciously to theories (i.e. that the weather affects their mood) even when those theories were wrong.

Research on the fundamental and ultimate attribution error, which is at the heart of cognitive social psychology, continues to throw light on common-sense understanding.

(5) The Taxonomisation of Explanations

Because it is assumed that common-sense explanations are of different levels or types researchers, particularly those interested in children, have attempted to categorise them. For instance, Obani and Doherty (1986) found children's reasons for the causes of handicap fell into four groups: naive realism (irrelevant, naive, tautological responses); inchoate realism (technically feasible but biologically fallacious); physical realism (focuses entirely on physical damage) and comprehensive realism (a full understanding). Looking at explanations in general, Soloman (1986) came up with a rather different list: reaffirming that things are as they are, looking for the purposes of events, trying to find life-world synonyms for concepts, close comparison, seeking empirical causes and using distanced analogies.

10.6 Amateurs, Hobbyists and Avocational Scientists

The vast majority of people are not, of course, professional, pure or applied, natural or behavioural scientists, though their jobs may well involve apparatus, tools as well as concepts, derived from science. Nevertheless, many people choose to partake in leisure activities which are closely akin to those of scientists.

Stebbins (1980a) has attempted to describe how *amateurs* are linked to professionals (scientists) and a public, but are distinguished from hobbyists who are usually more passive and do not interact with professionals to the same extent. Stebbins (1980b) has in fact investigated avocational or amateur scientists (archaeologists and astronomers). He suggests that avocational scientists can be categorised into two broad groups: *observers* and *armchair participants*. The former, observers, are further sub-divided into: *Apprentices* — learners about procedures and instrumentation, and operate independently, but are generally incapable of contributing anything to the field; *Journeyman* — knowledgeable and reliable practitioners who can work independently within one or a few specialities, but is still attempting to grasp the discipline as a whole and developments in it, *Master* — a systematic collector of original data who has a grasp of the field as a whole and gaps in knowledge. These amateurs can, and do, make real contributions to knowledge.

Stebbins' studies had led him to suggest that amateurs are extremely serious about their pursuit precisely because it gives them an opportunity to guide their own enterprise:

> The system of values within avocational science supports this interpretation. The most honoured people are the masters who make original contributions to the science, have close associations with the professionals, and know well their speciality. Much independent work goes into reaching this exalted position. The value system in avocational science also stresses active data collection rather than passive reading. (Stebbins, 1980b, p. 47)

Clearly amateurs share completely the perspective of the scientist and are not likely to be epistemologically different. Just as it is frequently difficult to distinguish work from leisure so it is often difficult to distinguish amateurs from professionals.

10.7 The Lay Psychometrician

Popular magazines frequently print brief personality tests purporting to measure such things as anxiety, sexual preferences, work habits, etc. They are usually devised by laymen with little or no psychometric knowledge or skill, and although the tests may have high face validity there is no evidence of their reliability, concurrent, construct or predictive validity.

But how good are lay people at constructing tests? Most textbooks on test construction warn people that it is a skilful enterprise and that lay attempts will frequently result in failure. Ashton and Goldberg (1973) attempted to compare the ability of expert psychometricians, novice psychology students and lay people (non-psychology students) in their ability to devise 20-item scales to measure sociability, achievement and dominance. These scales were compared to those developed by experts and administered to students whose peer ratings had been obtained. They found the validity of the lay person scales well under that of the novices, whose tests were comparable to those of the experts. Furthermore, the most reliable scales constructed by the psychology students were of equal validity to one test measure (PRF) and of considerably higher validity than another (PI).

However, in the devising of questionnaires lay people fall into numerous traps: asking double-barrel questions (Are you scared of cats and dogs?); ambiguous questions (What time do you usually take tea?); non-discriminating questions (Are you in favour of world peace?). Any experienced psychometrician who has seen the first (or even fifth) draft of a novice's questionnaire usually would have little doubt that most lay people do not understand some of the most simple, but important, concepts, such as reliability, validity, multi-dimensionality, discriminability, etc.

10.8 Lay Theories and Memory

There is an extensive and diffuse literature showing how prior knowledge, prototypes, scripts or "theories" affect judgement, recognition and recall (Cantor and Mischel, 1977; Hirt and Sherman, 1985).

For over 50 years psychological research has demonstrated that an individual's conceptual schemata, that is their belief systems of attitudes, stereotypes and theories, have a direct effect on how they encode and recall information. Bartlett (1932), in his watershed book subtitled "A study of experimental and social psychology", argued "Remembering is a constructive justification of attitude" (p. 208) and later, "Whenever strong, preferred persistent, social tendencies are subject to any form of social control, social remembering is very apt to take on a constructive and inventive character, either wittingly or unwittingly" (p. 267).

One idea emerging from schemata theory is the selective recall hypothesis. This suggests that people remember more information if it is congruent with their attitudes or theories, because they act as an organising framework that helps in the encoding and retrieval of attitude supportive material. That is, facts or arguments that challenge pre-established attitudes are lost in memory because to encode and retrieve antithetical information casts doubts on the beliefs themselves. Studies investigating the selective recall hypothesis have used a wide variety of stimulus material and have generally tended to support the selective recall hypothesis but not all have been successful. For instance, Furnham and Procter (1987), asked nearly 60 subjects to read a report of approximately 500 words presenting both pro- and anti- attitudes to nuclear technology. Two hours prior to this they completed the Nuclear Attitudes Questionnaire. Subjects were given free and cued recall tests approximately five minutes after reading the report. The results supported the selective recall hypothesis, particularly with respect to the free recall of anti-nuclear information.

Not all the research supports the selective recall hypothesis or related ideas like script theory. Nevertheless, the idea that lay theories affect memory provides one with another interesting way of investigating lay theories.

10.9 Errors in Lay Thinking: The Art of Doubt

Psychologists from various specialisms have long been puzzled by lay people's interest and belief in the psychic and the occult and "non-scientific" phenomena like astrology, graphology, etc. However, studies on why people believe in these phenomena have proved very illuminating, both in terms of explaining the techniques of astrologers, graphologists, etc., and also in showing people's pre-scientific theories.

(1) The Barnum Effect

Although people are frequently unhappy to complete and/or are dubious of the validity of properly psychometrised psychological tests they appear to enjoy and seek out the feedback of astrologers and graphologists.

In 1949 Forer wrote a critical paper questioning the validity of personality interpretations and measuring instruments, posing the problem of the gullibility or suggestibility of subjects when evaluating these feedback statements. He argued that there was a "fallacy of personal validation", in that because people frequently accept as correct generalised, vague, bogus descriptions of themselves which have high base-rate occurrence in the general population, their acceptance of the accuracy of personality interpretations in general cannot be used to support the validity of an instrument. Meehl (1956), who borrowed the concept from his colleague D. G. Patterson, later labelled this the "Barnum effect", after the famous phrase "there's a sucker born every minute"; a phenomenon whereby subjects accept personality feedback as true, whether it is universally valid or trivial, because it is supposedly derived from personality assessment procedures. Since then researchers have explored various aspects of the phenomenon and have generally confirmed early findings, which, it is argued, partly explains why people believe horoscopes and other quasi-scientific personality assessment procedures (graphology, tarot cards) to be true (Tyson, 1982).

Research has shown that although there is limited support for client (subject) or clinician (experimenter) characteristics, such as neuroticism or gullibility, explaining this phenomenon, what appears to explain the Barnum effect is the nature of the feedback and the test situation. If people are given *general feedback* (universally valid applying to nearly all the population) that is by-and-large *favourable* (that is positive) they will tend to believe it specifically true of them. Furthermore, if the assessment device is complicated and mystical (e.g., the use of a Rorschach; dream analysis) clients are likely to have even more faith in the procedure. The famous Barnum statements are shown in Table 10.1 and show the results from a study by Stagner (1958) who used personnel managers as subjects.

Furnham and Schofield (1987) have reviewed the, by now extensive, literature on the Barnum effect. Although it is true that early studies suggested that client acceptance of feedback was usually high if they were gullible, insecure and unsophisticated yet dealing with a high status consultant who delivered briefs, ambiguous, positive feedback supposedly developed for a *specific* client; more recent studies, however, have shown that clients (i.e. lay people) are not as gullible as previously thought, in that they can frequently pick out their profile from others; do realise that the feedback is general; and can discriminate between accurate and inaccurate feedback.

Nevertheless, it is still relatively easy to demonstrate the Barnum effect with lay people, which explains (in part) why they continue to seek out astrologers, graphologists and the like. That is, unless lay people are aware of the techniques of gathering highly specific information (e.g. exact place and time of birth) and then giving bland, general, favourable feedback, they can too easily be fooled by the perspicacity of those selling them bogus feedback.

(2) Bogus "Psychologists" and their Techniques

At various points in time, people "demonstrate" various psychic powers from spoon bending to remote viewing. Where these have been investigated, nearly all have proved to be unreplicable or explicable in terms of "trickery" or conventional scientific explanations. Marks and Kammann (1980) have sceptically analysed and appraised claims about ESP, precognition, clairvoyance, telepathy, psychokenesis and other related phenomena. They conclude their book with an appendix called "Modes for rationals or the art of doubt". These maxims are attempts to prevent lay people being fooled by bogus "psychic phenomena". The 10 rules are:

1. *If-what-then-what* — make the theorist be specific by asking what the theory predicts.

TABLE 10.1. *Evaluations of Items by 68 Personnel Managers, when Presented as a Personality Analysis*

Item	Judgement as to accuracy of item; percent choosing				
	Amazingly accurate	Rather good	About half and half	More wrong than right	Almost entirely wrong
You have a great need for other people to like and admire you	39	46	13	1	1
You have a tendency to be critical of yourself	46	36	15	3	0
You have a great deal of unused capacity which you have not turned to your advantage	37	36	18	1	4
While you have some personality weaknesses, you are generally able to compensate for them	34	55	9	0	0
Your sexual adjustment has presented problems for you	15	16	16	33	19
Disciplined and self-controlled outside, you tend to be worried and insecure inside	40	21	22	10	4
At times you have serious doubts as to whether you have made the right decision or done the right thing	27	31	19	18	4
You prefer a certain amount of change and variety and become dissatisfied when hemmed in by restrictions and limitations	63	28	7	1	1
You pride yourself as an independent thinker and do not accept others' statements without satisfactory proof	49	31	12	4	4
You have found it unwise to be too frank in revealing yourself to others	31	37	22	6	4
At times you are extroverted, affable, sociable, while at other times you are introverted, wary, reserved	43	25	18	9	5
Some of your aspirations tend to be pretty unrealistic	12	16	22	43	7
Security is one of your major goals in life	40	31	15	9	5

Not all percentages add to 100%, because of omissions by an occasional subject.
Reproduced with permission from Stagner, R. (1958). The gullibility of personnel managers. *Personal Psychology, 50*, 145–147.

2. *Disprovability* — ask the theorist what piece of evidence would be required to disprove his theory.
3. *Burden of proof* — it is for the theorist to prove or substantiate his belief in the theory, rather than your disbelief.
4. *Alternative thinking* — it is possible that other phenomena (i.e. mediating variables) explain the theorist's evidence, just as well as the phenomena he cites.
5. *Missing negative cases* — very often negative cases (those which "disprove" a theory) are omitted, so making the data look stronger. These need to be sought out.
6. *Personal observation* — subjective validations are not sufficient unless accompanied by detailed recorded observations.
7. *Testimonials* — personal experience is poor evidence because often people are not fully aware of forces acting upon them or their real needs and motives.
8. *Sources* — it is worth examining the credibility of the source of a theory, i.e., where it is published, debated, etc., as these sources are frequently dubious.
9. *Emotional commitment* — the more a person is ego-involved in a theory the less rationally and sceptically it may be assessed.
10. *Ad hominen technique* — "First a believer may hold certain authorities to be infallible, and quote their opinions as evidence. Second, he may try to place contrary believers into a category of bad people and thus reject their arguments out of hand. Third, he may turn against you, accusing you of bad motives or stupidity. All of these arguments are fallacious, and it is not only important to recognise them, but also not to use them. The object is to learn, not to win" (Marks and Kamman, 1980, p. 226).

10.10 The Self-Presentation of Lay Theories

No doubt specific situational factors, such as the number and type of people present, influence both the content and style of the public presentation of lay theories (Argyle *et al.* 1981). However, there are other more open forums where lay people express their views. These include such things as writing letters to the newspapers, writing letters of recommendation, as well as such things as book reviews. Some researchers have actually studied public letter writing. Cryns (1975) monitored the editorial columns of two daily American newspapers in a town that had seen campus unrest and prison riots. Over 120 letters were written; about 60 of these were content-analysed for their salience and whether they expressed favourable, unfavourable, or mixed reactions (according to four criteria). Some of the letter writers were then contacted and sent (under a realistic guise) various questionnaires measuring such things as their beliefs about human nature (anomie, authoritarianism and striving). Letter writers who were unfavourable to the campus unrest and prison riots had more pessimistic and simplistic views of human nature and were more positive about the past than authors favourably disposed to the students and prisoners. The sex of the author and the topic addressed (prison or campus) made no difference.

Similarly Furnham (1986b) studied over 50 letters to the Editor of *The Times* (of London) on the Burt scandal. Letters from lay people proved particularly interesting in the way in which they revealed their thinking on the heredity–environment issue. However, Furnham (1986b) argued that using these letters as data to study lay beliefs or theories is problematic for a number of reasons.

> First, newspaper readership is highly specific in terms of age, class, and geographic area. As it is perhaps most likely that people would write to a paper they read (and subscribe to), the demographic variables associated with writers are likely to be specific, homogeneous, and unrepresentative. Second, not all letters submitted to a newspaper are printed. Indeed, only a very small proportion of the letters that reach the editor may end up in the columns. Journalists may choose to accept letters using all sorts of criteria — brevity, style, balance, humor, or authorship — over which the researcher has neither control nor knowledge. Furthermore, letters are often cut by editors. In addition, the precise motive for the letter and sometimes the authorship (which may be multiple, anonymous, or pseudonymous) may be obscure and may reflect the views of a pressure group or otherwise interested party, rather than the attitudes of the signed individual. (p. 922)

Others have looked at letters of recommendations or references which also no doubt contain various lay theories about human nature. Baxter *et al.* (1981), who looked at the value of letters of recommendation (testimonials, references), found a pattern of nondiscriminative, nonconsensual and non-differentiating descriptions of people and found that the actual letter was more directly a function of the writers' idiosyncrasies than the students' qualities.

Similarly, book reviews offer an insight into people's beliefs. In a very interesting study of book reviews Amabile (1983) has shown that only pessimism sounds profound; optimism sounds superficial. If people are aware of this and want to present themselves as profound, they may be tempted to present negative, critical points in the press rather than positive ones, and the letters may not accurately reflect their opinions. It seems that intellectually insecure individuals exhibit and admire negative criticism more than praise, and that there is no logical reason to attribute higher intelligence to negative evaluations. Thus, as Furnham (1986e) has argued, book reviews frequently tell us more about the reviewer than the book. He notes:

> Thus, because book reviewers are identified by name, they may well be lead to self-presentational strategies that are presumably less apparent in anonymous journal article reviewers. In fact, some reviewers (of books, plays, music) are proud of their notoriously cutting, critical, sarcastic, negative reviews. While these may make amusing reading, they do not always sufficiently inform the reader of the contents, strengths and weakness, etc. of the book. (p. 31)

In other words, the forum or medium in, or through which, people express their lay theories may partly determine the form these theories take. It is

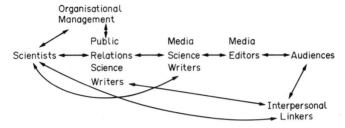

FIGURE 10.1. A Model of Science Communication Behaviours and Interactions.

possible that various attributional and self-presentation strategies mean that people may be more cynical or optimistic about human nature, or more damning or praising about the effort or merit of others. Thus one should be aware of the fact that lay theories may be offered in subtly different forms given the medium or context in which they are expressed.

10.11 The Communication of Scientific Information to Non-scientists

Lay people often base their theories on popular science magazines, books and pamphlets, which often attempt to make complicated scientific ideas and terminology interpretable for the lay person. But frequently, because of a number of intermediaries, each with different briefs and objectives, these ideas become distorted.

Grunig (1980) has developed a simple interactive model of this process.

He argues that there are two broad factors in this process — the individuals concerned and the interactions between them. Studies on science writers, editors, scientists, have shown how and where various errors arise. Similarly, systematic biases in the interactions between scientists and science writers, as well as many others, lead to specific problems.

Isaacs and Clark (1987) studied experimentally how experts and novices accommodate to their differences. As may be expected, experts assess and then supply specialised knowledge which is rapidly acquired by novices in order to make interaction more efficient.

The image of science in popular magazines frequently does as much to mystify and obfuscate as it does to clarify and explain. Furthermore, there is considerable difference between clarification and simplification. Often because a piece of writing or a concept passes through so many hands (but not always heads) it becomes distorted and it is thus incorrect or biased material which is held up as scientific fact. No wonder then that lay people do not always understand scientific theories.

10.12 Selling and Marketing Pet Theories

Academics and policy-makers know that they must "market" their "pet" theories for them to be adopted by a significant portion of the popular reading public — perhaps the simplest but clearest criterion of success. Lay people, too, try to convert their friends, family, peers and often a wider audience, to their point of view.

In order to understand how "scientific", and presumably lay, theories become accepted, popular and employed, Peter and Olson (1983) considered the marketing of scientific theories. A theory, they argue, is like a product, in that when it appears as a manuscript or book it takes on product-like characteristics or attributes. Theories that are easiest to understand and research, and which cover big areas or problems, are most frequently adopted. Secondly, the professional credentials and status of inventor or perpetrator determine popularity. Also, theories drawn from familiar fields using familiar words, and consistent with current socio-political values, are more likely to be adopted. The extent to which the theory has empirical support seems to be more relevant to scientists than to lay people.

As scientific theories are test marketed among colleagues, friends and interest groups in the "invisible college", so lay theories are tried out on family, friends and depending on the feedback, pursued. Scientific theories are distributed through a wide variety of channels — books, journals, conference proceedings, departmental papers. Lay theories are, however, rarely formally printed and circulated in this way. Scientific theories are "promoted" or advertised in trade magazines and journals, and in this capacity may actually become incorporated into lay theories. The price of theories determines their market — easily accessible new theories consistent with the prevailing world view are cheap, but ones that may cause a scientific revolution are expensive and, therefore, may not be adopted. High-priced theories may be risky, too counter-intuitive or demand too long a time-horizon commitment to be useful.

There are all sorts of markets for scientific and lay theories which may predict how effectively or quickly they are accepted, developed and spread. Zealous, committed individuals who have invested most in the theory are, not unsurprisingly, the most keen to perpetrate lay theories.

According to Peter and Olson (1983) there are often three objectives for marketing theories: the noble goal of furthering knowledge and understanding; curiosity in determining reactions; and self-serving goals of personal gain.

They tend to opt for the relativist/constructionist view and offer various recommendations to further that view. They include scientific training in formulating, rather than simply testing hypotheses; evaluating the truthfulness as much as the validity of data; admitting that science is a joint social activity and admitting that many findings are culture and situation specific.

What their work does alert one to is how theories are sold — packaged, advertised and marketed. Political theories are most frequently marketed on the media as are economic theories, but much less so theories of statistics or mental health. Clearly, how, where and why theories are marketed have

TABLE 10.2. *Major Differences between Positivistic/Empiricist and Relativistic/Constructionist Views of Science*

Positivistic/empiricist science	Relativistic/constructionist science
Science discovers the true nature of reality	Science creates many realities
Only the logic of justification is needed to understand science	The processes by which theories are created, justified, and diffused throughout a research community are needed to understand science
Science can be understood without considering cultural, social, political and economic factors	Science is a social process and cannot be understood without considering cultural, social, political and economic factors
Science is objective	Science is subjective
Scientific knowledge is absolute and cumulative	Scientific knowledge is relative to a particular context and period of time in history
Science is capable of discovering universal laws that govern the external world	Science creates ideas that are context-dependent, i.e. relative to a frame of reference
Science produces theories that come closer and closer to absolute truth	Truth is a subjective evaluation that cannot be properly inferred outside of the context provided by the theory
Science is rational since it follows formal rules of logic	Science is rational to the degree that it seeks to improve individual and societal well-being by following whatever means are useful for doing so
There are specific rules for doing science validly (e.g. falsification)	There are many ways of doing science validly that are appropriate in different situations
Scientists subject their theories to potential falsification through rigorous empirical testing	Scientists seek supportive, confirmatory evidence in order to market their theories
Measurement procedures do not influence what is measured	Nothing can be measured without changing it
Data provided objective, independent benchmarks for testing theories	Data are created and interpreted by scientists in terms of a variety of theories, and thus are theory laden.

Reprinted with permission from the *Journal of Marketing*, published by the American Marketing Association. Peter, J. and Olson, J. (1983). Is Science Marketing? *Journal of Marketing*, **47**, 111-125.

extremely important implications for their adoption and eventual implementation.

10.13 Choosing, Using and Formulating Theories

It was argued in the first two chapters that there are a number of criteria whereby one can choose a theory (to adopt to formulate hypotheses or to explain phenomena) such as parsimony, consistency, validity, flexibility, etc. Few lay people undertake a formal evaluation of theories, preferring a more pragmatic evaluation. However, this is often fraught with difficulties — it may be difficult to translate the theory into action or observable data, it is frequently problematic in establishing the criteria of success or failure. There is also the problem, bound up with dissonance reduction, of investing so much time and energy in comprehending a theory that people are loath to discard it in the face of considerable evidence that it is false. Alternatively, abandoning the terminology and jargon of a theory as well as respect, friendship and support of a believer group may be so threatening and difficult that it is rarely done.

Thus, once they have chosen a theory, people tend to stick with it. Further, the theory tends to predispose the follower to observe and accept facts compatible with the theory, and it becomes the core feature in group allegiances and social discourse. What is being suggested, then, is that the choosing and using of theories can be very dangerous, even if they are substantially true, because they need to be constantly and dispassionately evaluated.

For most phenomena people adopt theoretical positions they may imperfectly understand. Thus one finds vulgar Marxists, vulgar Freudians and, more recently, vulgar socio-biologists who having grasped some of the basic concepts of a theory seek minimal confirmatory evidence and, worse still, apply the theory to the explanation of phenomena it was never designed to explain.

However, there are probably even more dangers involved if a person actually formulates their own unique theory, which does occur. Because so much more is invested in the theory, originators are likely to be even more susceptible to the traps outlined above. The history of science is littered with stories of scientists who persist in the face of overwhelming disconfirmatory evidence. Also, modern business schools set exercises which encourage groups to adopt theoretical explanations and then see how they react to a mixture of confirmatory, disconfirmatory and irrelevant information.

The moral is simply this: there are various dangers in the choosing, using or formulating of theories. It is infrequently a disinterested, patient, passive, presuppositionless inquiry and hence there may be important psychological, rather than rational, principles that dictate when, how or why lay theories are adopted (Klayman and Ha, 1987).

References

Able, G., Blanchard, E. and Becker, J. (1976) Psychological treatment of rapists. In: S. Brodsky and Walker, M. (Eds.), *Sexual Assault.* New York Lexicon: MA, pp. 46–71.

Ahmed, S. and Viswarathan, P. (1984) Factor analytical study of Nunnally's scale of popular concepts of mental health. *Psychological Reports,* **54**, 455–461.

Albee, G. (1982) The politics of nature and nurture. *American Journal of Community Psychology,* **10**, 4–36.

Albee, G. (1983) Political ideology and science: A reply to Eysenck. *American Psychologist,* **38**, 965–966.

Allen, V. (1970) *Psychological factors in poverty.* Chicago: Markham.

Allsop, J. and Feldman, M. (1976) Personality and antisocial behaviour in schoolboys. *British Journal of Criminology,* **16**, 337–351.

Amabile, T. (1983) Brilliant but cruel: Perceptions of negative evaluations. *Journal of Experimental Social Psychology,* **19**, 146–156.

Antaki, C. (Ed.) (1981) *The psychology of explanations,* London: Academic Press.

Argyle, M., Furnham, A. and Graham, J. (1981) *Social situations.* Cambridge: Cambridge University Press.

Asch, S. (1946) Forming impressions of personality. *Journal of Abnormal and Social Psychology,* **41**, 258–290.

Ashton, and Goldberg, L. (1973) In response to Jackson's challenge: The comparative validity of personality scales constructed by the external (empirical) strategy and scales developed intuitively by experts, novices and laymen. *Journal of Research in Personality,* **7**, 1–20.

Ashton, H. and Stepney, R. (1982) *Smoking: Psychology and Pharmacology.* London: Tavistock.

Austin, W., Walster, E. and Utne, M. (1976) Equity and the law: The effect of harmdoer's "suffering in the act" on liking and assigned punishment. In: L. Berkowitz and E. Walster (Eds.), *Advances in experimental social psychology,* New York: Academic Press, pp. 163–190.

Bacon, M. and Ashmore, R. (1985) How mothers and fathers categorize descriptions of social behaviour attributed to daughters and sons. *Social Cognition,* **3**, 193–217.

Balch, P. and Ross, A. (1975) Predicting success in weight reduction as a function of locus of control: A unidimensional and mutidimensional approach. *Journal of Consulting and Clinical Psychology,* **43**, 119.

Banks, C., Maloney, E. and Willcock, H. (1975) Public attitudes to crime and the penal system. *British Journal of Criminology,* **15**, 228–240.

Banner, C. (1979) Child-rearing attitudes to mothers of under-, average- and over-achieving children. *British Journal of Educational Psychology,* **49**, 150–155.

Baron, R. (1983) *Behaviour in organizations: Understanding and managing the human side of work.* Boston: Allyn & Bacon.

Baron, R. and Byrne, D. (1981) *Social psychology: Understanding human interaction.* Boston: Allyn & Bacon.

Bar-Tal, D. and Guttman, J. (1981) A comparison of teachers', pupils' and parents' attributions regarding pupils' academic achievements. *British Journal of Educational Psychology,* **51**, 301–311.

Bar-Tal, D., Goldberg, M. and Knaani, A. (1984) Causes of success and failure and their dimensions as a function of SES and gender: A phenomenological analysis. *British Journal of Educational Psychology*, **54**, 51–61.

Bar-Tal, D., Raviv, A., Raviv, A. and Levit, R. (1981) Teachers' reactions to attributions of ability and effort and their predictions of students' reactions. *Educational Psychology*, **3**, 231–240.

Bartlett, Sir F. (1932) *Remembering: A study of experimental and social psychology*. Cambridge: Cambridge University Press.

Barton, K. and Garbach, T. (1985) Teachers' and school psychologists' perceptions of school psychologists. *Perceptual and Motor Skills*, **60**, 1003–1009.

Baxter, J., Brook, B., Hall, P. and Roselle, R. (1981) Letters of recommendation: A question of value. *Journal of Applied Psychology*, **66**, 296–301.

Beard, G. (1880) *A practical treatment of nervous exhaustion (neurasthenia): Its symptoms, nature, sequences and treatment*. New York: Wood.

Becker, M. (1974) The Health Belief Model and personal health behaviour. *Health Education Monographs*, **2**, 328–335.

Beckman, L. (1979) Beliefs about the causes of alcohol-related problems among alcoholic and non-alcoholic women. *Journal of Clinical Psychology*, **35**, 663–670.

Beez, W. (1972) Influence of biased psychological reports on teacher behaviour and pupil performance. In: A. Morrison and D. McIntyre (Eds.), *Social psychology of teaching*. Harmondsworth: Penguin.

Belson, W. (1975) *The public and the police*. London: Harper & Row.

Bem, D. (1967) Self-perception: An alternative interpretation of cognitive dissonance phenomena. *Psychological Review*, **74**, 183–200.

Bentz, W. and Edgerton, J. (1970) Consensus on attitudes toward mental illness. *Archives of General Psychiatry*, **22**, 468–473.

Berry, J. (1984) Towards a universal psychology of cognitive competence. *International Journal of Psychology*, **19**, 335–361.

Berti, A., Bombi, A. and Lis, A. (1982) The child's conception about means of production and their owners. *European Journal of Social Psychology*, **12**, 221–239.

Best, J. (1982) Misconceptions about psychology among students who perform highly. *Psychological Reports*, **51**, 239–244.

Biggs, J., Fitzgerald, D. and Atkinson, S. (1972) Convergent and divergent abilities in children and teachers' ratings of competence and certain classroom behaviours. *British Journal of Educational Psychology*, **42**, 277–286.

Blease, D. (1983) Teacher expectations and the self-fulfilling prophesy. *Education Studies*, **9**, 123–129.

Bord, R. (1971) Rejection of the mentally ill: Continuities and further developments. *Social Problems*, **18**, 496–509.

Boyle, C. (1970) Differences between patients' and doctors' interpretation of some medical terms. *British Medical Journal*, **2**, 286–289.

Blackmore, S. and Troscianko, T. (1985) Belief in the paranormal: Probability, judgements, illusory control and the "chance baseline shift". *British Journal of Psychology*, **76**, 459–468.

BPS (1979) *Report of the society's working party on corporal punishment in schools*. Leicester.

Braun, J. and Linder, D. (1979) *Psychology today*. New York: Random House.

Broadbent, D. (1961) *Behaviour*. London: Eyre & Spottiswoode.

Breubeck, C. (1971) *Social foundations of education*. New York: John Wiley.

Brickman, P. (1980) A social psychology of human concerns. In: R. Gilmour and S. Duck (Eds.), *The development of social psychology*. London: Academic Press.

Brooks-Gunn, J. (1985) The relationship of maternal beliefs about sex-typing to maternal and young children's behaviour. *Sex Roles*, **14**, 21–35.

Brown, M. (1970) *What economics is about*. London: Weidenfeld & Nicolson.

Brown, R. and Brown, N. (1982) Bias in psychology and introductory psychology textbooks. *Psychological Reports*, **51**, 1195–1204.

Bruner, J. and Taguiri, R. (1954) The perception of people. In: G. Lindzey (Ed.), *The handbook of social psychology*. Reading, MA: Addison-Wesley.

Budd, R. and Spencer, C. (1986) Lay theories of behavioural intention: A source of response bias in the theory of reasoned action? *British Journal of Social Psychology*, **25**, 109–117.

Burbeck, E. and Furnham, A. (1985) Police officer selection: A critical review of the literature.

Journal of Police Science and Administration, **13**, 58–69.

Burdsal, C. and Bardo, T. (1986) Measuring students perceptions of teaching: Dimensions of evaluation. *Educational and Psychological Measurement,* **46**, 63–79.

Burns, R. (1977) Teachers' beliefs on the relative effectiveness of reforms for motivating pupils and alleviating behaviour problems. *Educational Studies,* **3**, 185–190.

Burton, A. (1986) Programming common sense: Analytic consequences of Heider's naive analysis of action. *Human Relations,* **39**, 725–744.

Buss, A. (1966) *Psychopathology.* New York: John Wiley.

Butler, R. (1986) The role of generalized expectancies in determining causal attribution for success and failure in two social classes. *British Journal of Educational Psychology,* **56**, 51–63.

Calhoun, A., Pearce, J. and Dawes, A. (1973) Attribution theory concepts and outpatients' perceptions of the causal basis of their psychological problems. *Journal of Community Psychology,* **1**, 52–58.

Callaghan, C. and Manstead, A. (1983) Causal attributions for task performance: The effects of performance outcome and sex of subject. *British Journal of Educational Psychology,* **53**, 14–23.

Calnan, M. (1984) The health belief model and participation in programmes for the early detection of breast cancer: A comparative analysis. *Social Science and Medicine,* **19**, 823–830.

Cantor, N. and Mischel, W. (1977) Traits as prototypes: Effects of recognition memory. *Journal of Personality and Social Psychology,* **35**, 38–48.

Cantor, N., Mischel, W. and Schwartz, J. (1982) Social knowledge: Structure, content, use and abuse. In: A. Hastor and A. Isen (Eds.), *Cognitive social psychology.* New York: Elsevier.

Caro, I., Miralles, A. and Rippere, V. (1983) What's the thing to do when you're feeling depressed? A cross cultural replication. *Behaviour Research and Therapy,* **21**, 477–483.

Carr, W. (1986) Theories of theory and practice. *Journal of Philosophy of Education,* **20**, 177–186.

Carraher, T., Carraher, D. and Schliemann, A. (1985) Mathematics in the street and in the schools. *British Journal of Developmental Psychology,* **3**, 21–29.

Cattell, R. (1965) *The scientific analysis of personality.* Harmondsworth: Penguin.

Ceci, S. and Liker, J. (1986) A day at the races: A study of IQ, expertise and cognitive complexity. *Journal of Experimental Psychology,* **115**, 255–266.

Chalmers, A. (1986) *What is this thing called science?* Milton Keynes: Open University Press.

Child, I. (1968) Socialization. In: E. Lindzey (Ed.), *Handbook of social psychology.* Reading, MA: Addison-Wesley.

Christie, R. and Geis, F. (Eds.) (1970) *Studies in Machiavellianism.* New York: Academic Press.

Clare, A. (1979) The causes of alcoholism. *British Journal of Hospital Medicine,* **4**, 103–110.

Cohen, L. (1982) Are people programmed to commit fallacies? Further thoughts about the interpretation of experimental data on probability judgement. *Journal for the Theory of Social Behaviour,* **12**, 251–273.

Coleman, J., Butcher, J. and Carson, R. (1980) *Abnormal psychology and modern life.* London: Scott, Foresman.

Colman, A. (1984) *What is psychology?* London: Kogan Page.

Compas, B., Adelman, H., Freundl, P., Nelson, P. and Taylor, L. (1982) Parent and children causal attributions during clinical interviews. *Journal of Abnormal Child Psychology,* **10**, 77–84.

Conklin, E. (1919) Superstitious belief and practice among college students. *American Journal of Psychology,* **30**, 83–102.

Cook, M. (1979) *Perceiving others: The psychology of interpersonal perception.* London: Methuen.

Cook, M. (1984) *Levels of Personality.* London: Holt, Rinehart and Winston.

Cooper, H. (1979) Pygmalion grows up: A model for teacher expectation communication and performance influence. *Reviews of Educational Research,* **49**, 389–410.

Cornish, P. (1978) *Gambling: A review of the literature and its implications for policy and research.* London: HMSO.

Cryns, A. (1975) Public letter writing in response to campus unrest and prison riots. *Journal of Personality and Social Psychology,* **31**, 516–521.

Custer, R. (1976) *Description of compulsive gambling.* Unpublished paper.

D'Andrade, R. (1974) Memory and the assessment of behaviour. In: H. M. Blalock Jr. (Ed.), *Measurement in the social sciences.* Chicago: Aldine-Atherton.

Dann, H-D. (1986) *Reconstruction and validation of teachers' interaction-relevant subjective theories.* Paper presented at the Third European Conference on Personality. Gdansk: Poland.

Darley, J. and Goethals, G. (1980) People's analyses of the causes of ability-linked performances. In: L. Berkowitz (Ed.), *Advances in experimental social psychology.* New York: Academic Press.

Davidson, C. and Gaitz, C. (1974) Are the poor different? A comparison of work behaviour and attitudes between the urban poor and non poor. *Social Problems*, **22**, 229–245.

Devereaux, E. (1968) Gambling in psychological and sociological perspective. *International Encyclopedia of the Social Sciences*, **6**, 53–62.

Dielman, T., Leech, S., Lorenger, B. and Horvath, W. (1984) Health locus of control and self-esteem as related to adolescent health behaviour and intention. *Adolescence*, **19**, 935–950.

Doring, A. (1984) Beliefs about the employed and the unemployed held by senior High School students in North Queensland. *Australian Journal of Psychology*, **28**, 78–88.

Douglas, J. (1974) *Understanding everyday life.* London: Routledge & Kegan Paul.

Downey, M. and Kelly, A. (1980) *Theory and practice of education.* London: Harper & Row.

Edwards, D. (1984) Perception of personality and social behaviour in different racial groups by black and white university students. *South African Journal of Psychology*, **14**, 79–81.

Effler, M. (1984) Attribution theories or lay epistemology? *European Journal of Social Psychology*, **14**, 431–437.

Einhorn, H. (1980) Overconfidence in judgement. In: R. Schweder (Ed.), *Fallible judgement in behavioural research.* San Francisco: Jossey-Bass.

Einhorn, H. and Hogarth, R. (1978) Confidence in judgement: Persistence of the illusion of validity. *Psychological Review*, **85**, 395–416.

Einhorn, H. and Hogarth, R. (1986) Judging probable cause. *Psychological Bulletin*, **99**, 3–19.

Eiser, J. and van der Pligt, J. (1983) Actors' and observers' attributions, self-serving bias and positivity bias. *European Journal of Social Psychology*, **13**, 95–104.

Eiser, J., Sutton, S. and Wober, M. (1977) Smokers, non-smokers and the attribution of addictions. *British Journal of Social and Clinical Psychology*, **16**, 329–336.

Eiser, J., Sutton, S. and Wober, M. (1978a) Smokers' and non-smokers' attribution about smoking: A case of actor–observer differences? *British Journal of Social and Clinical Psychology*, **17**, 189–190.

Eiser, J., Sutton, S. and Wober, M. (1978b) "Consonant" and "Dissonant" smokers and the self-attribution of addiction. *Addictive Behaviours*, **3**, 99–106.

Elkind, A. (1982) Changes in the smoking behaviour, knowledge and opinion of medical students, 1972–1981. *Social Science and Medicine*, **16**, 2137–2143.

Ellis, N. and Richard, H. (1977) Evaluating the teaching of introductory psychology. *Teaching of Psychology*, **4**, 128–132.

Elvin, L. (1977) *The place of commonsense in educational thought.* London: Allen & Unwin.

Epstein, Y. and Babad, E. (1982) Economic stress: Notes on the psychology of inflation. *Journal of Applied Social Psychology*, **12**, 85–99.

Erskine, H. (1974) The polls: Causes of crime. *Public Opinion Quarterly*, **38**, 288–295.

Evans, J. and Bradshaw, H. (1986) Estimating sample-size requirements in research design: A study of intuitive statistical judgement. *Current Psychology Research*, **5**, 10–19.

Eysenck, H. (1947) Primary social attitudes — I. The organisation and measurement of social attitudes. *International Journal of Opinion and Attitude Research*, **1**, 49–84.

Eysenck, H. (1957) *Sense and nonsense in psychology.* Harmondsworth: Penguin.

Eysenck, H. (1960) The place of theory in psychology. In: H. Eysenck (Ed.), *Experiments in personality.* London: Routledge & Kegan Paul.

Eysenck, H. (1964) *Crime and punishment.* London: Routledge & Kegan Paul.

Eysenck, H. (1965) *Smoking, health and personality.* London: Weidenfeld & Nicolson.

Eysenck, H. (1978) *You and neurosis.* Glasgow: Collins.

Eysenck, H. (Ed.) (1981) *A model for personality.* Berlin: Springer.

Eysenck, H. (1982) The sociology of psychological knowledge, the genetic interpretation of the IQ, and Marxist–Leninist ideology. *Bulletin of the British Psychological Society*, **35**,

449–451.

Eysenck, H. and Eysenck, S. (1975) *Eysenck Personality Questionnaire manual*. London: Hodder & Stoughton.

Farb, P. and Armelagos, G. (1980) *Consuming passions: The anthropology of eating*. Boston: Houghton Mifflin.

Farley, F. and Goh, D. (1976) PENmanship: faking the P-E-N. *British Journal of Social and Clinical Psychology*, **15**, 139–148.

Farina, A. (1981) Are women nicer than men? Sex and the stigma of mental disorders. *Clinical Psychology Review*, **1**, 223–243.

Fawcett, B., Ingham, E., McKeever, M. and Williams, S. (1979) Social skills group for young prisoners. *Social Work Today*, **10**, 16–18.

Feagin, J. (1975) *Subordinating the poor*. Englewood Cliffs, NJ: Prentice-Hall.

Feather, N. (1974) Explanations of poverty in Australian and American samples: The person, society and fate. *Australian Journal of Psychology*, **26**, 199–216.

Feather, N. (1982) Unemployment and its psychological correlates: A study of depressive symptoms, self-esteem, Protestant ethic values, attributional style and apathy. *Australian Journal of Psychology*, **34**, 309–323.

Feather, N. (1983) Causal attributions and beliefs about work and unemployment among adolescents in state and independent secondary schools. *Australian Journal of Psychology*, **35**, 211–232.

Feather, N. (1985) Attitudes, values and attributions. Explanations of unemployments. *Journal of Personality and Social Psychology*, **48**, 876–889.

Feather, N. and Davenport, P. (1981) Unemployment and depressive effect: A motivational and attributional analysis. *Journal of Personality and Social Psychology*, **41**, 422–436.

Festinger, L. (1957) *A theory of cognitive dissonance*. Stanford: Stanford University Press.

Fincham, J. and Wertheimer, A. (1985) Using the health belief model to predict initial drug therapy defaulting. *Social Science and Medicine*, **20**, 101–105.

Fitzpatrick, R. (1984) Lay concepts of illness. In: R. Fitzpatrick, J. Hinton, S. Newman, G. Scambler and J. Thompson (Eds.), *The experience of illness*. London: Tavistock, pp. 11–30.

Finnegan, J., Larson, P. and Haag, H. (1945) The role of nicotine in the cigarette habit. *Science*, **102**, 94–96.

Fletcher, G. (1984) Psychology and common sense. *American Psychologist*, **39**, 203–213.

Flugel, J. (1947) An inquiry as to popular views on intelligence and related topics. *British Journal of Educational Psychology*, **17**, 140–152.

Fong, G., Krantz, D. and Nisbett, R. (1986) The effects of statistical training on thinking about everyday problems. *Cognitive Psychology*, **18**, 253–292.

Fontes, P., Kelleghan, T. Madaus, G. and Airasian, P. (1983) Opinions of the Irish public on intelligence. *Irish Journal of Education*, **2**, 55–67.

Foot, P. (1977) *Why you should be a socialist*. London: Socialist Workers Party.

Forgas, J., Morris, S. and Furnham, A. (1982) Lay explanations of wealth: Attributions for economic success. *Journal of Applied Social Psychology*, **12**, 381–397.

Forsyth, D. (1980) A taxonomy of ethical ideologies. *Journal of Personality and Social Psychology*, **39**, 175–184.

Forsyth, D. (1981) The influence of ethical ideology. *Personality and Social Psychology Bulletin*, **7**, 218–223.

Forsyth, D. and Berger, R. (1982) The effects of ethical ideology on moral behaviour. *Journal of Social Psychology*, **117**, 53–56.

Freedman, B., Rosenthal, L., Danahoe, C. and McFall, R. (1979) A social behavioural analysis of skills deficits in delinquent and non-delinquent adolescent boys. *Journal of Consulting and Clinical Psychology*, **46**, 1148–1163.

French, L. and Waites, S. (1982) Perceptions of sexual deviance: a bi-racial analysis. *International Journal of Offender Therapy and Comparative Criminology*, **26**, 242–249.

Frieze, I. (1979) *Women's beliefs about the causes of alcoholism in other women*. Unpublished paper, University of Pittsburgh.

Frieze, I. and Snyder, H. (1980) Children's beliefs about the causes of success and failure in school settings. *Journal of Educational Psychology*, **73**, 186–196.

Fry, P. and Ghosh, R. (1980) Attributions of success and failure: Comparisons of cultural differences between Asian and Caucasian children. *Journal of Cross-Cultural Psychology*,

11, 343–363.

Furnham, A. (1982a) Why are the poor always with us? Explanations for poverty in Britain. *British Journal of Social Psychology*, **20**, 311–322.

Furnham, A. (1982b) The Protestant work ethic and attitudes towards unemployment. *Journal of Occupational Psychology*, **55**, 277–285.

Furnham, A. (1982c) Explanations for unemployment in Britain. *European Journal of Social Psychology*, **12**, 335–352.

Furnham, A. (1982d) The perception of poverty among adolescents. *Journal of Adolescence*, **5**, 135–147.

Furnham, A. (1983a) Attributions for affluence. *Personality and Individual Differences*, **4**, 31–40.

Furnham, A. (1983b) Social psychology as common sense. *Bulletin of the British Psychological Society*, **36**, 105–109.

Furnham, A. (1983c) The A type behaviour pattern, mental health and health locus of control beliefs. *Social Science and Medicine*, **17**, 1569–1572.

Furnham, A. (1984a) Work values and beliefs in Britain. *Journal of Occupational Behaviour*, **5**, 281–291.

Furnham, A. (1984b) Lay conceptions of neuroticism. *Personality and Individual Differences*, **5**, 95–103.

Furnham, A. (1984c) Unemployment, attribution theory, and mental health: A review of British literature. *International Journal of Mental Health*, **13**, 51–67.

Furnham, A. (1984d) Personality, social skills, anomie and delinquency: A self-report study of a group of normal non-delinquent adolescents. *Journal of Child Psychology and Psychiatry*, **25**, 409–420.

Furnham, A. (1985a) A short measure of economic beliefs. *Personality and Individual Differences*, **6**, 123–126.

Furnham, A. (1985b) *School-leavers' knowledge of psychology*. Unpublished paper.

Furnham, A. (1985c) The determinants of attitudes towards social security recipients. *British Journal of Social Psychology*, **24**, 19–27.

Furnham, A. (1985d) Attitudes to, and habits of, gambling in Britain. *Personality and Individual Differences*, **6**, 493–502.

Furnham, A. (1985e) Just world beliefs in an unjust society: A cross cultural comparison. *European Journal of Social Psychology*, **15**, 363–366.

Furnham, A. (1986a) Response bias, social desirability and dissimulation. *Personality and Individual Differences*, **7**, 385–400.

Furnham, A. (1986b) Popular interest in psychological findings: *The Times* correspondence over the Burt scandal. *American Psychologist*, **87**, 922–924.

Furnham, A. (1986c) Medical students' beliefs about nine different specialities. *British Medical Journal*, **293**, 1607–1610.

Furnham, A. (1986d) Children's understanding of the economic world. *Australian Journal of Education*, **30**, 219–240.

Furnham, A. (1986e) Book reviews as a selection tool for libraries: Comments from a psychologist. *Collection Management*, **8**, 33–43.

Furnham, A. (1987) The proverbial truth: Reconciling the truthfulness of antonymous proverbs. *Journal of Language and Social Psychology*, **6**, 49–55.

Furnham, A. (1988a) *The Protestant work ethic*. London: Methuen.

Furnham, A. (1988b) Coping with inflation. *Applied Psychology*. In Press.

Furnham, A. And Alibhai, N. (1983) Cross-cultural differences in the perception of female body shapes. *Psychological Medicine*, **13**, 829–837.

Furnham, A. and Bland, K. (1983) The Protestant work ethic and conservatism. *Personality and Individual Differences*, **4**, 205–206.

Furnham, A. and Henderson, M. (1983a) The mote in my brother's eye and the beam in their own: Predicting one's own and others' personality test scores. *British Journal of Psychology*. **74**, 381–389.

Furnham, A. and Henderson, M. (1983b) Lay theories of delinquency. *European Journal of Social Psychology*, **13**, 107–120.

Furnham, A. and Henley, S. (1988) Lay beliefs about overcoming psychological problems. *Journal of Social and Clinical Psychology*, (in press).

Furnham, A. and Hesketh, B. (1988) Explanations for unemployment: A cross-national study. *Journal of Social Psychology*, (in press).

Furnham, A. and Lewis, A. (1986) *The economic mind*. Brighton: Wheatsheaf.

Furnham, A. and Lowick, V. (1984a) Lay theories of the causes of alcoholism. *British Journal of Medical Psychology*, **57**, 319-332.

Furnham, A. and Lowick, V. (1984b) Attitudes to alcohol consumption: The attributions of addiction. *Social Science and Medicine*, **18**, 673-681.

Furnham, A. and Pendred, J. (1983) Attitudes towards the mentally and physically disabled. *British Journal of Medical Psychology*, **56**, 179-187.

Furnham, A. and Procter, E. (1987) Memory for information about nuclear power: A test of the selective recall hypothesis. Unpublished paper.

Furnham, A. and Schofield, S. (1987) Accepting personality test feedback: A review of the Barnum effect. *Current Psychological Reviews and Research*, **6**, 162-178.

Furnham, A. and Singh, A. (1987) Memory for information about sex differences. *Sex Roles*, **15**, 479-486.

Furnham, A., Johnson, C. and Rawles, R. (1985) The determinants of beliefs in human nature. *Personality and Individual Differences*, **6**, 675-684.

Furth, H. (1980) *The world of grown-ups*. New York: Elsevier.

Gale, A. (1985) *What is psychology?* London: Edward Arnold.

Gallup, G. (1983) Gallup poll of the public's attitude toward the public schools. *Phi Delta Kappa*, **65**, 33-47.

Gammack, G. (1982) Social work as uncommon sense. *British Journal of Social Work*, **12**, 3-22.

Gans, H. (1972) The positive functions of poverty. *American Journal of Sociology*, **78**, 275-289.

Garfinkle, H. (1959) Aspects of the problem of common-sense knowledge of social structures. *Transactions of the Fourth World Congress of Sociology*, Louvain, Belgium.

Garofalo, J. and Lamb, J. (1982) The fear of crime: broadening our perspective. *Victimology: An International Journal*, **3**, 242-253.

Gendreau, P., Irvine, M. and Knight, S. (1973) Evaluating response set styles on the MMPI with prisoners: faking good adjustment and maladjustment. *Canadian Journal of Behavioural Science*, **5**, 183-194.

Gerbner, G. and Gross, L. (1976) Living with television: the violence profile. *Journal of Communications*, **26**, 173-199.

Gerbner, G., Gross, L., Elley, R., Jackson-Beeck, M., Jeffries-Fox, S. and Signomelli, N. (1977) Television violence profile No.8. The highlights. *Journal of Communication*, **27**, 171-180.

Gergen, K. (1980) Toward intellectual audacity in social psychology. In: R. Gilmour and S. Duck (Eds.), *The development of social psychology*. London: Academic Press.

Gergen, K. (1986) The social constructivist movement in modern psychology. *American Psychologist*, **40**, 266-275.

Giddens, A. (1987) *Social theory and modern sociology*. Worcester: Polity Press.

Gilbert, R. (1984) *Depression*. London: Lawrence Erlbaum.

Gill, R. and Keats, P. (1982) Elements of intellectual competence: Judgements by Australian and Malay university students. *Journal of Cross-Cultural Psychology*, **11**, 233-243.

Gilovich, R. and Douglas, C. (1986) Biased evaluations of randomly determined gambling outcomes. *Journal of Experimental Social Psychology*, **22**, 228-241.

Goodnow, J. (1980) Everyday concepts of intelligence and its development. In: N. Warren (Ed.), *Studies in cross-cultural psychology*. London: Academic press.

Goodnow, J. (1984) Parents' ideas about parenting and development: A review of issues and recent work. In: M. Lamb, A. Brown and B. Rogoff (Eds.), *Advances in developmental psychology*, Vol.3. Hillsdale, NJ: Lawrence Erlbaum.

Goodwin, L. (1973) Middle-class misperceptions of the high life, aspirations and strong work ethic held by the welfare poor. *American Journal of Orthopsychiatry*, **43** 554-564.

Gray, J. (1972) Self-rating and Eysenck Personality inventory estimates of neuroticism and extraversion. *Psychological Report*, **30**, 213-214.

Greenberg, H. (1980) Psychology of Gambling: In: J. Kaplan *et al.* (Eds.), *Comprehensive textbook of psychiatry*, Vol. III. London: Williams & Williams.

Gregory, C. (1975) Changes in superstitious beliefs among college women. *Psychological Reports*, **37**, 939-944.

Gruman, J. and Sloan, R. (1983) Disease as justice: Perceptions of the victims of physical illness. *Basic and Applied Social Psychology*, **4**, 49–56.

Grunig, J. (1980) Communication of scientific information to non-scientists. Unpublished paper.

Gudjonsson, G. (1984) Attribution of blame for criminal acts and its relationship with personality. *Personality and Individual Differences*, **5**, 53–58.

Gunter, B. and Wakshlag, J. (1986) *Television viewing and perception of crime among London residents*. Unpublished paper.

Gurney, R. (1981) Leaving school, facing unemployment and making attributions about the causes of unemployment. *Journal of Vocational Behaviour*, **18**, 79–91.

Hall, C. and Lindzey, G. (1957) *Theories of personality*. New York: John Wiley.

Hall, L. and Tucker, C. (1985) Relationships between ethnicity, conceptions of mental illness, and attitudes associated with seeking psychological help. *Psychological Report*, **57**, 907–916.

Hampson, S. (1982) *The construction of personality: An introduction*. London: Routledge & Kegan Paul.

Hansen, R. (1980) Commonsense attribution. *Journal of Personality and Social Psychology*, **39**, 996–1009.

Hardiker, P. and Webb, D. (1979) Explaining deviant behaviour: The social context of "action" and "infraction" accounts in the probation service. *Sociology*, **13**, 1–16.

Harding, C., Eiser, J. and Kristiansen, C. (1982) The representation of mortality statistics and the perceived importance of causes of death. *Journal of Applied Social Psychology*, **12**, 169–181.

Hargreaves, D. (1981) Common-sense models of action. In A. Chapman and D. Jones (Eds.), *Models of man*. Leicester: British Psychological Society, pp. 215–225.

Harré, R. (1984) *Pesonal being*. Oxford: Blackwell.

Harris, M. and Smith, S. (1982) Beliefs about obesity: Effects of age, ethnicity, sex and weight. *Psychological Reports*, **51**, 1047–1055.

Harrison, N. and McLaughlin, R. (1969) Self-rating validation of Eysenck Personality Inventory. *British Journal of Social and Clinical Psychology*, **8**, 315–330.

Harrod, D. (1983) *Making Sense of the Economy*. Oxford: Martin Robertson.

Harvey, O., Prather, M., White, B. and Hoffmeister, J. (1968) Teachers' beliefs, classroom atmosphere, and student behaviour. *American Educational Research Journal*, **5**, 151–165.

Hayes, J. and Nutman, P. (1981) *Understanding the unemployed*. London: Tavistock.

Heider, F. (1958) *The psychology of interpersonal relations*. New York: John Wiley.

Helman, C. (1984) *Culture, health and illness*. Bristol: Wright.

Henley, S. and Furnham, A. (1988) The attribution of cure. *British Journal of Clinical Psychology*, in press.

Herzlich, C. (1973) *Health and illness*. London: Academic Press.

Hesketh, B. (1984) Attribution theory and unemployment: Kelley's covariation model, self-esteem and locus of control. *Journal of Vocational Behaviour*, **24**, 94–109.

Hewstone, M. (Ed.) (1983) *Attribution theory: Social and functional extensions*. Oxford: Blackwell.

Hey, R. (1977) Some findings concerning beliefs about alcoholism. *British Journal of Medical Psychology*, **50**, 227–235.

Hindelang, M. (1974) Public opinion regarding crime, criminal justice and related topics. *Journal of Research in Crime and Delinquency*, **10**, 101–116.

Hirst, P. (1960) A study of education. In: J. Tibble (Ed.), *A study of Education* London: Routledge & Kegan Paul.

Hirst, P. and Peters, R. (1975) *The logic of education*. London: Routledge & Kegan Paul.

Hirt, E. and Sherman, S. (1985) The role of prior knowledge in explaining hypothetical events. *Journal of Experimental Social Psychology*, **21**, 519–543.

Hogan, R. and Schroeder, D. (1981) Seven biases in psychology. *Psychology Today*, **15**, 8–14.

Hogarth, J. (1971) *Sentencing as a Human Process*. Toronto: University of Toronto Press.

Hoghughi, M. and Forrest, S. (1970) Eysenck's theory of criminality: An examination with approved schoolboys. *British Journal of Criminology*, **10**, 240–254.

Hollin, C. and Howells, K. (1987) Lay explanations of delinquency: Global or offence specific? *British Journal of Social Psychology*, **26**, 203–210.

Horowitz, L., Wright, J., Lowenstein, E. and Parad, H. (1981a) The prototype as a construct in abnormal psychology — I. A method for deriving prototypes. *Journal of Abnormal Psychology*, **90**, 568–574.

Horowitz, L., Post, D., French, R., Wallis, K. and Siegelman, E. (1981b) The prototype as a construct in abnormal psychology — II. Clarifying disagreement in psychiatric judgements. *Journal of Abnormal Psychology*, **90**, 575–585.

Hough, M. and Mayhew, P. (1985) *Taking account of crime*. London: HMSO.

Houston, J. (1983) Psychology: A closed system of self-evident information? *Psychological Reports*, **52**, 203–208.

Houston, J. (1985) Untutored lay knowledge of the principles of psychology: Do we know anything they don't? *Psychological Reports*, **57**, 567–570.

Howard, G. (1985) The role of values in the science of psychology. *American Psychologist*, **40**, 255–265.

Huber, J. and Form, W. (1973) *Income and ideology*. New York: Free Press.

Hull, C. (1943) *Principles of behaviour*. New York: Appleton-Century-Crofts.

Hull, C. (1952) *A behaviour system*. New Haven: Yale University Press.

Huxley, T. (1902) *Collected essays*. London: Methuen.

Inner London Education Authority (ILEA) (1985) *Educational opportunities for all?* Mimeograph.

Irvine, S. (1969) Factor analysis of African abilities and attainments: Constructs across cultures. *Psychological Bulletin*, **71**, 20–32.

Isaacs, E. and Clark, H. (1987) References in conversation between experts and novices. *Journal of Experimental Psychology*, **116**, 26–37.

Jackson, P. (1968) *Life in classrooms*. London: Holt, Rinehart & Winston.

Jahoda, G. (1979) The construction of economic reality by some Glaswegian children. *European Journal of Social Psychology*, **9**, 115–127.

Jahoda, G. (1981) The development of thinking of an economic concept: The bank. *Cahiers de Psychologie Cognitive*, **1**, 55–70.

Jahoda, G. and Woerdenbagch, A. (1982) The development of ideas about an economic institution: A cross-national replication. *British Journal of Social Psychology*, **21**, 337–338.

Jaspars, J. (1983a) The process of causal attribution in common sense. In: M. Hewstone (Ed.), *Attribution theory: Social and functional extensions*. Oxford: Blackwell.

Jaspars, J. (1983) Attribution theory and research: The state of art. In: J. Jaspars, F. Fincham and M. Hewstone (Eds.), *Attribution theory and research*. London: Academic Press.

Jensen, G. (1981) *Sociology of delinquency: Current issues*. London: Sage.

Johnson, S. (1984) Knowledge, attitudes, and behaviour: Correlates of health in childhood diabetes. *Clinical Psychology Review*, **4**, 503–524.

Kahneman, D. and Tversky, A. (1973) On the psychology of prediction. *Psychological Review*, **80**, 237–251.

Kahneman, D. and Tversky, A. (1982) Variants of uncertainty. *Cognition*, **11**, 143–157.

Karnlol, R. (1987) Not all failures are alike: Self-attribution and perception of teachers' attributions for failing tests in liked and disliked subjects. *British Journal of Educational Psychology*, **57**, 21–25.

Katona, G. (1971) Consumer durable spending: Explanation and prediction. *Brooking Papers on Economic Activity*, 234–239.

Katona, G. (1975) *Psychological economics*. Amsterdam: Elsevier.

Kellaghan, T., Madaus, G., Airasian, P. and Fontes, P. (1981) Opinions of the Irish public on innovation in education. *Irish Journal of Education*, **1**, 23–40.

Keller, H., Miranda, D. and Gauda, G. (1984) The naive theory of the infant and some maternal attitudes: A two-country study. *Journal of Cross-Cultural Psychology*, **15**, 165–179.

Kelley, H. (1973) The process of causal attribution. *American Psychologist*, **23**, 107–128.

Kelley, G. (1955) *A theory of personality: The psychology of personal constructs*. New York: Norton.

Kennedy, L. and Silverman, R. (1985) Significant others and fear of crime among the elderly. *International Journal of Aging and Human Development*, **20**, 241–256.

Kerlinger, F. (1973) *Foundations of behavioural research*. New York: Holt, Rinehart & Winston.

Kidder, L. and Cohn, E. (1979) Public views of crime and crime prevention. In: I. Frieze, D. Baral and J. Carroll (Eds.), *New approaches to social problems*. San Francisco: Jossey-Bass.

Kimble, G. (1984) Psychology's two cultures. *American Psychologist*, **39**, 833–839.

King, J. (1983) Health belief in the consultation. In: D. Pendleton and J. Hasler (Eds.), *Doctor–patient communication*. London: Academic Press, pp. 109–125.

King, J., Pendleton, D. and Tate, P. (1985) *Making the most of your doctor*. London: Methuen.

Kirton, M., Hollin, C. and Radford, J. (1983) *School pupils' "image of psychology" — I. General knowledge and opinions*. Unpublished paper.

Kisker, G. (1964) *The disorganized personality*. New York: McGraw-Hill.

Klayman, J. and Ha, Y-W. (1987) Confirmation, discomfirmation and information in hypothesis testing. *Psychological Review*, **94**, 211–228.

Klein, R., Freeman, H. and Millett, R. (1973) Psychological test performance and indigeneous conception of intelligence. *Journal of Social Psychology*, **84**, 219–222.

Kleinke, C., Staneski, R. and Meeker, F. (1983) Attribution for smoking behaviour: Comparing smokers with non-smokers for predicting smoker's cigarette consumption. *Journal of Research in Personality*, **17**, 242–255.

Kline, P. (1972) *Fact and fantasy in Freudian theory*. London: Methuen.

Koenig, E. and Juni, S. (1981) Attitudes toward policewomen: A study of interrelationships and determinants. *Journal of Police Science and Administration*, **9**, 463–474.

Kohler, W. (1947) *Gestalt psychology*. New York: Luralight.

Knapp, J. and Delprato, D. (1980) Willpower, behavior therapy, and the public. *Psychological Record*, **30**, 477–482.

Knapp, J. and Karabenick, S. (1985) Overcoming problems: The perceived importance of willpower and other contributors. *Cognitive Therapy and Research*, **9**, 343–354.

Kraepelin, E. (1915) *Psychiatric: Ein Lehrbuch fur Studieriche und Artze*. Leipzig: Barth.

Krasner, L. and Houts, A. (1984) A study of the "value" systems of behavioural scientists. *American Psychologist*, **39**, 840–850.

Kristiansen, C., Harding, C. and Eiser, J. (1983) Beliefs about the relationship between smoking and causes of death. *Basic and Applied Social Psychology*, **4**, 253–261.

Kruglanski. A. (1980) Lay epistemologic-process and contents: Another look at attribution theory. *Psychological Review*, **87**, 70–87.

Kruglanski, A. (1984) Contents, logic and motivation in the process of knowledge acquisition: A reply to Effler. *European Journal of Social Psychology*, **14**, 439–446.

Kruglanski, A., Friedland, N. and Farkash, E. (1984) Lay persons' sensitivity to statistical information: The case of high perceived applicability. *Journal of Personality and Social Psychology*, **46**, 503–518.

Kunda, Z. and Nisbett, R. (1985) The psychometrics of everyday life. Paper presented at the Annual BPS Conference, Wales, 1985.

Lacey, A. (1976) *A dictionary of philosophy*. London: Routledge & Kegan Paul.

La France, M. and Cicchetti, C. (1979) Perceived responsibility and blame for economic success and failure: Social class and employment status comparisons. *Journal of Applied Social Psychology*, **9**, 466–475.

Lakoff, G. and Johnson, M. (1980) The metaphysical structure of the human conceptual system. *Cognitive Science*, **4**, 195–208.

Lalljee, M., Lamb, R., Furnham, A. and Jaspars, J. (1984) Explanations and information search: Inductive and hypothesis-testing approaches to arriving at the explanation. *British Journal of Social Psychology*, **23**, 201–212.

Lamiell, J., Foss, M., Larser, R. and Heupel, A. (1983) Studies in intuitive personology idiothetic point of view: Implications for personality theory. *Journal of Personality*, **51**, 438–467.

Lau, R. (1982) Origins of health locus of control beliefs. *Journal of Personality and Social Psychology*, **42**, 322–334.

Lawton, J., Schuler, S., Fowell, N. and Madsen, M. (1984) Parents' perceptions of actual and ideal child-rearing practices. *Journal of Genetic Psychology*, **145**, 77–87.

Lemkau, P. and Crocetti, G. (1962) An urban population's opinion and knowledge about mental illness. *American Journal of Psychiatry*, **118**, 692–700.

Lentz, W. (1966) Social status and attitudes towards delinquency control. *Journal of Research into Crime and Delinquency*, **3**, 147–154.

Lerner, M. (1980) *The belief in a just world: A fundamental delusion*. New York: Plenum Press.

Lerner, M. and Miller, D. (1978) Just world research and the attribution process: Looking back and ahead. *Psychological Bulletin*, **85**, 1030–1051.

Lesieur, W. (1977) *The chase: Careers of the compulsive gambler*. New York: Anchor Books.

Levi, M. (1981) *Economics deciphered: A survival guide for non-economists*. London: Basic Books.

Levine, M. (1977) Sex differences in behaviour ratings: Male and female teachers rate male and female pupils. *American Journal of Community Psychology*, **5**, 347–353.

Levine, I., Faraone, S. and McGraw, J. (1981) The effects of income and inflation on personal satisfaction. *Journal of Economic Psychology*, **1**, 303–318.

Levitt, E. (1952) Superstitions: twenty-five years ago and today. *American Journal of Psychology*, **65**, 443–449.

Lewis, A. (1981) Attributions and politics. *Personality and Individual Differences*, **2**, 1–4.

Lewis, A. and Furnham, A. (1986) Reducing unemployment: Lay beliefs about how to reduce current unemployment. *Journal of Economic Psychology*, **6**, 75–85.

Lewis, A., Snell, M. and Furnham, A. (1987) Lay explanations for the cause of unemployment in Britain: Economic, individualistic, societal or fatalistic? *Political Psychologys*, **8**, 427–439.

Lewontin, R., Rose, S. and Kamin, L. (1982) Bourgeois ideology and the origins of biological determinism. *Race and Class*, **24**, 1–16.

Lillie, (1973) Conservatism, psychiatry and mental distress. In: G. Wilson (Ed.), *The psychology of conservatism*. London: Academic Press, pp. 225–236.

Lindgren, H. and Harvey, J. (1981) *An introduction to social psychology*. St. Louis: Mosby.

Linsky, A. (1972) Theories of behaviour and the social control of alcoholism. *Social Psychiatry*, **7**, 47–52.

Little, A. (1963) Professor Eysenck's theory of crime: an empirical test on adolescent young offenders. *British Journal of Criminology*, **4**, 152–163.

Little, A. (1985) The child's understanding of the causes of academic success or failure. *British Journal of Educational Psychology*, **55**, 11–23.

Lloyd-Bostock, S. (1981) Do lawyers' references to "common sense" have anything to do with what ordinary people think? *British Journal of Social Psychology*, **20**, 161–163.

Lloyd-Bostock, S. (1983) Attributions of causes and responsibility as social phenomena. In: J. Jaspars, F. Fincham and M. Hewstone (Eds.), *Attribution theory and research*. London: Academic Press.

Lloyd-Bostock, A. (1984) Legal literature, dialogue with lawyers, and research on practical legal questions: Some gains and pitfalls for psychology. In: G. M. Stephenson and J. Davis (Eds.), *Progress in applied social psychology*, Vol. 2. New York: John Wiley, pp. 265–292.

Loker, B. (1982) Heavy smokers', light smokers', and nonsmokers' beliefs about cigarette smoking. *Journal of Applied Psychology*, **67**, 616–622.

Ludenia, K. and Denham, G. (1983) Dental outpatients: Health locus of control correlates. *Journal of Clinical Psychology*, **39**, 854–858.

MacDonald, A. (1971) Correlates of the ethics of personal conscience and the ethics of social responsibility. *Journal of Consulting and Clinical Psychology*, **37**, 443.

MacFadyen, H., Evans, F. and MacFadyen, A. (1984) Economic satisfaction as a function of inflation, raise and economic knowledge. *Journal of Economic Psychology*, **5**, 31–47.

Mackay, D. (1975) *Clinical psychology: Theory and therapy*. London: Methuen.

Madaus, G., Fontes, P., Kelleghan, T. and Airasian, P. (1979) Opinions of the Irish public on the goals and adequacy of education. *Irish Journal of Education*, **2**, 87–125.

Maddi, S. (1976) *Personality theories: A comparative analysis*. Homewood, Il: Dorsey Press.

Makridakis, S., Wheelwright, S. and McGee, P. (1983) *Forecasting: Methods and application*. New York: John Wiley.

Marks, D. and Kammann, R. (1980) *The psychology of psychic*. New York: Prometheus Books.

Marx, M. (1970) *Learning theories*. New York: Macmillan.

Marx, M. (1976) Formal theory. In: M. Marx and F. Goodson (Eds.), *Theories in contemporary psychology*. New York: Macmillan.

Maslow, A. (1969) *The psychology of science: A reconnaissance*. Chicago: Henry Regnery.

Matas, M., el-Guebaly, N., Peterkin, A., Green, M. and Harper, D. (1985) Mental illness and the media: An assessment of attitudes and communication. *Canadian Journal of Psychiatry*, **30**, 12–17.

McCann, E. (1978) Children's perceptions of corporal punishment. *Educational Studies*, **4**, 167–172.

McCarthy, B. and Furnham, A. (1986) Patients' conceptions of psychological adjustment in the normal population. *British Journal of Clinical Psychology*, **25**, 43–50.

McCartney, J. and O'Dowd, P. (1981) The perception of drinking roles by recovery problem drinkers. *Psychological Medicine*, **11**, 747–754.

McFather, R. (1978) Sentencing strategies and justice: Effects of punishment philosophy on sentencing decisions. *Journal of Personality and Social Psychology*, **36**, 1490–1500.

McGregor, D. (1960) *The human side of enterprises*. New York: McGraw-Hill.

McHugh, M. (1979) *Causal explanations of alcoholics, non alcoholics, and college students for male and female alcoholism*. Unpublished Thesis, University of Pittsburgh.

McHugh, M., Beckman, L. and Frieze, I. (1980) Analysing alcoholism. In: I. Frieze, D. Bar-Tal and J. Carroll (Eds.), *New approaches to social problems*. San Francisco: Jossey-Bass, pp. 186–208.

McKeachie, W. (1960) Changes in scores on the northwestern misconceptions test in six elementary psychology courses. *Journal of Education Psychology* **51**, 240–244.

McKeachie, W. and Doyle, C. (1966) *Psychology*. Reading, MA: Addison-Wesley,

McKennell, A. and Thomas, R. (1967) *Adults' and adolescents' smoking habits and attitudes*. London: HMSO.

McLoughlin, C. (1985) Utility and efficacy of knowledge of behavioural principles as applied to children. *Psychological Reports*, **56**, 463–467.

Meehl, P. (1956) Wanted — A good cook-book. *American Psychologist*, **11**, 262–272.

Meertens, R., Koomen, W., Delpeut, A. and Hager, G. (1984) Effects of hypothesis and assigned task on question selection strategies. *European Journal of Social Psychology*, **14**, 369–378.

Meighan, R. (1981) *A sociology of education*. London: Holt, Rinehart & Winston.

Michaelis, W. and Eysenck, H. (1971) The determination of personality inventory factor patterns and intercorrelations by changes in real life motivation. *Journal of Genetic Psychology*, **118**, 223–234.

Milgram, S. (1974) *Obedience to authority*. London: Tavistock.

Miralles, A., Caro, I. and Rippere, V. (1983) What makes depressed people feel worse? A cross-cultural replication. *Behaviour Research and Therapy*, **21**, 485–490.

Mischel, W. and Mischel, H. (1980) *Children's knowledge of psychological principles*. Unpublished, Stanford University.

Moore, P. (1980) *Reason by numbers*. Harmondworth: Penguin.

Morgan, C. (1961) *Introduction to psychology*. New York: McGraw-Hill.

Moscovici, S. (1981) On social representation. In: J. Forgas (Ed.), *Social cognition: Perspectives on Everyday Understanding*. London: Academic Press.

Mosley, P. (1983) Popularity function and the role of the media: A pilot study of the popular press. *British Journal of Political Science*, **14**, 117–133.

Mulford, H. and Miller, D. (1961) Public definitions of the alcoholic. *Quarterly Journal of Studies on Alcohol*, **25**, 72–125.

Mulford, H. and Miller, D. (1964) Measuring public acceptance of the alcoholic as a sick person. *Quarterly Journal of Studies on Alcohol*, **29**, 314–323.

Musgrove, F. and Taylor, P. (1969) *Society and the teacher's role*. London: Routledge & Kegan Paul.

Neisser, V. (1979) *Cognition and reality*. New York: Freeman.

Ng, S. (1983) Children's ideas about the bank and shop profit: Developmental stages and the influence of cognitive contrasts and conflict. *Journal of Economic Psychology*, **4**, 209–221.

Nicholls, J., Patashnick, M. and Nolen, S. (1985) Adolescents' theories of education. *Journal of Educational Psychology*, **77**, 683–692.

Nicholson, J. and Lucas, M. (Eds.) (1984) *All in the mind: Psychology in action*. London: Methuen.

Nieradzik, K. and Cochrane, R. (1985) Public attitudes towards mental illness — the effects of behaviour, roles and psychiatric labels. *International Journal of Social Psychiatry*, **31**, 23–33.

Nisbett, R. and Wilson, T. (1977) Telling more than we know: Verbal reports on mental processes. *Psychological Review*, **84**, 231–259.

Nisbett, R. and Kunda, Z. (1985) Perception of social distributions. *Journal of Personality and Social Psychology*, **48**, 297–311.

Nisbett, R., Krantz, D., Jepson, C. and Kunda, Z. (1983) The use of statistical heuristic in everday inductive reasoning. *Psychological Review*, **90**, 339-363.

Nixon, H. (1925) Popular answers to some psychological questions. *American Journal of Psychology*, **36**, 418-423.

Norman, D. (1963) Toward an adequate taxonomy of personality attributes: replicated factor structure in peer nomination personality ratings. *Journal of Abnormal and Social Psychology*, **66**, 574-583.

Norman, D. (1980) Twelve issues for cognitive science. *Cognitive Science*, **4**, 1-32.

Nowicki, S. and Hopper, A. (1974) Locus of control correlated in an alcoholic population. *Journal of Consulting and Clinical Psychology*, **42**, 735.

Nunnally, J. (1961) *Popular conceptions of mental health*. New York: Holt, Rinehart & Winston.

Obani, T. and Doherty, J. (1986) The development of concepts of handicaps in adolescence: A cross-cultural study. *Educational Studies*, **12**, 191-212.

O'Hagan, F. and Edmunds, G. (1982) Pupils' attitudes towards teachers' strategies for controlling disruptive behaviour. *British Journal of Educational Psychology*, **52**, 331-340.

O'Hagan, F. and Swanson, W. (1986) Teachers and psychologists: A comparison of views. *Research and Education*, **36**, 1-36.

Oliver, R. (1953) Attitudes to education. *British Journal of Educational Studies*, **2**, 31-41.

Orcutt, J. (1976) Ideological variations in the structure of deviant types: A multivariate comparison of alcoholism and heroin addicts. *Social Forces*, **55**, 415-437.

Osgood, C. (1962) *An alternative to war or surrender*. Urbana: University of Illinois Press.

Panday, T., Sinha, T., Prakash, A. and Tripalhi, R. (1982) Right-left political ideologies and attributions of the causes of poverty. *European Journal of Social Psychology*, **12**, 327-331.

Parcel, G. and Meyer, M. (1978) Development of an instrument to measure children's health locus of control. *Health Education Monographs*, **6**, 149-159.

Parker, G. and Brown, L. (1982) Coping behaviours that mediate between life events and depression. *Archives of General Psychiatry*, **39**, 1386-1391.

Pastore, N. (1949) *The nature - nurture controversy*. New York: Kings Crown.

Paulus, D. (1983) Sphere-specific measures of perceived control. *Journal of Personality and Social Psychology*, **44**, 1253-1265.

Payne, M. and Furnham, A. (1985) Explaining the causes of poverty in the West Indies: A cross-cultural comparison. *Journal of Economic Psychology*, **6**, 215-229.

Pearlin, L. and Schooler, C. (1978) The structure of coping. *Journal of Health and Social Behaviour*, **19**, 2-21.

Pendleton, D. (1983) Doctor-patient communication: A review. In: D. Pendleton and J. Hasler (Eds.), *Doctor-patient communication*. London: Academic Press, pp. 5-53.

Pervin, L. (1984) *Current controversies: Issues in personality*. New York: John Wiley.

Peter, J. and Olson, J. (1983) Is science marketing? *Journal of Marketing*, **47**, 111-125.

Peters, R. (1960) *The Concept of Motivation*. London: Routledge & Kegan Paul.

Peterson, C. and Beach, I. (1967) Man as an intuitive statistician. *Psychological Bulletin*, **68**, 29-46.

Phares, E. (1984) *Clinical Psychology: Concepts, methods and profession*. Homewood, IL: 4:6 Dorsey.

Pill, R. and Stott, N. (1982) Concepts of illness causation and responsibility: some preliminary data from a sample of working class mothers. *Social Science and Medicine*, **16**, 43-52.

Pill, R. and Stott, N. (1985) Choice or chance: further evidence on ideas of illness and responsibility for health. *Social Science and Medicine*, **20**, 981-991.

Plowman, D. and Leytham, G. (1957) How university entrants see psychology. *Bulletin of the British Psychological Society*, **10**, 34-43.

Power, R. and MacRae, K. (1977) Characteristics of items in the Eysenck Personality Inventory which affect responses when students simulate. *British Journal of Psychology*, **68**. 491-498.

Price, J., Price, J., Shanahar, P. and Desmond, S. (1986) Elderly persons' perceptions and knowledge of Alzheimer's disease. *Psychological Reports*, **58**, 419-424.

Pulman, D. and Kilbride, P. (1980) *A relativistic understanding of intelligence: social intelligence among the Songhay of Mali and the Samia of Kenya*. Unpublished paper.

Putnins, A. (1982) The Eysenck Personality Questionnaire and delinquency prediction. *Personality and Individual Differences*, **3**, 339-340.

Rabkin, J. (1974) Public attitudes towards mental illness: A review of the literature. *Schizophrenia Bulletin*, **10**, 9–33.

Ramsey, G. and Seipp, M. (1948) Attitudes and opinions concerning mental illness. *Psychiatric Quarterly*, **22**, 428–444.

Raven, J. (1977) *Education, values and society*. London: H. K. Lewis.

Raviv, A., Bar-Tal, D., Raviv, A. and Bar-Tal, Y. (1980) Causal explanations of success and failure by advantaged integrated, and disadvantaged pupils. *British Journal of Educational Psychology*, **50**, 137–146.

Raviv, A., Bar-Tal, D., Raviv, A. and Levit, R. (1983) Students' reactions to attributions of ability and effort. *British Journal of Educational Psychology*, **53**, 1–13.

Rees, D. (1985) Health beliefs and compliance with alcoholism treatment. *Journal of Studies on Alcohol*, **4**, 517–524.

Reicher, S. and Potter, J. (1985) Psychological theory as intergroup perspective: A comparative analysis of "scientific" and "lay" accounts of crowd events. *Human Relations*, **38**, 167–189.

Reichman, W. (1964) *Use and abuse of statistics*. Harmondsworth: Penguin.

Reid, W. and Holly, B. (1974) The factor structure of teacher attitudes to sixth form education. *British Journal of Educational Psychology*, **43**, 65–73.

Reuterman, N. (1978) The public's view of delinquency causation: A consideration in comprehensive juvenile justice planning. *Juvenile and Family Court Journal*, **29**, 39–45.

Reuterman, N. and Cartwright, D. (1976) Practitioners' views of delinquency causations: A consideration in comprehensive juvenile justice planning. *Criminal Justice and Behaviour*, **3**, 67–84.

Rice, M. and Chapman, T. (1979) Social skills training for hospitalized male arsonists. *Journal of Behaviour Therapy and Experimental Psychiatry*, **10**, 105–108.

Richard, G. and Burley, P. (1978) Alcoholic's beliefs about and attitude to controlled drinking and total abstinence. *British Journal of Social and Clinical Psychology*, **17**, 159–163.

Richmond, W. (Ed.) (1968) *Readings in education*. London: Methuen.

Richmond, W. (1975) *Education and schooling*. London: Methuen.

Rim, Y. (1984) Explanations for poverty: Personality aspects. *Personality and Individual Differences*, **5**, 123–124.

Rippere, V. (1977) Some cognitive dimensions of antidepressive behaviour. *Behaviour Research and Therapy*, **15**, 57–62.

Rippere, V. (1979) Scaling the helpfulness of antidepressive activities. *Behaviour Research and Therapy*, **17**, 439–449.

Rippere, V. (1980a) Predicting consensus about propositions concerning depression and antidepressive behaviour: Another cognitive dimension of commonsense knowledge. *Behaviour Research and Therapy*, **18**, 79–86.

Rippere, V. (1980) Predicting frequency, intensity and deviation of other people's self-reported depression. *Behaviour Research and Therapy*, **18**, 259–264.

Rippere, V. (1981a) How depressing: Another cognitive dimension of commonsense knowledge. *Behaviour Research and Therapy*, **19**, 169–181.

Rippere, V. (1981b) Depression, commonsense and psychological evolution. *British Journal of Medical Psychology*, **54**, 379–387.

Rippere, V. (1981c) The survival of traditional medicine in lay medical man: An empirical approach to the history of medicine. *Medical History*, **25**, 411–414.

Roberts, M., Bendleman, W. and Wurtele, S. (1981) Children's perceptions of medical and psychological disorders in their peers. *Journal of Clinical Child Psychology*, **10**, 76–78.

Robinson, D. (1976) *From drinking to alcoholism: A sociological commentary*. New York: John Wiley.

Rock, P. (1979) Another commonsense conception of deviancy. *Sociology*, **13**, 75–88.

Roediger, H., Rushton, J., Capaldi, E. and Paris, S. (1984) *Psychology*. Toronto: Little, Brown & Compass.

Rosenberg, S. and Sedlak, A. (1972) Structural representations of implicit personality theories. In L. Berkowitz (Ed.), *Advances in experimental social psychology*, Vol. 6. New York: Academic Press.

Rosenfield, S. (1982) Sex roles and societal reactions to mental illness: The labeling of "deviant" deviance. *Journal of Health and Social Behaviour*, **23**, 18–24.

Rosenthal, R. (1966) *Experimenter effect in behavioral research*. New York: Appleton-Century-

Crofts.

Rosenthal, R. and Jacobson, L. (1968) *Pygmalion in the classroom: Teacher expectation and pupil's intellectual development*. New York: Holt, Rinehart & Winston.

Rosenstock, I. (1974) Historical origins of the health belief model: Origins and correlates in psychological theory. *Health Educations Monographs*, **2**, 336–353.

Ross, L. (1977) The intuitive psychologist and his shortcomings: Distortions in the attribution process. In: L. Berkowitz (Ed.), *Advances in experimental social psychology*, Vol. 10. New York: Academic Press.

Rotenberg, G. (1974) Conceptual and methodological notes on affective and cognitive role taking: An illustrative experiment with delinquent and non-delinquent boys. *Journal of Analytic Psychology*, **125**, 177–185.

Rotter, J. (1966) Generalized expectancies for internal versus external control of reinforcement. *Psychological Monographs*, **80**, No. 609.

Rubin, Z. and Peplau, A. (1973) Beliefs in a just world and reaction in the national draft lottery. *Journal of Social Issues*, **29**, 73–93.

Rubin, Z. and Peplau, A. (1975) Who believes in a just world? *Journal of Social Issues*, **31**, 65–89.

Rushton, J. and Chrisjohn, R. (1981) Extraversion, neuroticism, psychoticism and self-reported delinquency. *Personality and Individual Differences*, **21**, 11–20.

Russell, J. and Steiger, J. (1982) The structure of persons' implicit taxonomy of emotions. *Journal of Research in Personality*, **16**, 447–469.

Ryckman, R., Burns, M. and Robbins, M. (1986) Authoritarianism and sentence strategies for low and high severity crimes. *Personality and Social Psychology Bulletin*, **12**, 227–235.

Ryle, G. (1949) *The concept of mind*. London: Hutchinson.

Sackett, P. (1982) The interviewer as hypothesis tester: The effects of impressions of an applicant on interviewer questioning strategy. *Personnel Psychology*, **35**, 789–804.

Sadava, S. and Weithe, H. (1985) Maintenance and attributions about smoking among smokers, nonsmokers and ex-smokers. *International Journal of Addictions*, **20**, 1533–1544.

Salas, R. (1968) Fakability of responses on the Eysenck Personality Inventory. *Journal of Psychology*, **20**, 55–57.

Saltzer, E. (1982) The weight locus of control (WLOC) scale: A specific measure for obesity research. *Journal of Personality Assessment*, **46**, 620–628.

Sarbin, T., Taft, R. and Bailey, D. (1960) *Clinical Inference and cognitive theory*. New York: Holt, Rinehart & Winston.

Satterly, D. and Hall, H. (1983) Personality differences and the effects of success and failure on causal attributions and expectancies of primary school children. *Educational Psychology*, **3**, 245–258.

Schweder, R. (1980) Factors and fictions in person perception: A reply to Lamiell, Foss and Lawrence. *Journal of Personality*, **48**, 74–81.

Schwieso, J. (1984) What is common to common sense. *Bulletin of the British Psychological Society*, **47**, 43–45.

Selltiz, C., Wrightsman, L. and Cook, S. (1959) *Research methods in social relations*. New York: Holt, Rinehart & Winston.

Semin, G. and Krahé, B. (1987) Lay concepts of personality: Eliciting tiers of a scientific conception of personality. *European Journal of Social Psychology*, **17**, 199–210.

Semin, G. and Strack, F. (1980) The plausibility of the implausable: A critique of Snyder and Swann. *European Journal of Social Psychology*, **10**, 379–388.

Semin, G. and Chassein, J. (1985) The relationship between higher order models and everyday conceptions of personality. *European Journal of Social Psychology*, **15**, 1–15.

Semin, G., Rosch, E. and Chassein, J. (1981) A comparison of the common-sense and "scientific" conceptions of extraversion-introversion. *European Journal of Social Psychology*, **11**, 77–86.

Serpell, R. (1974) Estimates of intelligence in a rural community of eastern Zambia. *Human Development Research Unit Report*, No. 25. University of Zambia.

Shapland, J., Rushton, J. and Campbell, A. (1975) Crime and personality: further evidence. *Bulletin of the British Psychological Society*, **28**, 66–68.

Sharp, F. (1898) An objective study of some moral judgements. *American Journal of Psychology*, **9**, 198–234.

Sharteau, J. and Nagy, G. (1984) Information integration in person perception: theory and application. In M. Cook (Ed.), *Issues in personal perception*. London: Methuen, pp. 48–86.

Sherman, S., Zehner, K., Johnson, J. and Hirt, E. (1983) Social explanation: The role of timing, set and recall on subjective likelihood estimates. *Journal of Personality and Social Psychology*, **44**, 1127–1143.

Shoemaker, D. (1984) *Theories of delinquency: An examination of explanations of delinquent behaviour*. Oxford: Oxford University Press.

Shotter, J. and Burton, A. (1985) Common sense accounts of human action: The descriptive formulations of Heider, Smedslund and Ossomo. In: L. Wheeler and P. Shaver (Eds.), *Review of personality and social psychology*, Vol. 4. London: Sage.

Siegal, M. (1981) Children's perception of adult economic needs. *Child Development*, **52**, 379–382.

Sigelman, L. (1981) Is ignorance bliss? A reconsideration of the folk wisdom. *Human Relations*, **34**, 965–974.

Sillars (1980) Attributions and interpersonal conflict resolution. In: J. Harvey, W. Ickes and R. Kidd (Eds.), *New directions in attribution research*. Vol. 3. Hillsdale, NJ: Erlbaum.

Sillars, A. (1982) Attribution and communication. In: M. Roloff and C. Berger (Eds.), *Social cognition and communication*. Beverly Hills: Sage, pp. 73–106.

Silverman, R. and Kennedy, L. (1986) Loneliness, satisfaction and fear of crime. *Canadian Journal of Criminology*, **27**, 1–13.

Silverman, M., Smith, L., Nelson, C. and Dembo, R. (1984) The perception of the elderly criminal when compared to adult and juvenile offenders. *Journal of Applied Gerontology*, **3**, 97–104.

Simon, H. and Newell, A. (1956) Models: their uses and limitations. In: L. White (Ed.), *The state of the social sciences*. Chicago: Chicago University Press.

Singh, S. and Vasudeva, P. (1977) A factorial study of the perceived reasons for poverty. *Asian Journal of Psychology and Education*, **2**, 51–56.

Six, B. and Krahé, B. (1984) Implicit psychologists' estimates of attitude — behaviour consistencies. *European Journal of Social Psychology*, **14**, 79–86.

Sjöberg, L. (1982) Logical versus psychological necessity: A discussion of the role of common sense in psychological theory. *Scandinavian Journal of Psychology*, **23**, 65–78.

Skarzynska, K. (1975) How teachers are influenced by advanced information on student abilities. *Polish Psychological Bulletin*, **6**, 45–53.

Skinner, B. (1972) *Beyond freedom and dignity*. London: Jonathan Cape.

Skinner, B. (1985) Cognitive science and behaviourism. *British Journal of Psychology*, **76**, 291–301.

Skov, R. and Sherman, S. (1986) Information-gathering processes: Diagnosticity, hypothesis-confirmatory strategies, and perceived hypothesis confirmation. *Journal of Experimenal Social Psychology*, **22**, 93–121.

Slenker, S., Price, J. and O'Connell, J. (1985) Health, locus of control of joggers and non-exercisers. *Perceptual and Motor Skills*, **61**, 323–328.

Sloan, R. and Gruman, J. (1983) Beliefs about cancer, heart disease and their victims. *Psychological Report*, **52**, 415–424.

Smedslund, J. (1978) Some psychological theories are not empirical: Reply to Bandura. *Scandinavian Journal of Psychology*, **19**, 101–102.

Smedslund, J. (1979) Between the analytic and the arbitary: A case study of psychological research. *Scandinavian Journal of Psychology*, **20**, 129–140.

Smedslund, J. (1982a) Common sense as psychosocial reality: A reply to Sjoberg. *Scandinavian Journal of Psychology*, **23** 79–82.

Smedslund, J. (1982b) Revising explanations of common sense through dialogue: Thirty-six psychological theories. *Scandinavian Journal of Psychology*, **23**, 299–305.

Smedslund, J. (1982c) Seven common sense rules of psychological treatment. *Journal of the Norwegian Psychological Association*, **19**, 441–449.

Smedslund, J. (1986) How stable is common sense psychology and can it be transcended? Reply to Valsiner. *Scandinavian Journal of Psychology*, **27**, 91–94.

Smith, T. (Ed.) (1982) *Macmillan guide to family health*. London: Bookclub.

Smith, P. and Casbolt, D. (1984) Sixth-formers and psychology: Fifteen years on. *Bulletin of the British Psychological Society*, **37**, 334–337.

Smith, P., Ashton, P., Elliott, J., Freeland, C., Jones, W., McKinnon, A., Simpson, S. and Stroy, R. (1969) Sixth-formers and psychology: *A survey. Bulletin of the British Psychological Society*, **22**, 205–212.

Snyder, M. (1979) Self-monitoring processes. In: L. Berkowitz (Ed.), *Advances in experimental social psychology*, Vol. 12. New York: Academic Press.

Snyder, M. (1984) When beliefs creates reality: In: L. Berkowitz (Ed.), *Advances in experimental social psychology*, Vol. 17. London: Academic Press.

Snyder, M. and Campbell, B. (1980) Testing hypotheses about other people: The role of hypothesis. *Personality and Social Psychology Bulletin*, **6**, 421–426.

Snyder, M. and Skryprek, B. (1981) Testing hypotheses about the self: Assessment of job suitability. *Journal of Personality*, **49**, 193–211.

Snyder, M. and Swann, W. (1978) Hypothesis-testing processes in social interaction. *Journal of Personality and Social Psychology*, **36**, 1202–1212.

Snyder, M., Cambell, B. and Preston, E. (1982) Testing hypotheses about human nature: Assessing the accuracy of social stereotypes. *Social Cognition*, **1**, 256–272.

Soloman, J. (1986) Children's explanations. *Oxford Review of Education*, **12**, 41–51.

Spence, S. (1981) Differences in social skills performance between institutionalized juvenile male offenders and a comparable group of boys without offence records. *British Journal of Clinical Psychology*, **20**, 163–172.

Stacey, B. (1978) *Political Socialization in western society*. London: Edward Arnold.

Stacey, B. (1985) Economic socialization. *Annual Review of Political Science*, **2**, 114–128.

Stacey, B. and Singer, M. (1985) The perception of poverty and wealth among teenagers. *Journal of Adolescence*, **8**, 231–241.

Stagner, R. (1958) The gullibility of personnel managers. *Personnel Psychology*, **50**, 145–147.

Stebbins, R. (1980a) "Amateur" and "Hobbyist" as concepts for the study of leisure problems. *Social Problems*, **27**, 413–417.

Stebbins, R. (1980b) Avocational science: The amateur routine in archeology and astronomy. *International Journal of Comparative Sociology*, **21**, 34–48.

Sternberg, R. (1982) Who's intelligent? *Psychology Today*, **4**, 30–39.

Sternberg, R. (1985) Implicit theories of intelligence, creativity and wisdom. *Journal of Personality and Social Psychology*, **49**, 607–627.

Sternberg, R., Conway, B., Ketron, J. and Bernstein, M. (1981) People's conceptions of intelligence. *Journal of Personality and Social Psychology*, **41**, 37–55.

Stewart, R. (1983) Beliefs about human nature held by young people in the South Pacific. *Social Behaviour and Personality*, **11**, 125–132.

Strickland, B. (1978) Internal-external expectances and health-related behaviours. *Journal of Consulting and Clinical Psychology*, **46**, 1192–1211.

Stroebe, W. (1980) Process loss in social psychology: Failure to exploit? In: R. Gilmour and S. Duck (Eds.), *The development of social psychology*. London: Academic Press, pp. 181–205.

Sullivan, H. (1947) *An interpersonal theory of psychiatry*. New York: Norton.

Sullivan, T., Thompson, K., Wright, R., Gross, G. and Spady, D. (1985) *Social problems: Divergent perspectives*. New York: John Wiley.

Super, C. (1982) Cultural variations in the meaning and uses of children's "intelligence". In: J. Deregowski, S. Dziurawiec and R. Annis (Eds.), *Explorations in cross-cultural psychology*. Amsterdam: Swets & Zetlinger.

Sutton, R. (1962) Behaviour in the attainment of economic concepts. *Journal of Psychology*, **53**, 37–46.

Swede, S. and Tetlock, P. (1986) Henry Kissinger's implicit theory of personality. A quantitative case study. *Journal of Personality*, **54**, 615–646.

Teigen, K. (1983) Studies in subjective probability I & II. *Scandanavian Journal of Psychology*, **24**, 13–25, 27–33.

Thornton, D. and Kline, P. (1982) Reliability and validity of the Belief in Human Benevolence scale. *British Journal of Social Psychology*, **21**, 57–62.

Tiffany, D., Cowan, J. and Tiffany, P. (1970) *The unemployed: A social-psychological portrait*. Englewood Cliffs, NJ: Prentice-Hall.

Todman, J. and Farquharson, E. (1983) Primary teacher's attitudes to child-centred theory of education. *Educational Psychology*, **3**, 79–83.

Tolor, A. and Tamerin, J. (1975) The attitudes towards alcoholism instrument: A measure of attitudes towards alcoholism and the nature and causes of alcoholism. *British Journal of Addiction*, **70**, 223–231.

Trope, Y. and Bassok, M. (1982) Confirmatory and diagnosing strategies in social information gathering. *Journal of Personality and Social Psychology*, **43**, 22–34.

Trope, Y. and Bassok, M. (1983) Information-gathering strategies in hypothesis-testing. *Journal of Experimental Social Psychology*, **19**, 560–576.

Trope, Y., Bassok, M. and Alon, E. (1984) The questions lay interviewers ask. *Journal of Personality*, **52**, 90–106.

Tucker, C. (1979) Underutilization of mental health services by blacks: strategies for change. *University of Florida Psychological and Vocational Counseling Center Monograph Series*, **3** 1–5.

Tupper, V. and Williams, R. (1986) Unsubstantiated beliefs among beginning psychology students: 1925, 1952, 1983. *Psychological Reports*, **58**, 383–388.

Turnbull, W. (1981) Naive conceptions of free will and the deterministic paradox. *Canadian Journal of Behavioural Science*, **13**, 1–13.

Tversky, A. and Kahneman, D. (1974) Judgement under uncertainty: Heuristics and biases. *Science*, **185**, 1124–1131.

Tyson, G. (1982) People who consult astrologers: A profile. *Personality and Individual Differences*, **3**, 119–126.

Valentine, E. (1982) *Conceptual issues in psychology*. London: Allen & Unwin.

Valsiner, J. (1984) Conceptualizing intelligence: From an internal static attribution to the study of the process structure of organism-environment relationships. *International Journal of Psychology*, **19**, 363–389.

Valsiner, J. (1985) Between groups and individuals: Psychologists' and lay persons' interpretations of correlational findings. In: J. Valsiner (Ed.), *The role of the individual subject in scientific psychology*. New York: Plenum.

Valsiner, J. (1985) Common sense and psychological theories: The historical nature of logical necessity. *Scandinavian Journal of Psychology*, **26**, 97–109.

Vaughn, E. (1977) Misconceptions about psychology among introductory psychology students. *Teaching of Psychology*, **4**, 138–141.

Vecchio, R. (1981) Workers' beliefs in internal versus external determinants of success. *Journal of Social Psychology*, **114**, 199–207.

Viney, W., Waldman, P. and Barchilon, J. (1982) Attitudes toward punishment in relation to beliefs in free-will and determinism. *Human Relations*, **35**, 939–950

Vollmer, F. (1986) The relationship between expectancy and academic achievement — How can it be explained. *British Journal of Educational Psychology*, **56**, 64–74.

Waganaar, W. and Keren, G. (1985) Calibration of probability assessments by professional blackjack dealers, statistical experts and lay people. *Organizational Behavior and Human Decision Processes*, **36**, 406–416.

Wagner, R. (1987) Tacit knowledge in everyday intelligent behaviour. *Journal of Personality and Social Psychology*, **52**, 1236–1247.

Wagner, R. and Sternberg, R. (1985) Practical intelligence in real-world pursuits: The role of tacit knowledge. *Journal of Personality and Social Psychology*, **49**, 436–458.

Wallis, R. and Bruce, S. (1983) Accounting for action: Defending the common sense heresy. *Sociology*, **17**, 97–111.

Wallston, K. and Wallston, B. (1981) Health locus of control scales. In: H. Lefcourt (Ed.), *Research with the locus of control construct*, Vol. 1. New York: Academic Press.

Wallston, K., Wallston, B. and Develles, R. (1978) Development of the multidimensional health locus of control (MHLC) scales. *Health Education Monographs*, **6**, 160–169.

Walters, R., Cheyne, J. and Banks, R. (1972) *Punishment*. Harmondsworth: Penguin.

Warburton, F. (1956) Beliefs concerning human nature among students in a university department of education. *British Journal of Educational Psychology*, **26**, 156–162.

Wason, P. and Shapiro, D. (1971) Natural and contrived experience in a reasoning problem. *Quarterly Journal of Experimental Psychology*, **23**, 63–71.

Wehling, L. and Charters, W. (1969) Dimensions of teacher beliefs about the teaching process. *American Education Research Journal*, **6**, 7–30.

Weiner, B. (1985) An attributional theory of achievement, motivation and emotion. *Psychological Review*, **92**, 548–573.

Weiss, M. (1985) Children's attitudes towards mental illness as assessed by the opinions about mental illness scale. *Psychological Reports*, **57**, 251–258.

Weiss, M. (1986) Children's attitudes towards mental illness: A developmental analysis. *Psychological Reports*, **58**, 11–20.

Westland, G. (1978) *Current crisis of psychology*. London: Heinemann.

Whatley, C. (1958) Social attitudes towards discharged mental patients. *Social Psychology*, **6**, 313–320.

White, P. (1984) A model of the lay person as pragmatist. *Personality and Social Psychology Bulletin*, **10**, 333–348.

Williamson, J. (1974) Beliefs about the motivation of the poor and attitudes towards poverty policy. *Social Problems*, **18**, 634–648.

Williams, G. (1978) *The economics of everyday life*. Harmondsworth: Penguin.

Williams, R. and Defris, L. (1981) The roles of inflation and consumer sentiment in explaining Australian consumption and saving patterns. *Journal of Economic Psychology*, **1**, 105–120.

Wilson, G. (1973) *The psychology of conservatism*. London: Academic Press.

Wilson, J. (1979) *Fantasy and common sense in education*. Oxford: Martin Robertson.

Wilson, J. and Bill, J. (1976) The structure of Oliver's "Survey of Opinions about Education". *British Journal of Education*, **46**, 184–189.

Wilson, T., Laser, P. and Stone, J. (1982) Judging the predictors of one's own mood: Accuracy and the use of shared theories. *Journal of Experimental Social Psychology*, **18**, 537–556.

Wittgenstein, L. (1953) *Psychological investigations*. Oxford: Blackwell.

Wober, M. (1969) Distinguishing centri-cultural from cross-cultural tests and research. *Perceptual and Motor Skills*, **28**, 488.

Wober, M. (1978) Television violence and paranoid perception: The view from Great Britain. *Public Opinion Quarterly*, **42**, 315–321.

Wood, D. and Letak, J. (1982) A mental-health locus of control scale. *Personality and Individual Differences*, **3**, 84–87.

Wrightsman, L. (1964) Measurement of philosophies of human nature. *Psychological Report*, **14**, 743–751.

Wrightsman, L. (1974) *Assumptions about human nature: A social-psychological approach*. Monterey, CA:Brooks/Cole.

Wrightsman, L. and Satterfield, C. (1967) *Additional norms and standardization of the Philosophies of Human Nature Scale*. Mimeograph, George Peabody College.

Wurtele, S., Britcher, J. and Saslawsky, D. (1985) Relationships between locus of control, health value and preventive health behaviours among women. *Journal of Research in Personality*, **19**, 271–278.

Yin, P. (1980) Fear of crime among the elderly: Some issues and suggestions. *Social Problems*, **27**, 492–504.

Young, G. (1980) The attitudes of teachers in further education. *British Journal of Educational Psychology*, **50**, 181–185.

Young, G. and Martin, M. (1981) Processing of information about self by neurotics. *British Journal of Clinical Psychology*, **20**, 205–212.

Younger, J., Arrowood, A. and Hemsley, G. (1977) And the lucky shall inherit the earth: Perceiving the causes of financial success and failure. *European Journal of Social Psychology*, **1**, 509–515.

Zanna, M., Sheras, P., Cooper, J. and Shaw, C. (1975) Pygmalion and Galatea: The interactive effect of teacher and student expectation. *Journal of Experimental Social Psychology*, **11**, 279–287.

Zelko, F., Duncan, S., Barden, C., Garber, C. and Masters, J. (1986) Adults' expectancies about children's emotional responsiveness: Implications for the development of implicit theories of affect. *Developmental Psychology*, **22**, 109–114.

Zimbardo, P., Haney, C., Books, W. and Jaffe, P. (1973) Pirandellian prison: The mind is a formidable jailer. *New York Times Magazine*, April, 38–60.

Index

DE